HOW TO DETECT CONSTRUCTION FRAUD

HOW TO DETECT CONSTRUCTION FRAUD

BY

ROBERT LOUIS BECKER

WHAT TO LOOK FOR AND HOW TO RECOVER INAPPROPRIATE
CONTRACTOR BILLINGS ON LARGE CONSTRUCTION PROJECTS

*An examination of Contractor Practices, Contractor Profits, and Project Controls,
including an Invoice Format, a Lien Waiver Log, and Contractor Dispute Forms.*

Copyright © 2012 by Robert Louis Becker.

Library of Congress Control Number:		2012901487
ISBN:	Hardcover	978-1-4691-5758-0
	Softcover	978-1-4691-5757-3
	Ebook	978-1-4691-5759-7

All rights reserved. No part of this book may be reproduced or transmitted in any form or by any means, electronic or mechanical, including photocopying, recording, or by any information storage and retrieval system, without permission in writing from the copyright owner.

This book was printed in the United States of America.

To order additional copies of this book, contact:
Xlibris Corporation
1-888-795-4274
www.Xlibris.com
Orders@Xlibris.com
110902

DEDICATION

I would like to dedicate this book to my family and the reason for getting up each morning. To my wife Ruth, who has shared my joys and sorrows over the past 42 years. To my three children, Rob, Todd, and Stacy and to my eight grandchildren, who all keep me young.

I would also like to dedicate this book to my parents, Robert and Vera Becker. They taught me Religion, Honesty, and Morales, and provided me the opportunity to finish college and achieve my goals. They also provided me with the happiest childhood one could ever have.

TABLE OF CONTENTS

CHAPTER 1	Intro.	1
CHAPTER 2	Corporate Policies	19
CHAPTER 3	Contractor Profit	29
CHAPTER 4	Material	35
CHAPTER 5	Contractor's Construction Equipment	63
CHAPTER 6	Craft Labor	93
CHAPTER 7	Staff Salaries	119
CHAPTER 8	Contractor Insurance	129
CHAPTER 9	Lien Waivers	135
CHAPTER 10	Construction Project Controls	141
CHAPTER 11	Freight and Fuel Surcharges	147
CHAPTER 12	Fuel Taxes for Non-highway Use	151
CHAPTER 13	Travel Airline Tickets, Booking Class and Abbreviations	153
CHAPTER 14	Invoice Workbooks	155
CHAPTER 15	Invoice Audit Dispute Sheet Sample	171
CHAPTER 16	Lien Waiver Record Log	177
CHAPTER 17	Consumable Items	183
CHAPTER 18	Suggested Small Tools	203
CHAPTER 19	Glossary	217

CHAPTER 1 –
INTRO

There are Six Stages to every major construction project:

1. Camaraderie, Team Building, and Wild Enthusiasm
2. Misunderstandings, Schedule Delays, and Disputes
3. Budget Overruns and Disillusionment
4. Name Calling, Finger Pointing, and Search for the Guilty
5. Reassignment for the participants
6. Promotions for the incompetents

Opportunities abound for a good project to go bad because:

A. Time is of the essence
B. Absentee Owners
C. No defined work scope
D. Ambiguous contracts needing interpretation
E. No enforceability that protects the owner's best interest
F. Poor planning and poor controls
G. Lack of segregation of duties.

Millions of dollars are spent each year with unexplained cost overruns and few justifications provided by project management to the various stakeholders. By the time the Army of Attorneys and Accountants show up, the damage has been done, the contractors have demobilized, and it's almost impossible to recover funds from anyone involved.

The owner can avoid this outcome by having an enforceable contract, the right to audit as the project progresses, adequate controls in place prior to starting construction, and accurate drawings, plans, and specifications that avoid construction mistakes before they are made. This includes a well-defined scope of work, an experienced owner's oversight staff, and adequate reviews and approval of changes to the scope of work. More money can be saved by preventing mistakes before they occur than chasing after recovery of funds after they have been spent.

The contractor will have a dedicated staff focused on maximizing their profit on every project. Shouldn't the owner likewise have a sufficient staff to review the bills and actively participate in the project? The need to devote dedicated resources cannot be stressed enough, whether the owner uses his internal staff or hires consultants acting as project liaisons. This does not mean adding new responsibilities to an existing staff that is already overwhelmed and will monitor this new project on a part-time basis or as time allows.

The purpose of this book is to provide Government Agencies, Public and Private Project Owners, Certified Public Accountants, Construction Auditors, and Invoice Reviewers the tools needed to detect and dispute overcharges as well as provide guidance for Project Controls. Audit tools listed in this book will help detect unethical billing practices for any Agency or Company reimbursing contractors for craft labor, staff labor, material invoices, rental company invoices, or sub-tier-contractor invoices.

The author recovered over $7 million for the owner on a three year multi-million dollar project from contractors and subcontractors using techniques in this book.

LESSONS LEARNED

The author has audited many contractors over the past 30 years that have used various techniques to extract extra profits from the owner. These dubious business practices provided the motivation to write this book in an attempt to open the eyes of large corporations that have to expend large capital investments in real property. It was also written to assist Professional Auditors and others that may lack construction experience. The audit findings in this book were discovered during actual audits and have not been fabricated. When confronted with indisputable evidence, the contractor will never admit to any wrongdoing and will act bewildered as though they were unaware such a thing could happen.

This is not an accusation against every contractor in the construction industry. The drive to maximize profits is natural since there are so many unknowns in construction including if and when they will be awarded their next project. Nevertheless, the contractors I audited were some of the largest in their field with relatively good long term relationships with the project owner. Unfortunately the owner never conducted in-depth audits on prior projects. A significant amount of trust was earned over many years. I was amazed how belligerent the contractors became when confronted with these audit findings.

SOME DEFINITIONS

To assure that everyone has the same understanding of the construction terms used in this chapter there are some definitions that need to be explained. Other definitions can be found in the Glossary.

Contract - Firm Price – A total agreed to price the owner and contractor negotiate in advance in order to complete the project. A firm price does not require the same level of documentation for material costs, labor costs, or equipment costs like a Time and Material project. Under a firm price contract, the contractor assumes all risks for the project including escalating material costs, higher labor costs, labor strikes, bad weather, and unforeseen events. Fewer and fewer contractors are willing to accept these unforeseen risks.

Contract - Maximum Not to Exceed – An agreed to price with an incentive to share cost savings between the owner and contractor. The contractor is motivated and rewarded if final project costs are significantly below the maximum contract price.

Contract - Time and Material – A reimbursable contract for all direct and indirect costs associated with the project including all fees and adders. All expenditures need to be documented. This type of contract is also referred to as Cost plus Fee Agreement. The owner assumes the risk of project completion and the unforeseen delays such as strikes, inclement weather, or material shortages. The majority of this book focuses on this type of contract.

Fee - Overhead – A percentage adder, say 15%, that is calculated and added to each monthly billing as a percentage of all direct costs incurred at the project that recovers the contractor's home office overhead costs. This overhead fee compensates the contractor for his on-going business expenses such as home office staff, executive payroll, buildings, insurance, and taxes that are not directly billable to the project.

Fee – Profit – The agreed to percentage, say 10%, added to each monthly billing as a percentage adder of all direct costs incurred at the project that provides a profit to the contractor. Under a fixed fee contract, the profit fee could be paid based on a pre-scheduled monthly payout regardless of actual expenditures or percentage complete.

Retention – A contractual agreement for the owner to "hold back" or keep a portion of the money owed the contractor on each monthly progress payment to assure satisfactory acceptance of the work. Upon completion and acceptance of the project, the final retention is paid to the contractor (usually 10 percent of the contract total amount) after all punch list items and disputes have been resolved. Should the contractor default on the contract, the owner may use the retention held to obtain another contractor to complete the work.

DECEITFUL PRACTICES

There will be many audit areas listed in detail in various sections of this book that will provide guidance to determine if deceit has occurred. The following types of contractor charges were discovered during invoice audits.

STAFF LABOR

A. Salary and per diem payments to employees after their termination date from the project.
B. Home Office Personnel billed to the project but were not at the project.
C. Holidays, Vacations, and Sick Leave pay directly charged to the job that is also included in Staff Billing Rates.
D. Apartment Lease Deposits billed which will ultimately be refunded to the tenant and therefore not a project cost.
E. Staff rates include casual overtime for the first 10 hours per week but the project was directly billed for all overtime. Casual overtime is defined as hours worked exceeding 40 hours per week but less than 50 hours that are non-billable in the contract.
F. Billing staff overtime on two different contracts when the combined overtime for both contracts does not exceed 10 hours casual overtime. The contractor was billing for costs they did not incur.
G. Billing per diem for the entire month in advance when the employee voluntarily transfers to another project with the same contractor. When the employee transfers to another project, he is also paid per diem in advance at the new project. If the employee voluntarily leaves before the 15th of the month, the owner should negotiate return of at least half of the per diem.
H. Listing employees by first name and last name rather than last name first and then first name last. This allows for sorting by last name in alphabetical order in Excel spreadsheets for audit purposes. Listing employee names by first name and then last name is not typical for employee payroll records, so why is the contractor doing this?
I. Billing per diem for weekends when the employee is at home and not incurring per diem costs.
J. Cell phone costs were fixed at $720 per year based on 1,800 hours worked and a component ($.40) of the hourly straight time rate. Cell phones were billed on overtime hours worked.

CRAFT LABOR

A. Hidden payroll tax burden in craft payroll (charged 8% instead of 7.65% for Social Security Tax). Contractor admitted that it was an auto liability insurance component (non-reimbursable).
B. "Labor Pool Bonus" charged in craft labor distribution with no accountability for funds. This unauthorized adder could accumulate hundreds of thousands of dollars based on every hour worked and was contrary to prevailing wage rates. It provided funding for an employee bonus program not authorized by contract.
C. Overbilling of FICA, FUI, and SUI rates in favor of the contractor. Mandatory collection of Social Security, Federal Unemployment Insurance, and State Unemployment Insurance becomes a profit center for contractors after maximum limits have been satisfied.
D. Monthly safety incentive gas cards or gift cards with no accountability of the recipients. These payments represent taxable income to the recipient and should be reported as W-2 earnings.
E. Small tools allowance ($3.00 per labor hour) was billed on craft hours worked by Superintendents. Superintendents perform administrative functions and rarely use tools to perform their work. The contractor did not furnish tools to the Superintendents.
F. Paid time away from the project for "Apprenticeship School". Apprentices are not direct permanent employees of the owner. The owner will not receive any direct benefit after an Apprentice becomes a Journeyman. Apprenticeship School should be treated as anyone attending night school to attain a degree. They are allowed time away from work but are not paid wages or overtime while attending school. This should be specific in the contract.
G. Hidden fringe benefit adders include "Riding Boss" or a home office person that calls the Union Hall when additional craft are needed. This position is funded with the overhead adder.
H. Billing some craft supervisors for Holiday Pay, some of whom are not qualified to be paid per the National Maintenance Agreement.

SUBCONTRACTOR BILLING

A. Billing of subcontractor craft site lead person (Superintendent) for "Extra Work" when that person is expected to be on site as their company representative. Contractors attempt to shift administrative personnel to "Extras" while they do not incur any additional costs

for that person. He was already on site as part of his normal job responsibilities.
B. The prime contractor bills per diem pay for non-employees, such as subcontractor employees. The employee's direct employer should bill this as a payroll cost if it was actually incurred. Questions arise for reporting per diem payments to the IRS for a non-employee and did the employee actually receive this payment?
C. Prime contractors take little or no corrective action to administer and reject subcontractor's invoices billed in error. The prime contractor is paid an overhead fee to perform administrative reviews of subcontractor invoices. They are rewarded for overpayments to subcontractors through their fee adders and penalized for finding errors that reduce their fee adders, so why look?
D. "Adjustments" made on subcontractor invoices to prematurely bill the owner for retention in order for the prime contractor to "pocket" the retention until it is actually paid to the subcontractor.
E. When subcontractors have both Lump Sum and T&M jobs, look for transfer of overhead personnel, material, and equipment to the extra cost job.
F. Failure to enforce the same General Terms and Conditions of the Prime Contract with similar terms and conditions written in subcontracts.
G. Submitting for reimbursement from the owner duplicate daily timesheets on different invoices in sequential months.

MATERIAL PURCHASES

A. Contractors and subcontractors do not pass along material cash discounts when the owner provides cash advances prior to the current month. If contract is "actual cost", the discount reduces the material cost to actual cost and should be rendered to the owner.
B. No formal written purchase orders and no competitive bidding from three or more suppliers.
C. Favored material suppliers from contractor's home office town in another state that adds substantial shipping costs when material is readily available locally.
D. Substitution of material without reducing lump sum project cost.
E. No Receiving Reports that document material was received (quantity, date).
F. No accountability for lost material in storage and owner is billed for replacement material lost by contractor.

G. No record made of damaged material received that should be rejected.
H. Submitting for reimbursement from the owner the same material invoices in different consecutive monthly invoices.
I. No common stores for all contractors using the same items. Each subcontractor and the prime contractor buy and store their own common items such as lumber, hardhats, safety glasses, tools, and work gloves. This leads to multiple inventories and potential overstocking by each contractor.

TRAVEL, MEAL, AND MISCELLANEOUS EXPENSE

A. The contractor's office staff at the project believe they are entitled to a paid business lunch at a local restaurant every Friday to discuss business. They believe this should be billed to the owner as a project cost. Since the owner does not provide free employee meals, why would they provide a paid lunch to non-employees? The IRS has issued regulations that business meals are only reimbursable if they have been incurred for out of town overnight travel or to entertain a client. The meals were denied as reimbursable since these IRS requirements were not met. Let the contractor pay for these meals out of their overhead and profit. Can you imagine how much this would add to project costs over a three year project? Can you imagine how fast this practice stopped when the owner refused to pay for the meals?
B. The meal receipt submitted for reimbursement should be the actual restaurant receipt, not the credit card receipt. The actual restaurant receipt will reveal how many meals were served, what was served, and how much liquor was consumed. It will also show that sales tax was paid to the restaurant. A State Sales Tax Auditor may insist on the actual restaurant receipt as proof sales tax was paid to the restaurant, otherwise he may hold the owner liable for additional sales tax since the credit card receipt does not show any tax. Meals should also show the names of attendees and the purpose of the business meeting if it can be justified as reimbursable.
C. Travel expense reports should show the purpose of the trip. A contractor may send employees on business trips to submit bids on new projects but charge the travel to the current owner rather than absorb the cost themselves.
D. Undocumented tips – A subcontractor employee claimed he put $20 every week on his pillow as a tip for the motel maid. Have you ever heard

of padding your expense account? The tip was denied as reimbursable since there was no proof of payment.

E. The same individual listed above in item D lost all his meal receipts and the Superintendent told him to go to an office supply store and buy a blank restaurant receipt tablet and prepare his own receipts from memory. The tablet sheets were sequentially numbered, did not have any restaurant logo or address as the header, and were filled in by the individual. Both the contractor and owner agreed too much time was required to coach this individual for his carelessness and he was released from the project.

F. The owner was billed for the contractor's Christmas Party, which exceeded $5,000. The contractor considered this billable to the project. The contract was silent and did not address reimbursement for Christmas Parties. None of the owner's employees were invited, and the contractor did not obtain prior written approval from the owner. This expense was rejected by the owner.

The Orange County School Board

In the **Orlando Sentinel** dated Thursday, February 17, 2011, the Orange County School Board was criticized for not taking enough responsibility for turning around the District's Construction Department after a critical audit. The audit found the District's Construction Department allowed contractors to determine the price, scope, and timing of millions of dollars of work for the District. "The Department, which has a $1.3 billion budget, has skipped field reviews and has paid for work without assuring that it had been done properly."

The Orange County School Board shouldn't be so naïve to think the contractors have the best interests of the school district in mind when determining price, scope, or timing. When spending Other People's Money (OPM), the contractors have little or none of their own money at risk if the contract is Time and Material Cost Plus and every dollar spent is rewarded with fees paid to the contractor.

Let's face it. For every dollar spent on Time and Material (T&M) jobs, the contractor can recover all of his direct costs plus all of his indirect overhead cost plus fees (profits). If all costs are recovered plus a fee for their overhead and profit, the contractor has little incentive to save the owner's money and expedite the work in the most prudent manner. The longer the project is delayed, the longer the contractor's equipment can be rented, the more field office staff can be billed, and the more overtime that is worked all contributes to more profits. You get the picture.

As will be explained later, construction sites are more prone to fraud, overbilling, and lack of controls. Through proper construction oversight, there should be monitoring, accountability, and transparency for all transactions.

There are two simple rules to follow:

Rule Number 1: Never Assume Anything!

There has to be a reason when the contractor fails to provide required documentation such as staff salary component details, purchase orders, equipment lists, or contracts with subcontractors. Perhaps the missing documentation shows charges to a different project that should not have been billed to this owner. Perhaps the missing Purchase Order is a Lease-Purchase Option for equipment rentals with ownership of the item going to the contractor at the end of the lease but paid for by the owner. Perhaps the staff salary components have hidden markups included in the rate in addition to the contractual fees. The reviewer should always question why something doesn't look right.

Rule Number 2: Everything is Negotiable.

Disputes often arise during a large construction project because of ambiguity in the contract terminology. The contract is the "Meeting of the Minds" of both parties. An interpretation is often called for as to "What was the original intent of the contract language?" When every detail is not spelled out in the contract (which it never does), there should be a reasonableness test applied. The contractor is acting as agent for the owner to complete the project prudently and expeditiously. If an equipment item can be rented for $1,000 per month or $600 per week and the length of rental is unknown, is it prudent to enter into a lease that costs the most ($1,000 per month versus $2,400 per month after 4 weeks)?

What leverage does the owner have to negotiate? Each contract should have a dispute clause that provides guidance to resolve disagreements. Materiality of the dispute is also a consideration. There could be potentially more owner projects in the future where the contractor wants to participate. Is it worth it for the contractor to lose future business in new projects worth several million dollars over some interpretation of what defines a small tool?

WHY CONSTRUCTION AUDITING?

Most owners of large projects, such as utilities or refineries, are not staffed for large maintenance or construction projects even though they always seem to be building or modifying their facilities. Projects can be short lived and the owners don't need a permanent staff for specific projects where the staff cannot be reassigned after job completion. They rely on contractors to execute the work acting as the owner's agent, gather the necessary documents to request their monthly reimbursement, and provide one accurate invoice for payment.

The owner processes the bill as they would any other bill with perhaps a cursory review of the summary, a math verification of totals and some cross matching of labor rates, equipment rental rates, etc. Rarely is an in-depth review performed by a unique department such as Construction Audit but by the Accounts Payable Department. The Accounts Payable Department is usually understaffed and swamped with other bills needing to be paid within payment terms. They cannot dwell on one construction invoice while they have a daily quota of invoices to process. They cannot legally reject a one million dollar invoice due to a misunderstanding of rates or some missing pages. The Accounts Payable Department relies on the owner's site representative for reviewing the invoice and approving the payment.

However the owner's site representative rarely has time or the training to go into the details of material delivery, craft labor rates, or equipment rentals. They may perform a cursory review and the bill gets paid. The owner's site representatives usually build a working relationship with the contractor and would not want to disrupt the job progress to create animosity. There are typically team building events such as golf outings and evening dinners with spouses at nice restaurants that create friendships.

Internal Audit Departments are more focused with Internal Operational Audits or Sarbanes Oxley and not a short term project at a construction site.

As a result, invoices are paid in full, errors are undetected, and the process is repeated month after month. Contractor errors are not disputed and if the contractor "tests the system", they can learn what they can get away with and what they can't get away with.

A Site Construction Auditor provides the perfect third party scapegoat that the owner's site management can point to as not under their direction or control. They can remain on friendly terms with the contractor while the Site Auditor keeps an independent judgment. The Site Construction Auditor should have reporting responsibilities to Corporate and not to the owner's site project management. The owner's site project management should not direct, supervise, or prohibit the Site Auditor from auditing or reviewing any construction activity at the project.

This is not to say all contractors are dishonest. However, it has been the author's experience that contractor and sub-contractor invoices need to be scrutinized through a robust audit process. The owner's coffers can be literally stolen out the back door by contractors while safeguards and controls are posted at the front door for normal business operations. There are many consultants and audit firms specializing in the business of recovering construction funds for owners. They would not be in business if the need did not exist.

CONSTRUCTION FRAUD

Fraud is defined in Webster's dictionary as deception, an act by which the right or interest of another is injured, or a deliberate attempt to deceive.

Most auditors won't use the term "fraud" lightly because of the legal ramifications of lawsuits and professional ethics. Most auditors approach an assignment without bias until the evidence mounts persistently month after month, test sample after test sample. An honest mistake can randomly occur and go in either parties favor due to mistyping, transposition of numbers, inattention to detail, or inexperience by a new hire. A dishonest mistake usually occurs intentionally with no attempt to correct the error or previous errors. "If I get caught, O.K., we'll correct. If I don't get caught, who would ever know?" The reward outweighs the risk.

On a recent project, the Project Manager's Travel Expense Reports were missing from the invoice bundle provided by the contractor. At first, the Auditor or Invoice Reviewer can rationalize that the copy machine must have jammed, the copy fell on the floor, or it was missed when all documents were assembled. When the same monthly expense report for the same individual is not provided for several months but is always listed in the summary sheet for reimbursable costs, it arouses suspicions that the error isn't random but intentional. It raises the question, "What is listed on the Expense Report that the contractor doesn't want the owner to see?" Remember Rule #1?

The next question to ask is, "Why wasn't the document provided? Are they hoping it will be too immaterial to be questioned?" After all, why bother the contractor for this one item when they are too busy getting other work done? Do they want to be reimbursed but not have to explain why the charge was incurred? Does it fall outside the terms of the contract as non-reimbursable? Red flags should become evident to any auditor when the tone of the contractor's cooperation changes to "I'm too busy!" or "Why do you need that?"

In this particular example the contractor's Project Manager was responsible for two projects. One project was in Illinois on a Time and Material job. All expenses were reimbursed but had to be fully documented. The second project was in another state and quoted as Lump Sum. The airfare to the second project was erroneously billed to the Time and Material Job (and a different owner) in order for the contractor to avoid absorbing this cost out of his own pocket. By not providing a copy and hoping the auditor would miss this item as immaterial, the error can be repeated for many months. This is a perfect example of intentional fraud to the owner of the Time and Material Project. Anyone familiar with accounting would know these charges should be accurately charged to the appropriate project. Someone had to go out of their way to bill the wrong project and intentionally not provide proper documentation in the invoice bundle.

Missing documentation should always be required to assure only valid project costs are being submitted. There is usually a reason when the contractor is reluctant or slow to provide the requested information. Not requiring needed documentation usually sets a precedent for the rest of the project. Any missing documentation should be provided within a few business days and not be dragged out for several months. Documentation supporting project costs become a permanent record and may be scrutinized by External Auditors or Regulatory Commissions. There is no defense for paying bills without the supporting documents on Time and Material Projects. Comparing the Invoice Summary Sheet to the supporting documents and "ticking and tying" each line item is a necessity on Time and Material Projects.

SEGREGATION OF DUTIES

Let's compare material purchases for a manufacturing company payment process to a jobsite contractor payment process.

In a manufacturing assembly line, a raw material is needed to produce a final product. In our example let's say lumber is purchased. A requisition is initiated in the storeroom or through a minimum reorder point computer system. A requisition is approved to place a Purchase Order (PO). The Buyer solicits 3 bids, chooses the lowest price or justifies a different vendor due to availability, shipping, or other factors. The PO is approved and sent to the Vendor as well as the Accounts Payable Department. The lumber is delivered resulting in a Receiving Report prepared by the Storekeeper or Receiving Department. The Receiving Department documents the quantity and date received. This document is sent to the Accounts Payable Department. The Vendor sends an Invoice to the Accounts Payable Department.

Accounts Payable matches the Invoice to the P.O. and Receiving Report, and prepares a check after this three way match of Invoice, PO, and receiver. A check is issued by the Treasury Department. Due to the segregation of duties, it would take considerable collusion between multiple departments and personnel to falsify records and perpetuate a scam without someone talking.

Now let's assume a contractor at a major construction site needs lumber. Typically the organization at the construction site consists of a contractor's Project Manager, Office Manager, Craft Superintendents, Engineers, Schedulers, and of course Craft Personnel.

The Office Manager and his subordinates place orders for material, receive the material, and pay for the material. At some construction sites, there are no formal requisitions, purchase orders, receiving reports, a formal bidding process for competitive prices, or segregation of duties. Prices are not always sought from the lowest bidder and orders may be placed with a supplier that has performed well in the past. There is no audit trail to follow without the normal sequence of documentation.

The Office Manager is in a unique position to take advantage of this lack of controls. Not only could material be overpriced, short shipped, or lost in the storage yard but also can be returned for credit. Material can be returned to the Vendor and a Credit Memo issued to the contractor. If the contractor does not include the Credit Memo in his billing to the owner, the contractor has over-billed the owner for that transaction even if the contractor incurs a restocking charge. The contractor has billed the owner for material that will never be used! If the owner has no shipping documents or Auditors at the construction site, the contractor may never get caught unless there is a whistle blower.

MOM AND POP SUBCONTRACTORS

Now let's think about a Mom and Pop subcontractor performing a service such as painting that bills their service to the general contractor. Pop started as an apprentice years ago and slowly worked his way up through Journeyman, Foreman, General Foreman, and Superintendent. Business was good so he decided to go into business for himself with his spouse as bookkeeper.

So now we have an opportunity for billing mistakes made in Mom and Pop's favor with no one detecting the errors month after month. Most clerical personnel employed by a subcontractor and not related to either Mom or Pop would not directly benefit from overbilling. There is always the possibility this clerk may become a disgruntled employee and a whistle blower. Therefore the Mom and Pop subcontractor would directly benefit from undetected overbillings because these mistakes become their profits. Owner personnel should be cognizant of this potential flaw by examining the staff labor payroll for spouses billed to the project and their respective job responsibilities.

STAFF COMPETENCY – WHO DOES THE BILLING?

The assembly of documents to provide a monthly Time and Material invoice to the owner can be very time consuming and an unthankful task. Mistakes will be made and nobody is perfect. A one million dollar invoice can have over 600 pages of backup including material supplier invoices, daily timesheets, subcontractor charges, and equipment rentals.

It can be rationalized that when mistakes occur it was inattention to detail, the small contractor staff is overwhelmed, long hours of overtime are required, or someone was on vacation. All of these reasons can create mistakes for rendering an invoice that is over or under stated. Over time, when the errors are persistent in certain areas such as missing airfare receipts for a Project

Manager, one can conclude the error is intentional. Most random errors can be positive or negative to the contractor. When the errors usually favor the contractor collecting $5,000, $10,000, or $50,000 more for their mistakes, the errors are no longer randomly done at the clerk level.

Most contractors retain the same personnel over several years unless severe business conditions cause a reduction-in-force. When experienced personnel make significant billing errors in favor of the contractor, the auditor has no other recourse but to expand his sampling techniques and review more areas in detail that was previously assumed to be correct.

The contractor's Office Manager or whoever is responsible for the invoice preparation is not typically in a position of authority to intentionally falsify data. So the drive to maximize profits without appearing to be fraudulent must be directed from upper management. The Office Manager may only be doing what he is told. These tricks have succeeded in the past because most owners never take the time or trouble to review contractor invoices.

LUMP SUM AND TIME AND MATERIAL JOBS

A sub-tier subcontractor may be working at the owner's project under two different contracts. One **Lump Sum contract** may be an agreed price to provide and install all insulation. There is no requirement to provide timesheets or supplier invoices since one lump sum price was agreed to when the contract was signed and that amount pays for the insulation and the insulators to install.

A **Time and Material (T&M) contract** with the same subcontractor may provide for all scaffolding labor, lumber and scaffold material. This would be to install and remove all scaffolding needed to install the insulation. When a contractor has a choice of charging items to either job, which would he choose? If common items to both jobs can be fully reimbursed for every dollar spent, it makes no sense for the contractor to absorb these costs under the fixed price contract. Office trailers, pickup trucks, copier machines, cell phones, tools, equipment, or whatever can be rationalized as needed for the scaffold crews.

The auditor must scrutinize the contract and the bid proposals for overlapping costs of trailers, equipment, storage facilities, etc. There may also be a tendency of billing craft labor to both jobs as well. When the fixed price job requires no timesheets, the auditor should sample timesheets for Insulator craftsmen billed to the T&M job. Technically Insulators should report their time to the lump sum project and not to erect scaffold. Erecting scaffold is typically performed by Laborers and Carpenters in the building trades.

Time and Material contracts and Lump sum contracts should be avoided on most projects with the same contractor unless there is a distinct segregation of work scope such as one job is on site and another job is offsite at a remote area, for example. There is a good possibility to have the owner pay for the same item twice – once for items included in the lump sum price and again on the T & M job.

GAMES CONTRACTORS PLAY

If the owner has the Project Purchase Order broken down by line items of work scope with specific amounts of money designated by line item, the contractor should submit his monthly bill broken down by line item to show monthly progress on each phase. As the job progresses, line item amounts are billed and when they reach their maximum amount per the Purchase Order, the owner's Accounts Payable system should reject invoices where the cumulative billing amounts exceed the Purchase Order line items until more money is authorized or a Change Notice is approved.

Invoice payments are stopped because there is no authority to pay additional amounts on certain line items until a Change Order is written. The easy way around that for the contractor is to reallocate his billings to other available funded line items, whether actual work was performed or not on those line items. This may distort the total reporting of percentage complete for the project, which the contractor doesn't care about. He only wants to be paid and will do anything to get his money on time.

This method of identifying work scope items to specific Purchase Order line items is a control to identify areas that are exceeding their budgeted cost in a timely manner. As a result, corrective action can be taken to authorize more funding or identify reasons for the overrun before more money is spent.

1-800-FRAUD

The owner's management is responsible for designing and implementing systems and procedures for the prevention and detection of fraud. The project should establish and publish a hot line for anyone to report inappropriate transactions or behavior at the project. The identity of the caller should remain confidential and anonymous. This phone number should be conspicuously posted on project site bulletin boards. The person being called could be the owner's Manager of Internal Audit or someone not physically present at the project site. The caller may have information about the owner's own personnel.

The hot line also provides a means of reporting violations of safety issues such as workers reporting to work under the influence of alcohol or drugs. Fatal accidents can occur due to carelessness and inappropriate actions by these workers. The owner is ultimately responsible.

RIGHT TO AUDIT

Every contract should have a Right to Audit Clause in the contract stating the owner's authorized representative or designee shall have reasonable access to the contractor's facilities, and shall be allowed to interview all current or former employees to discuss pertinent matters to the performance of the contract.

A contractual clause should clearly state that the contractor's records shall be open to inspection and subject to audit and/or reproduction during normal business working hours. The owner or his designee may conduct such audits or inspections throughout the term of the contract and for a period of three years after final payment or longer if required by law.

REIMBURSEMENT OF AUDIT COSTS

One question I have often asked myself is why should the owner incur the audit costs to have an audit staff at the project to keep everyone honest? Ideally it is fiscally prudent to have assurance that the project costs are accurate and the auditor is also acting in the owner's best interest to facilitate audits by outside auditors and regulatory agencies.

Now what costs does the contractor incur to intentionally overcharge the project? What are the risks and rewards for committing fraud? If the contractor submits the same material invoice twice for reimbursement in the amount of $50,000 and is not caught, he is rewarded a profit of $50,000 plus fees. If he is caught, he admits to the "clerical "error and submits a credit memo as though nothing has happened. Naturally some low paid staff employee makes the perfect scapegoat.

So the risk of getting caught is nothing to the contractor other than being ashamed for a few minutes but it is doubtful he is going to lose much sleep over the matter. More than likely he is mad that he got caught and will attempt to pull off some other scheme to get even.

The contract should have a funding mechanism back to the owner for significant audit findings where the amount of the error exceeds say one percent (1%) of the invoice total or an error exceeding $10,000 on a one million dollar invoice. The reasonable actual cost of the owner's audit should be reimbursed to the owner. Small human errors are dismissed. Large errors should not be tolerated and should be at the expense of the contractor.

IRS GUIDELINES

The contract may not define a reimbursable meal or what is allowed for a mileage rate. When the contract is silent, I have relied on Federal IRS guidelines

HOW TO DETECT CONSTRUCTION FRAUD

to check the contractor's aggressiveness. If certain conditions have to be met to satisfy the IRS concerning reimbursable meals or the current mileage rate, then I have insisted that the contractors abide by the current law. The IRS also provides guidance concerning commuter mileage versus business mileage. Using this approach, I have been successful overturning "That's the way we have always done it" or "That has always been our Policy".

THE CASE FOR A SITE CONSTRUCTION AUDITOR

An experienced Construction Auditor at the project site acts as the eyes and ears of the owner. This individual can provide a valuable service that usually justifies his position with cost savings that offsets his salary many times. The owner's Engineers and Managers are usually focused on other construction details such as schedule, job completion, and target costs. The site Construction Auditor is focused elsewhere and perhaps can be an irritant to the contractors when he asks questions but he also raises awareness that contractors are being watched.

A site Construction Auditor can prevent costly mistakes. On an assignment where the Construction Auditor observed a fuel delivery by a gasoline suppler, the intent was to assure the proper number of gallons was actually offloaded for the amount being billed. How does anyone know if the fuel tanker with 7,000 gallons of fuel drives in and leaves with an empty tanker? During the fuel delivery, the site Construction Auditor prevented gasoline fuel from being loaded into the diesel fuel tanks at the fuel depot. Just imagine the cost of replacing all the diesel engines when gasoline is mistakenly put in their tanks? This error could have resulted in costly delays for the entire project.

DATA MINING OF ELECTRONIC INVOICE FORMATS

Monthly contractor invoices are usually submitted to the owner for payment in both PDF format and hard copy paper. These formats are cumbersome, require substantial storage space, are not easily retrievable, and do not lend themselves to sort and accumulate information for audit purposes.

With paper invoices, the reviewer has to sort through the various sections of the bill page by page and may not even know if the summary total listings are correct without running an adding machine tape to verify totals and cross footings. This is a cumbersome and time consuming task. The contractor may have hidden rows in his summary listing where the total exceeds the actual invoices shown.

When a monthly invoice is submitted in an electronic Excel format, formulas can be reviewed for each footing and there is no need to run an adding machine tape where even the reviewer may make a transposition error. Invoices submitted electronically in an Excel format expedite the audit review process and can detect significant audit findings. An electronic invoice also provides benefits for tracking Lien Waivers from suppliers and reduces errors when entering data into a Lien Waiver Log. As will be described later in this book, the owner should insist that monthly billings be submitted in Excel electronic formats in an Invoice Workbook.

RESOLVING DISPUTES

The Contract should provide remedies to resolve disputes. Contractor invoices are normally reimbursed in full within 30 – 45 days after rendition of the invoice. Disputes should be listed separately after the audit for resolution and not be directly deducted from the current invoice payment. It can be cumbersome to reconcile disputes and partial resolution of disputes when various amounts are short-paid to the contractor over several months. The cleanest bookkeeping method that allows tracking and resolution of disputes would be to resolve the dispute (through a dispute resolution format explained later) and have the contractor issue a Credit Memo for the amounts after the dispute is resolved that results in a refund to the owner. Contractor payments should not be withheld pending completion of the audit.

CHAPTER 2 -
CORPORATE POLICIES

Most company policies have evolved over many years or have been mandated by Federal and State regulations. Written policies provide guidelines for the general welfare of all employees that should be uniformly enforced without providing exceptions to certain personnel.

On Time and Material projects, an owner should require the written policies of all contractors and subcontractors working on the project. **While the administration of all policies is the responsibility of each respective employer, the cost of those policies may ultimately be paid for by the owner.** The contractor's payroll cost flows through to the owner and may include non-billable excused absences. It is up to the owner to review adherence with policies. If the contractor fails to provide written policies, perhaps they aren't written. Administering policies inconsistently can lead to discrimination lawsuits, which could also ultimately cost the owner. Written policies should be requested prior to awarding the contract.

Every company has Corporate Policies that provide a written and defined guidance for employee benefits such as the following:

- Staff Vacation Policy and Accrued Vacations
- Holiday Policy
- Long Term Sick Leave Policy
- Sexual Harassment Policy
- Non Smoking Policy
- Personal Use of Company Equipment and Tools
- Business Ethics Policy
- Relocation Policy
- Per diem Policy
- Company Business Travel Policy
- Automobile Reimbursement Policy
- Termination for Cause Policy

STAFF VACATION POLICY

When a contractor's staff employee take paid vacation for 3 weeks, it is assumed they have been a long term employee who has earned their vacation allowance through continuous employment that exceeds a minimum of say 5 years. While this should be a given, the owner is assuming the financial responsibility for this payroll obligation unless the contract provides that excused absences are non-billable. If excused absences are directly billable, the owner should expect that all policies are strictly followed. Since these costs are "passed through" to the owner, the contractor could be quite generous with the owner's funds and pay out extra vacation days, bonus pay, termination pay, or anything not defined by contract or policy.

The owner has the right to request original hire dates for staff employees and the vacation each employee has accrued. While staff employees may be considered "salaried" and receive 40 hours of pay each week regardless of actual hours worked, the vacation hours actually taken should be known and possibly coded on the payroll register provided to the owner with the billing. Many contractors do not require a weekly timecard to be prepared by staff personnel that is signed and approved by both employee and their respective supervisor. Many projects have no documentation for staff excused absences. As will be explained later, the staff billing rates may include a component for vacation hours and therefore the contractor should not directly bill for these hours.

In addition to providing the contractor's vacation policy, there should be an understanding that avoids key personnel from taking their vacations at the same time in order for the project to progress during their absence.

ACCRUED VACATION

Let's say a staff employee transfers from a previous job where he worked overtime to meet specific completion milestones. The employee postponed any and all vacations last year for the benefit of the previous project and now transfers to the new project with 3 weeks of unused vacation plus 3 weeks of vacation for the current year billable to the new owner. Is the current project liable for six weeks of vacation because he did not "cash out"? More than likely his payroll costs will be included in billings to the new project because the contractor does not have any mechanism to cut him a check other than through his current project. It is up to the new owner's project management to challenge the payment and request a refund. Does the contactor have a vacation policy regarding unused and accrued vacation for staff terminations? How would an owner know if he is being ripped off without adherence to a written policy? If it is unwritten, the contractor can interpret employee benefits literally without any recourse from the owner. The unused vacation should be absorbed by the contractor's overhead and fee that was billed to the previous project.

HOLIDAY POLICY

The contractor should provide a list of paid holidays and if there are any floating holidays for those companies that do not recognize Dr. Martin Luther King's Birthday or the day after Thanksgiving. The owner should be aware of any conflicts with his own recognized holidays. Holiday pay is provided to staff employees plus one top craft general foreman of each discipline such as one electrical general foreman, one painter general foreman, etc. based on the National Maintenance Agreement. The contractor should provide a list of those individuals that qualify. Normally none of the craft employees receive paid Holiday Pay unless they work on that day at double time rates.

LONG TERM SICK LEAVE POLICY

A written policy should define the length of a long term illness or the number of weeks of paid leave. When did the owner assume this liability since this person is not a direct employee? This paid leave should be defined by contract as reimbursable or non-reimbursable or perhaps paid from the overhead adder billed by the contractor with every invoice. Maternity leave is usually defined by law for the number of allowed weeks and is usually a reimbursable project cost billable to the owner for staff employees.

SEXUAL HARASSMENT POLICY

Federal and State laws are very clear about defining sexual harassment and corrective actions concerning sexual harassment in the work place. It should not be tolerated. It may be difficult for management to oversee everything at a construction work site but that is seldom an excuse. Both males and females can work long hours of overtime. The employees will spend more time together than with their own families. Friendships may start that blossom into relationships. Typically harassment is unwelcomed advances, sexual suggestions, or inappropriate touching. The sexual harassment policy should be posted on all site bulletin boards with the consequences up to and including termination.

Management may be defenseless against this occurring at work. However when it is brought to their attention, swift action should address the problem. It becomes an even bigger problem when it is ignored and then management is blamed for a "good old boy" atmosphere and even condoning a hostile workplace.

NON SMOKING POLICY

A construction site can have flammable liquids moved in small temporary containers and stored at various locations that change from day to day. Smoking should only be allowed in clearly marked locations. This policy should be explained during employee orientation and strictly enforced.

PERSONAL USE OF COMPANY EQUIPMENT AND TOOLS

Employees may desire to borrow company equipment or tools for a weekend project at home with the intent of returning the item on Monday. There should be no lending of tools to employees because of the paperwork, the potential of having the item broken or stolen, or not having the item available when needed. This should be clearly stated to all employees. Therefore any company equipment or tool found in the employee's possession when leaving the project could be considered theft. This policy also eliminates any potential claim of personal injury caused by a company tool away from the project.

BUSINESS ETHICS POLICY

Every major corporation should have established written Corporate Business Ethics Policies for directors, employees, and vendors. However, many smaller contractors have no shareholders and have no written policies regarding how employees should deal with owners, other contractors, and suppliers. Without written policies and some guidelines, some contractor employees may interpret situations that could reward their own wallets. After all, "No one said I couldn't do it."

Owners should have high ethical expectations with all their contractors and their employees. It is doubtful that owners can impose their policies on outside contractors that have no written policies. However, contractors should know the reputation of the owner. Likewise the owner can usually limit his contract bid invitations to only those reputable contractors with a history of performance. Unfortunately the owner may have limited experience with second and third tier subcontractors working for the prime contractor.

Example of a Corporate Compliance Policy

A. All Company Directors and employees must exercise the highest standards of personal conduct in their dealings with the Company, its customers and suppliers, government officials and other employees. To the extent that a Director or an employee feels uncertainty regarding the interpretation or application of laws and regulations, questions should be directed to the Company's Legal Department.

Improper Receipts and Payments
- B. All Company transactions are to be based on merit. No Director or employee shall accept funds, in-kind gifts or other items of value that might tend to influence or compromise his or her business judgment.
- C. Directors and employees are prohibited from giving anything of value to Public Officials as an inducement to have a law or regulation enacted, defeated, or to affect the outcome of any governmental proceeding or matter.

Accounting, Internal Accounting Controls, or Auditing
- D. All accounting entries, books, and records shall properly and fairly reflect its assets, liabilities, and results of operations. No fund shall be created or maintained for any purpose that is not properly reflected in its books and records. All employees shall account for every transaction by or with the Company in accordance with the Company's prescribed accounting policies and procedures.

Compliance with Laws, Rules, and Regulations
- E. Directors and employees should respect and comply with all the Laws, Rules, and Regulations of the Federal, State, and Local Governments in which the Company conducts its business.

Conflict of Interest
- F. The Company has the right to expect undivided loyalty from its Directors and employees. Directors and employees must avoid situations where their personal interests could conflict or even appear to conflict with the interests of the Company. Company personnel are prohibited from holding any financial interest or engaging in any business relationship that impairs or prevents the proper discharge of his or her duties to the Company.

Gifts and Gratuities
- G. Directors and employees are prohibited from seeking or accepting, directly or indirectly, personal gain from anyone soliciting or doing business with the Company or from any person or firm in business competition. The only exception would be items of nominal value and then only if the director's or employee's objectivity to perform in the Company's best interest will not be adversely affected.

Company Sensitive Information

H. Directors and employees shall not use confidential information for personal benefit. All proprietary data and technology shall be kept confidential, both during and after the term of employment. Directors and employees have an obligation and duty to protect and safeguard all confidential Company information.

Corporate Opportunities

I. Directors and employees are prohibited from (1) taking for themselves personal opportunities that are discovered through the use of Company property, information or position; (2) using Company property, information, or position for personal gain; (3) directing Company businesses, contracts, funds or other property to family members without fully disclosing the relationship to the Company; and (4) competing with the Company.

Contractors should take reasonable actions to prevent any conditions which could result in a conflict with owner's best interests. These obligations should apply to the activities of contractor employees, agents, subcontractors, etc. Contractors agree to notify an appropriate owner representative such as the Director of Internal Audit, within 48 hours of any instance where the contractor becomes aware of a failure to comply with these previsions.

The owner should have written guidelines for companies that do not conform to a Business Ethics Policy. When irrefutable evidence is uncovered during the course of the project that any business has not complied with this policy, the owner can take action to prevent that business from bidding on future work. This "No-Bidder's List", if condoned by the owner's Legal Department, should be circulated to all procurement and contracting personnel. This should be an action of last resort.

RELOCATION POLICY

This policy should define the contractor personnel who qualify for relocation, the number of house hunting trips allowed, the number of days of temporary living expenses provided, provisions for a temporary rental car, if necessary, airport parking, etc. Any policy exceptions for non-salaried craft workers such as key superintendents or anyone who does not qualify for this policy, should be requested in writing and provided prior written approval from the owner.

A contractor had a policy of paying employees $300 to compensate them for new drapes, house plants, utility deposits, and other out-of-pocket expenses during their move. These expenses do not have to be documented with receipts.

Because of the loose terminology in the contract, the contractor paid both the husband and his wife the $300 or $600 total since the policy stated "employee". Both were employees of the contractor. It wasn't the contractor's money and beside the contractor gets fees on every dollar spent.

It was the auditor's viewpoint that the benefit was intended to be paid per household, not per employee when both work for the contractor. Why would a married couple, both of whom were also employees, incur twice the cost for houseplants, drapes, utility deposits, etc.?

While the owner cannot re-write policies for the contractor, there should be some "reasonableness" concerning employee benefits. While not all disputes are easily resolved, it appeared that the contractor did not consider married couples being paid twice for this benefit as employees. The policy was amended after the owner disputed the payment. Everything, although small, is negotiable. Apparently this policy was never questioned on previous projects. Several married couples were paid for this allowance and it was not just $300 in question.

PER DIEM POLICY

Per diem is understood to include the additional expenses incurred living away from home or basically having two residences. To qualify for per diem, the project should be at least seventy-five miles from the employee's tax home, and require an overnight stay. The IRS code does not specify the number of miles but it is commonly accepted that a distance of 75 miles as a reasonable distance to justify payment of per diem allowance. Information on per diems and the IRS published rates for various cities in the U.S. can be found at www.gsa.gov and www.irs.gov.

The term per diem is Latin for "per day" and the policy should provide a defined amount of money that an individual can spend per day to cover living and traveling expenses related to work. When the per diem amount is agreed to, there is usually no need to submit actual receipts for hotel and meal reimbursements. This is considered a Non-Accountable plan. The policy should also define when the daily allowance is not paid such as vacations, holidays, or days when the employee is at his tax home and not incurring these costs. The policy should clearly state the job classifications that are entitled to per diem.

Many projects will pay the full seven days even if the employee does not work on Saturday or Sunday but is home. Employees may argue that they have to reserve the motel room for the full seven days even though they are not there on weekends. If they vacate their room on the weekend, it may be rented to someone else and they won't have a place to stay the following week. Therefore, they argue, the per diem should be compensated based on seven days.

The owner is not forcing anyone to live in a motel. One could point out that $105 per day for a 30 day month is $3,150 and an apartment rental is considerably cheaper. The employee makes the decision of where to live, which may also be based on the length of the assignment. After all, the employee knew where the job was located when he took it and he should have considered his own accommodations if per diem payments would be limited.

Some projects will have technical support vendors, consultants, Safety and Quality Assurance personnel, and others that are entitled to per diem pay. Some of these personnel do not have to be at the project every day and may arrange to work 4 days per week at 10 hours each day. An auditor may dispute paying per diem for seven days each week when temporary living costs are incurred for only four days. The per diem Policy should address these situations.

Personnel on per diem may be required to attend meetings or training at a city away from the project as part of their job responsibilities. They submit a trip expense report for the lodging and meals while attending these meetings. It could be argued that part of their per diem payment already includes a provision for meals and therefore they are not entitled to a second reimbursement for meals. Is this an example of double dipping?

The biggest heartburn for any auditor regarding per diem is paying this allowance to employees when the employee incurs no out of pocket expenses. If the contract is "Cost Plus", the actual cost to the employee is zero when he is at home. Per diem has been paid to employees for vacation weeks, Holidays, Christmas week through New Year's Day, weekends at home, and beyond his/her termination date. There should be a clear understanding what the owner will allow for reimbursable per diem.

The terminology in an employee per diem policy could be phrased as follows:

> "Contractor agrees to reimburse employee/consultant $_____ per day worked, up to a maximum of five (5) days per week, for qualifying per diem expenses working for contractor on a temporary basis (expected duration of less than 12 month) at its Client _____. Employee is required to provide evidence of work on days for which per diem payments are made. Employee further agrees that, should employee receive per diem payments in excess of the deemed substantiated amount, employee will notify the contractor and return any excess amounts."

The same per diem policy for the prime contractor should apply to all subcontractors and any exceptions taken by the subcontractors should be clearly stated at any pre-bid meeting.

COMPANY BUSINESS TRAVEL POLICY

The contract should define what business travel is reimbursable by the owner and should require an expense report stating dates of travel, purpose for traveling, and all supporting documentation that is requesting reimbursement for travel including airfare tickets (not itineraries), rental cars receipts, airport parking, actual meals receipts, etc. The Travel Policy should state when spouses and families are allowed to travel at company expense. It should also clearly limit travel to immediate spouses and children and not grandparents, aunts, uncles, relatives, etc.

Reimbursable mileage by car should be defined, which is usually the allowable per mile rate set yearly by the Internal Revenue Service. Long term car leases should require the prior approval of the owner.

Itineraries can be prepared by an airline or travel agency and are available on the Internet. Itineraries are not adequate documentation that the trip actually occurred. Itineraries may provide some supporting documentation but actual receipts are required.

The owner should not reimburse for first class airfare unless there are some unique extenuating circumstances or only if prior approval is given.

The owner should not reimburse for rental car refueling services. This is a service where the renter returns the car without refueling and the rental company, such as Avis or Hertz, bills the fuel at perhaps twice the going rate for gasoline to compensate for this service. The renter should refuel the car near the airport at the market price for gasoline.

AUTOMOBILE REIMBURSEMENT POLICY

The contract or bid documents should provide the mileage rate for company reimbursed trips for those personnel who use their personal vehicles and do not have company cars or trucks. The mileage rate typically is the same as the IRS allowance that can change two or more times per year. The policy should also state what mileage is considered reimbursable such as monthly trips home to the employee's permanent residence and reimbursable business trips.

TERMINATION FOR CAUSE POLICY

Every project will have rule infractions that are serious enough to merit termination. Employees have the right to know the rules and they should be clearly stated and posted at the project to provide consistent guidance. While it doesn't seem necessary to publish common sense infractions, our society and our legal system requires published warnings.

Reasons an employee could be terminated for cause include, but are not limited to:

1. An intentional act of fraud, embezzlement, theft, or any other material violation of law.
2. Intentional damage to company assets.
3. Intentional disclosure of company's confidential information contrary to company policies.
4. Intentional breach of any company policy.
5. Willful conduct that is materially injurious to the company, monetarily or otherwise.
6. Intentional and willful violation of safety rules that may cause serious injury or death to co-workers.
7. Falsification of records.
8. Excessive absenteeism and tardiness.
9. Failing a drug or alcohol test.
10. Insubordination

All company policies should be clearly explained and be provided in writing to all new employees at orientation with a signed statement from the employee that they have read, discussed, and understood all company policies as a condition of their employment.

CHAPTER 3 -
CONTRACTOR PROFIT

Contractors are in business to make money on each project. They wouldn't be in business if it weren't for their projects. Everything they do therefore is attributable to the "Project". As a result of this thinking from a contractor's point of view, everything is billable to the project, including overheads that may be provided for in their fee structure. If a contractor bills 15% overhead fee plus 10% profit fee on all direct costs, they are recovering all their indirect costs such as their home office buildings and maintenance, executive salaries, and general office expenses as well as making a profit. However, the more items they can directly bill to the owner means the contractor spends less of their 15% overhead allowance. As a result, more dollars flow to their bottom line – the Profit and Loss Statement.

Any reviewer should have a keen eye for any home office costs such as executive cars, gasoline for executive cars, copier rentals, fax machines, and cell phones charged to the owner that are at the Home Office. Any direct cost billed to the owner should be directly attributable for the benefit of the owner's project in order to be reimbursable.

MISSING DOCUMENTATION

On large Time and Material Cost Plus projects, all expenditures by the contractor should be supported with a receipt, a subcontractor's invoice, a material supplier invoice, a payroll report, etc. There must be something tangible to document that the transaction took place. "No ticket, no laundry."

It would not be unusual that a receipt copy was not printed because the printer jammed due to staples, the copy was illegible because of poor toner cartridges, the receipt was lost, or the amount of detail is too voluminous to include in the invoice package, such as 100 daily weight scale tickets at a rock quarry.

The contractor may be testing the owner's auditor or reviewer to see what documentation won't be challenged. If the reviewer only randomly samples the documents, the contractor may never be asked for documents on certain expenses. If the dollar amount is immaterial, both parties may agree not to provide copies in the invoice bundle but provide arrangements to review documents for audit purposes at the contractor's Home Office or at the project. Such arrangements may save not only substantial and unnecessary copying costs but also the staff labor each month to make copies.

The reviewer should "tick and tie" the invoice summary to the supporting detail to assure listed expenses are legitimate. Missing documentation should be questioned and be provided when administrating Cost Plus contracts.

FEE ON FEE

Let's say a prime contractor is working with the owner on a $200 million Time and Material Cost Plus project. The contract allows 5% fees to the prime contractor on sub-tier contractor work. The prime contractor is responsible for all aspects of the project to include scheduling, execution, and co-ordination of sub-tier contractors.

Now let's say a significant portion of the work worth $45 million is performed by an Insulation sub-tier contractor. The sub-tier contractor coordinates his work with the prime contractor and mobilizes as the work is ready to proceed after being notified by the prime contractor. The majority of the insulator's daily work is independent of the prime contractor. The sub-tier insulator also is entitled to overhead and profit fees.

The prime contractor includes the sub-tier insulator billings in his costs and collects a 5% profit fee of $2,250,000 on an aspect of the work where he has little responsibility, oversight, or management. The owner is paying fees to the prime contractor that could be saved if the sub-tier insulator were designated as a general contractor reporting directly to the owner and not through the prime contractor. The prime contractor has done little or nothing to deserve collecting such a large fee. By setting up this arrangement, the owner saves $2,250,000 for fees (5% of $45 million) paid to the prime contractor.

The owner should consider directly contracting large portions of the work as well as purchasing major equipment items that will be installed in order to avoid paying the contractor for functioning as a purchasing agent. The owner should also consider providing some items and services to the project that will avoid paying additional fees to the contractor each month for such common items as electrical and water service, trash removal, office trailers, portable toilets, gang boxes, and common construction items such as hard hats, safety glasses, etc.

DIRECT COST OF THE WORK

The Direct Cost of the Work is defined as costs incurred by the contractor in the performance of the Work at rates not higher than the standard paid at the place of the Project except with the prior consent of the owner.

- **Labor Costs** – Prevailing wages and benefits defined by union labor agreements of construction workers directly assigned and employed by the contractor at the site or, with the prior owner's approval, at off-site prefabrication workshops.
- **Salaries of supervisory and administrative personnel** – authorized personnel performing their duties at the job-site location directly for the benefit of the project. All contractor personnel providing service or advice from time to time will be considered covered by the contractor's fee.

Project staff working at the field office includes project management, site superintendents, project engineering, project accounting, and administrative and secretarial services. The project field offices are located at the jobsite. From small to mid-sized projects, the on-site staff will be limited to the General Superintendent, and possibly the Area Superintendents and trade Foremen. For projects that are large and complex, different degrees of project administrative personnel will also be located at the site. These staff positions may include the Project Manager, Project Office Manager, Project Engineer, Project Accountant, and Project Secretary. Regardless of the project size be it $1 million or $25 million, the plans and technical specifications will be different but the language, procedures, and policies are virtually the same. The specific mix of responsibilities will have more to do with the individual's disposition, talent, and experience than with any formal job description.

Support personnel – Those staff employees defined as purchasing, expediting, or transporting of materials or equipment required for the project but only for the time required to support the project.

- **Indirect Labor costs** – defined as workmen's comp insurance, taxes, contributions, assessments, and benefits required by law or collective bargaining agreements and other benefits required by law such as sick leave, vacations, holidays, medical and health benefits, and pensions provided they are directly attributable to the project labor costs.
- **Overtime premiums for hourly workers** – the incremental cost of overtime or shift differential with the advance written approval of owner. If the contractor incurs overtime costs as a result of an inexcusable

delay or re-work that is the contractor's fault, the overtime premium or shift differential expense portion of the payroll expense may be considered non-reimbursable, depending on contract language.
- **Subcontract costs** – payments made by the prime contractor to the subcontractor based on the requirements of the subcontracts.
- **Material and equipment installed in the project** – Material, such as lumber, concrete, steel beams and equipment, such as that used or installed as the scope of work for the project. This material and equipment may be sales tax exempt if it adds to productive capacity or output of an assembly plant, increases the megawatt output of an electrical generating plant, or is used to meet the Clean Air Act requirements, for example. These sales tax exemptions vary by state.
- **Material and equipment temporarily used in the project** – Material that is consumed or rendered useless for the purpose of building the project may be rendered as scrap at project completion. It is not part of the final structure or scope of work defined by the project. Equipment may include air compressors used to operate air powered tools and will be returned to the contractor's storeroom and used on their next project.
- **Miscellaneous costs** – Other items not included above that are necessary for the construction to proceed such as building permits, insurance premiums, tools, safety supplies, hardhats, safety glasses, etc. A clear definition of miscellaneous costs should be defined by the contractor and owner and who is responsible for providing certain items.

COSTS NOT DIRECTLY ATTRIBUTABLE TO THE WORK

These exceptions should be defined by contract to avoid later disputes where the contractor bills the owner and is surprised when exceptions are disputed. This is only a brief sample of abuses that could occur.

1. Salaries and other compensation of contractor's personnel assigned to their principal office or at other locations other than the project site.
2. Expenses of the contractor's principal home office and other offices other than at the project site.
3. Cost of home office expenses to include home office computer services and other services such as payroll support, general ledger and job cost accounting, estimating, scheduling, and payroll processing not directly attributable to owner's project.
4. Rental costs of equipment and machinery at the contractor's home

office to include home office trucks and automobiles for executive staff.
5. Staff overtime billed to owner but not actually paid to employees.
6. Overtime worked without owner's prior approval except in the case of emergencies to save life or loss of property.
7. Self-insurance unless it can be directly attributable to owner's project and owner is named beneficiary. In no case should self-insurance costs exceed the comparable cost of purchasing conventional insurance.
8. Employee bonuses will not be considered directly reimbursable but are considered to be covered by the contractor's fee.
9. First class air fare or the use of company owned private airplanes. Contractor is to exercise prudence when incurring costs attributable to the project.
10. Safety awards, attendance awards, gas cards, gift cards or other incentives not previously approved by owner without specific measureable milestones and an acceptable Safety Policy.
11. Trip home policy should state the number of trips allowed per qualified employee per month when a staff member's permanent residence is over, say 200 miles from the project. Reimbursable expenses include air fare, parking at the project's airport, and defined expenses directly related to the trip. Home meal expenses and car rentals at the home destination are not allowed. The policy should identify which employees are qualified per company policy.
12. Hotel room service, in room movies, entertainment costs for contractor staff, contractor Christmas parties, or New Year's Eve parties are not billable.

Every project has allowed expenses based on industry practice and established contractor policies, which should be provided to the owner before signing the contract. The contractor's policies and benefits should be part of the contractor's bid package.

Unfortunately the auditor has to interpret the contract and existing policies to determine what is reasonable and prudent for the owner to reimburse. Very seldom will the contract provide enough details for gray areas concerning employee travel, overtime, and bonuses for every situation. Rarely does the owner's Auditor have input or access to the contract terms and conditions before the contract is signed. It has been the author's experience that the contractor is very liberal when spending Other People's Money and he will not seek prior approval before spending it. He would rather plead his case after the fact knowing most owners will give in.

MANAGEMENT SUPPORT

The Auditor or Reviewer should have the full management support from upper management when disputing invoices. If the owner does not support the Auditor and consistently sides with the contractor, the Auditor will soon start letting expenses slide through because, "What's the point? It will get reimbursed anyway."

All the Auditor can do is to bring to Management's attention the results of his audit based on his interpretation of the contract and why there is a contract dispute. Upper Management will have the final authority and responsibility to explain the project's success or failure.

CHAPTER 4 -
MATERIAL

The following chapter discusses several ways permanent material and equipment can be overcharged to a project. The owner's responsibility is to deter fraud and reduce inflated material costs by imposing adequate controls.

ORIGINAL VENDOR INVOICES

The prime contractor will purchase items to be installed by placing orders with vendors. Likewise, the subcontractors will also purchase material they are responsible for under their respective contracts. The vendors will ship the item(s) and render the original invoice to each respective contractor. The contractor will pay the original invoice from his funds and provide a copy of the original invoice in his monthly invoice bundle when he seeks reimbursement plus his fees. The owner will not normally receive the original invoice but only copies of originals when working with a Time and Material Contract.

A good internal control for any business, including the contractors, would be to stamp "VOID" and record their voucher number on the original invoice when processing payments for material, rentals, and subcontractors. This voucher number and date would provide an audit trail and prevent that same original invoice from being copied multiple times and be submitted to the owner for reimbursement in consecutive months. Rarely would an owner's Accounts Payable clerk compare the previous month's supporting documentation with the current month's billing for duplicate charges. Most contractors do not indicate the voucher number, payment date, or any indication of payment on the original invoice. They may record an accounting stamp with the correct accounting distribution charged to various cost codes. The point is that the owner could potentially reimburse the contractor several times for the same material invoice submitted in consecutive months unless there are controls in place to prevent these errors. One method for detecting these duplicate invoices is discussed later in this chapter.

Ideally the owner should insist on the same internal controls for the contractors as the owner has for his business when buying material – segregation of duties and a three way match of the Invoice, Purchase Order, and Receiving Report submitted with each request for payment. The contractors may refuse to provide this amount of documentation because they don't have the manpower, the monthly billings for reimbursement bundles would be too voluminous, or they don't prepare formal Purchase Orders or Receiving Reports. The owner must determine the acceptable amount of risk when contractors refuse to change their normal business policies or procedures to satisfy the owner's requests.

BOGUS INVOICES

The owner should always be aware of potential bogus companies set up by someone as a valid business that provides a product or service to the project. These bogus companies will render an invoice that may not have an invoice number, a post office box instead of a street address, no phone number, no Company Logo, and no tax identification number. Perhaps a name similar to an employee's name on the contractor's staff will be the company's name or have the employee's mailing address. The Yellow Pages or the Internet should be searched for potential bogus companies where the invoice appears to be suspicious.

Another indication of a bogus invoice is a product or service that cannot be verified as being received or a hand written invoice that is illegible. Most ethical companies provide a computer generated invoice indicating shipping dates, specific descriptions such as part numbers, ship to addresses, and correct math extensions. The contractor(s) should use pre-numbered Purchase Orders and pre-numbered Receiving Reports that can be traced and accounted for.

ALTERED INVOICES

A contractor buys material on behalf of the owner and submits a copy of the material invoice as proof of payment along with other monthly expenditures that are summarized on his monthly invoice to the owner. The owner typically has 30 days to review the contractor's invoice and reimburse the contractor.

Adjustments by the contractor on a supplier invoice may have been made because of quantity shipped differences, retention not deducted, sales tax rate errors, or pricing errors. These adjustments may be penciled changes to the invoice with no initials indicating who made the changes. When an adjustment or deduct is made, the amount paid to the supplier may be different than the original invoice. As a result, the supplier's "Accounts Receivable" will always show a "Past Due" balance until he creates a Credit Memo or he receives payment from the contractor.

The contractor makes penciled changes to the invoice to expedite his reimbursement from the owner rather than requiring a corrected invoice. The reasons for the penciled changes may not be evident and the reviewer is left to wonder why any changes were made in the first place. The changes eventually have to be reconciled before the supplier provides a final Release of Lien Waiver. When the Vendor receives his second check for another purchase, he may apply the payment to the oldest invoice first and therefore shows other transactions as past due. The application of payments to invoices creates a nightmare of reconciliation back to where the problem started. The contractor should provide a clear audit trail that can easily be followed by any reviewer rather than creating a mystery for everyone by adding or deleting amounts with pencils. It should be remembered that any amounts not paid in full may be subject to a late payment penalty that the owner may have to pay.

THE OWNER IS ENTITLED TO A CORRECT INVOICE- PERIOD!

The original invoice is a permanent record of project costs that should be clearly legible. The owner should not tolerate penciled changes or adjustments made (by whomever) that cannot be explained from material suppliers, rental companies, or subcontractors. The best way to avoid disputes that can linger for months or years is to insist on correct invoices before payment. Both sets of books for the Vendor (an Accounts Receivable) and contractor (Accounts Payable) should agree. Trying to recreate payments after changes have been deducted and repaid is an exercise in frustration and time consuming for everyone.

Let's say a subcontractor invoices for his first monthly progress payment without deducting $10,000 for retention. The prime contractor deducts the retention before processing and pays only 90 percent to the subcontractor. Each subsequent invoice has to be "adjusted" for retention and previous payments. The 10 percent retention is contractual and should be corrected by the subcontractor after notification. The final release of retention has to be invoiced by the subcontractor, who has already billed 100 percent. As far as he is concerned, his system cannot generate another bill for a completed contract to recognize previous deductions taken by the prime contractor. Then the prime contractor has to input a modified subcontractor invoice (designated with a letter -A after the invoice number) to obtain his final 10 percent from the owner. Other deductions to invoices may be for sales taxes, cash discounts, math error extensions, returned material, etc. The point is that all invoices should be contractually correct and no modifications should be necessary.

A Final Release of Lien Waiver should be obtained from all major contractors, subcontractors, equipment dealers, and material suppliers that validates that all their invoices have been paid and no outstanding disputes remain.

OWNER PROVIDED VERSUS CONTRACTOR PROVIDED

Major permanent plant equipment for the project like furnaces, presses, tanks, and air quality equipment installed have to be purchased by someone, such as the owner, the contractor, or perhaps the design engineering firm. These major items are the identified scope of work items in the contract. It must be remembered that the contractor bills for actual cost plus overhead fee and profit fee markup. Say their overhead fee is 15% of direct cost plus 10% profit of direct cost. The contractor collects $1,250,000 in fees for a piece of equipment costing $5,000,000 by merely placing a Purchase Order. This may be an extreme example but the owner can save this amount by providing the item directly through his own Purchasing Department. Owners should always be aware of these saving possibilities.

OWNER PROVIDED CASH ADVANCES

When an owner provides funding to the contractor in a monthly advance, the contractor is said to be cash neutral during the month. The contractor is using the owner's money to pay the bills and therefore avoids borrowing funds on large construction projects. This advance can be included in the monthly bill or billed on a separate invoice at the end of each month for payment purposes and reversed with a Credit Memo the following month. In this way the separate invoice and Credit Memo for advances cancel each other out and the actual invoice reflects the net additional amount due or credit above or below the Advance per the following:

January Actual Spent	$5,425,325.00
Plus February Advance	+$5,000,000.00
Total	$10,425,325.00
Less January Advance	-$4,000,000.00
Current Amount Due	$6,425,325.00

The actual amount spent by the contractor in January was $1,425,325 more than his January advance. This shortfall is being billed plus an additional $5,000,000 to spend during February.

The contractor should plan his next month's expenditures when submitting his advance. If the contractor consistently overestimates his advances each month and underestimates actual expenses (over $1,000,000), he has collected too much money from the owner to pay his bills. The owner has an obligation to review these reconciling amounts each month to gauge how well the contractor is forecasting his work. Bear in mind this over collection is interest free money for the contractor. If the contractor is experiencing slow economic times, he may be financing his cash requirements with the owner's money. The goal is to have a relatively small payment due the contractor after all his bills for the project are paid. The owner should have accurate cash flow projections throughout the project.

MATERIAL CASH DISCOUNTS

On time and material jobs, the contractor is the Purchasing Agent for the project and may place orders that provide cash discounts for prompt payment, usually less than 30 days. These cash discounts should be passed back to the owner as credits against material costs. If the contractual terms state "actual costs" are reimbursable, the material cash discounts represent a reduction of material costs. Not passing the discounts back to the owner means the material was priced higher to the owner than actual cost. Contractors want to retain these funds for themselves because of their due diligence to expediently process payments. However paying bills on time is an expected business practice and the owner is also funding all payroll costs to perform this function. This provision should be made clear at bid awards to avoid any confusion.

Contractors have little incentive to capture cash discounts if they cannot pocket these funds. In order for them to process payments within 15 days to qualify for the discounts, the invoice process may have to be expedited between the project and their home office where the checks are written. As a result of this extra effort and stress, the contractors may negotiate payment terms of net 30 with suppliers that eliminate cash discounts. This may be especially true if a "Monthly List of Discounts Lost" is furnished to the owner that makes the contractor look bad. After all, higher material costs mean contractors collect higher fees and profits. When these tactics become obvious, the owner may express his dissatisfaction with these business practices by lowering any incentive bonuses included in a Key Performance Indicator Bonus or a Customer Satisfaction Bonus in the contract.

MATERIAL SUBSTITUTION

Owners should be aware of being billed for a higher quality of material than was actually received. Vendors may deliver products which do not meet the plans or specs. An owner's representative should periodically verify material receipts on a sample basis.

Some welding rods used for certified welding material need to be stored correctly in storerooms with controlled temperature. Welding ovens provide this protection for welding rods. Quality Control Certification is provided by the manufacturers and suppliers. An owner's representative or QA/QC personnel should periodically verify this documentation and if this material was correctly installed at critical locations.

Some contract change orders may be written as an alteration to the original project scope where work was eliminated and therefore material is not needed that was previously purchased. Was the owner given proper credit for the lesser quality material or material returned to suppliers? Was the material returned to the contractor's warehouse for use on another project without giving the owner proper credit?

MATERIAL DELIVERED TO ALTERNATE ADDRESSES

Most material invoices from vendors indicate the "Ship To" address on the invoice. Some invoices may indicate shipment to the contractor's home office or an unknown address. Unless the contractor has fabrication shops at his home office, there should be little reason for a vendor to ship material to a contractor's home office, unload it, and have it re-shipped to the jobsite by the contractor. If this is commonly used material that could be used on any jobsite such as lumber, the owner may be paying for material used on other projects. The owner should question this practice of double handling of any material.

MATERIAL RETURNED FOR CREDIT

Some invoices may have notations on the receipts that the material was damaged in shipment and is being returned to the vendor. Look for any indications of refusal to accept the material because of quality or quantity mistakes. A contractor may include the bill in the current month in order to be compensated and may not include the Credit Memo the following month. If the transaction is being disputed, the contractor should not include the bill for reimbursement until all items are resolved.

An unscrupulous contractor may buy material, bill the owner, and subsequently return the material in order to receive a credit. The owner may never know items have been returned and has no way of validating credit due the project. Any reviewer should be aware of unusual quantities continuously being billed that far exceed reasonable quantities. A Material Return Log, which summarizes pre-numbered material return transaction forms, should be approved by an owner representative for each shipment returned to vendors and the reason in order to track expected credit memos. Poor performing vendors should be disqualified from future business.

Remember that an invoice reviewer or auditor can only make a judgment of appropriate project costs based on documentation provided by the contractor. If the contractor intentionally fails to provide a credit memo or pass the credit to the owner, there is no way of detecting this oversight unless the auditor is present at the jobsite daily and is knowledgeable about material returns from the warehouse. Project management and on site auditors should be aware of any trucks remaining at the warehouse after normal receiving hours of operations or activity occurring on weekends when the warehouse staff is minimal.

INVOICE DATES

Vendor invoices submitted with the current month's billing should have current dates from the current or immediately preceding month. If invoices are dated older than 3 months prior, there is a good possibility it may have been submitted in a prior billing to the owner. Any outdated invoices should be a red flag for reviewers to question why the bill was misplaced.

FAVORED VENDORS

Some contractors win bids because of their expertise in construction and/or they submitted the lowest bid. Sometimes these contractors are from another state. Over the years they develop relationships with suppliers from their home town and continue to do business with them at each project. Commonly supplied items such as piping, electrical cable, and paint can be procured locally. The contractors may award Purchase Orders with their home town buddies because they play golf together and not because they offer the lowest prices. When freight, which may be billed separately from the material, is added to the cost of the material, the low prices may no longer be a bargain. The reviewer should consider the buying practices of the contractors if they are not favorable to the owner. These favored suppliers may also be providing kickbacks or incentives to the contractor for doing business with them. Prices can be verified on the Internet for most construction items and the contractor can be challenged to justify their procurement practices.

UNAUTHENTIC INVOICES

One contractor sent a Purchase Order through in their monthly billing instead of an invoice. This is not acceptable documentation since a Purchase

Order can be cancelled. The excuse they provided was to allow a cash flow to the contractor in anticipation of the invoice and have cash in hand before having to pay the bill.

Reviewers should always be conscious of the format of the documentation to assure they are valid invoices. Both the invoice and the Purchase Order may have similar formats with quantities, descriptions, and dollar amounts. The only problem is that Purchase Orders do not have Invoice numbers, shipment dates, or a sales tax amount added.

MATERIAL FROM AFFILIATED COMPANIES OR CONTRACTOR'S CENTRAL WAREHOUSE

A contractor may provide common safety items such as hard hats, welding supplies, or safety vests from his warehouse at his home office. The "Invoice" charging for these items may be nothing more than an Excel spreadsheet listing quantity, description, price, and total bill. The contract may provide some latitude to obtain supplies at considerable savings compared to third party vendors. The owner assumes that costs will be competitive or lower than if provided by third party suppliers. The contractor can have this material delivered on a weekly basis with no shortages or delays to the construction schedule but there can be significant flaws with this procurement process.

Most companies have a "material handling" charge or internal fees to cover storeroom overheads. This hidden cost may be buried in other parts of the invoice under labor so the cost of the material does not reflect its' true cost. When the contractor says the material is being provided at their "cost" doesn't mean the price they paid for it but what another division of the company charged them including the inter-company fees.

Forklift drivers and truck drivers at the home office charge their labor to bring this material to the jobsite. The contractor is shifting his "overheads" to the project rather than absorbing these labor hours himself. These costs are hidden elsewhere within the invoice and may not be reflected in the unit price shown on the invoice to compare to other suppliers.

Was the material actually received in the quantity billed? The owner is asked to pay for material that may or may not have been delivered. A Receiving Report should be signed by an owner representative on the date of receipt, otherwise the contractor is writing himself a blank check based on some ink spots on a piece of paper. Some owners may say its' not worth the time or effort to track small items such as gloves, safety glasses, or untraceable supplies but these items can add significant costs over a three year project. This is a situation where there is no audit trail for the transaction.

Sales taxes paid on material from the contractor's warehouse may also be a concern for the owner and any State Tax Auditor. Was State Sales Tax paid on the items at the time of original purchase or should tax be collected from this project since the owner is the end user? The owner may be held liable for any additional Sales Tax found during a Tax Audit. State Auditors will require proof that Sales Tax was paid on the original transaction or was the material bought tax exempt for resale and the final transfer of title was between this contractor and this owner and therefore tax is due on the final sale? The contractor will not pay these additional taxes out of their pocket as a result of an audit but claim it as an additional project cost subject to fees and markup.

What benefit does the owner obtain by procuring material from the contractor? Is the contractor providing outdated scrapped items left over from other projects in order to clean out his warehouse? If material is returned to the contractor's warehouse, will the project receive a Credit Memo? What record exists for material returns? Are unusually large quantities being shipped to the job near project completion to extract even more profit?

Whenever a contractor provides material from sources that cannot be verified, a cautious auditor should ask the question, "Why is the project getting such a good deal?" Maybe it's not such a good deal after all.

MATERIAL/SUPPLIES BILLED TWICE TO THE PROJECT

The contractor submits all supporting documentation monthly to request reimbursement for his expenditures on large Cost Plus projects. If this information is provided with vendor invoice copies and/or a pdf file, most reviewers would be sure to scan the copies to assure there is no missing documentation. However what if the same invoice for lumber is submitted in two different months and therefore billed twice to the owner? How would anyone catch this mistake since most invoices are reviewed independently each month with little or no time to refer back to previous bills? Unless the reviewer has a photographic memory that reminds him of seeing that invoice before or unless the invoice dates are not in the current billing period, these payments are easily overlooked and the contractor profits by collecting additional money that he did not spend based on what appears to be a "clerical error".

The following steps may detect duplicate vendor invoices that were billed to the owner in two or more different months. If the contractor submits all of his supporting documentation in an Excel format, all the payments made to vendors would be listed by vendor name, vendor invoice number, vendor invoice date, and amount in a format that is easy to audit.

ROBERT LOUIS BECKER

A. Material Invoice Billing on Excel Spreadsheet- Not Sorted

	A	B	C	D	E	F	G
		Prime Contract Invoice No.	Date	Vendor	Invoice No.	Amount	
	1	65053	1/5/xx	Acme Co.	04321	$45,000	
	2	65053	1/5/xx	Ace Supply	1569	$235	
	3	65053	1/5/xx	Lamar & Sons	5625	$8,365	
	4	65053	1/5/xx	Claude's Tools	1469	$9,666	
	5	65054	2//xx8	Home Depot	8536	$444	
	6	65054	2/8/xx	Lumber Liq.	9935	$44,005	
	7	65054	2/8/xx	Blake's Safety'	7533	$15,000	
	8	65064	3/11/xx	AB Lumber	69325	$35,000	
	9	65064	3/11/xx	Turner	3428	$9,500	
	10	65064	3/11/xx	Safety R Us	8346	$750	
	11	65065	4/5/xx	Rex's	65043	$422	
	12	65065	4/5/xx	Blake's Safety	7533	$15,000	
	13	65065	4/5/xx	Turner	3428	$9,500	
	14	65065	4/5/xx	Zack's Gas	4582	$1,355	
	15	65065	4/5/xx	Lamer & Sons	5625	$8,365	
	16	65065	4/5/xx	Acme Co.	04321	$45,000	
	17	65065	4/5/xx	Office Depot	9632	$935	
	18	65065	4/5/xx	Taylor Parts	2317	$19,000	

The above short table is a small example that could represent hundreds of invoices submitted for reimbursement over a period of several months or years.

Steps:
1. Merge monthly contractor or subcontractor invoice material summaries into one Excel file and label the first file tab as "Universe". This tab represents the entire sample selected.
2. Create and insert a column in column A and label as "Prime Contractor's Invoice Number". This identifies each line item to a source billing document. This is essential to provide an audit trail for anyone else to verify the audit findings. Copy the source billing invoice number down to each respective line entry in the worksheet.

3. Copy "Universe Tab 1" to Tab 2 and save. This preserves the original documentation (Tab 1) for later reference and tab 2 becomes the working copy.
4. On Tab 2, eliminate any subtotals, text, or unnecessary information that was included in the original data. This new spreadsheet on Tab 2 should be one continuous listing in rows of all invoices from suppliers for this test sample.
5. It is sometimes beneficial to highlight different months in different colors (like yellow) to review the sorted data later. After sorting, the highlighted color differences will help locate the duplicates compared to visually scanning an otherwise white worksheet.
6. Capture all data in the worksheet by clicking the mouse and holding while dragging the mouse through all the data from the top left to the bottom right of the worksheet for sorting. This is the entire worksheet that will be sorted. Then, at the top of the spreadsheet, click on **Data, Sort, Ascending**, and select a column for sorting in ascending order, such as invoice numbers. The column to be sorted may be by invoice number, invoice date, vendor name, or amounts. After the sort, save the file. This sort will arrange whatever data needs to be reviewed in rows from top to bottom of the worksheet. When sorting data, it is important to highlight all the data to assure everything was sorted.

B. Sample Material Invoice Billing Excel Spreadsheet- Sorted by Invoice Number

A	B	C	D	E	F	G
	Prime Invoice No.	Invoice Date	Vendor Name	Vendor Invoice No.	Amount	Formula
1	65053	10/5/xx	Claude's Tools	1469	$9,666	
2	65053	10/5/xx	Ace Supply	1569	$235	=If(e2=e1,"True")
3	65065	1/5/xx	Taylor Parts	2317	$19,000	=If(e3=e2,"True")
4	65064	12/3/xx	Turner	3428	$9,500	=If(e4=e3,"True")
5	65065	1/5/xx	Turner	3428	$9,500	=If(e5=e4,"True")
6	65053	10/5/xx	Acme Co.	04321	$45,000	=If(e6=e5,"True")
7	65065	1/5/xx	Acme Co.	04321	$45,000	=If(e7=e6,"True")
8	65065	1/5/xx	Zack's Gas Co.	4582	$1,355	=If(e8=e7,"True")
9	65053	10/5/xx	Lamar & Sons	5625	$8,365	=If(e9=e8,"True")
10	65065	1/5/xx	Lamar & Sons	5625	$8,365	=If(e10=e9,"True")

11	65054	11/8/xx	Blake's Safety	7533	$15,000	=If(e11=e10, "True")
12	65065	1/5/xx	Blake's Safety	7533	$15,000	=If(e12=e11, "True")
13	65064	12/3/xx	Safety R Us	8346	$750	=If(e13=e12, "True")
14	65054	11/8/xx	Home Depot	8536	$444	=If(e14=e13, "True")
15	65065	1/5/xx	Office Depot	9632	$935	=If(e15=e14, "True")
16	65054	11/8/xx	Lumber Liq.	9935	$44,005	=If(e16=e15, "True")
17	65065	1/5/xx	Rex's	65043	$422	=If(e17=e16, "True")
18	65064	12/3/xx	AB Lumber	69325	$35,000	=If(e18=e17, "True")

7. In a far right hand column, insert the formula: =IF (e2=e1, "True"). This formula compares all data in column e (which are invoice numbers, for example), row by row with the previous row. This formula simplifies the search for duplicate numbers.
8. Copy and paste this formula to the bottom of the worksheet and it should change the comparison with the next row to the preceding row as you copy, i.e., e3=e2.
9. When both data rows are identical, a "True" statement will appear. In other words, all identical dates, identical invoice numbers, or identical amounts will show as "True" in their respective columns.

C. **Sample Material Invoice Billing Excel Spreadsheet- Sorted by Invoice Number Revealing Duplicate invoices submitted for payment on different Prime Contractor Invoices.**

A	B	C	D	E	F	G
	Prime Contractor Invoice No.	Invoice Date	Vendor Name	Vendor Invoice No.	Amount	Formula
	65053	10/5/xx	Claude's Tools	1469	$9,666	
	65053	10/5/xx	Ace Supply	1569	$235	FALSE
	65065	1/5/xx	Taylor Parts	2317	$19,000	FALSE
	65064	**12/3/xx**	**Turner**	**3428**	**$9,500**	FALSE
	65065	**1/5/xx**	**Turner**	**3428**	**$9,500**	**TRUE**
	65053	10/5/xx	Acme Co.	04321	$45,000	FALSE
	65065	**1/5/xx**	**Acme Co.**	**04321**	**$45,000**	**TRUE**
	65065	1/5/xx	Zack's Gas Co.	4582	$1,355	FALSE
	65053	**10/5/xx**	**Lamar & Sons**	**5625**	**$8,365**	FALSE

65065	1/5/xx	Lamar & Sons	5625	$8,365	TRUE
65054	11/8/xx	Blake's Safety	7533	$15,000	FALSE
65065	1/5/xx	Blake's Safety	7533	$15,000	TRUE
65064	12/3/xx	Safety R Us	8346	$750	FALSE
65054	11/8/xx	Home Depot	8536	$444	FALSE
65065	1/5/xx	Office Depot	9632	$935	FALSE
65054	11/8/xx	Lumber Liq.	9935	$44,005	FALSE
65065	1/5/xx	Rex's	65043	$422	FALSE
65064	12/3/xx	AB Lumber	69325	$35,000	FALSE

Each True statement should be reviewed for identical numbers in sequential months and why the True statement appeared. Perhaps a typo mistake occurred in the data. List the exceptions and review the original invoices to verify the exceptions. Copy the invoices as documentation for your work papers. Write the prime contractor's invoice number and date on their respective copies to indicate the source of the billing that was rendered to the owner.

Repeat these steps on tabs 3 and 4 of the Excel worksheet for sorting by different criteria like identical dollar amounts. This could potentially identify the same payments if the invoice numbers have been altered or transposed in the data. Also be aware of any names that were changed from one month to the next such as AB Chance changed to Chance, AB. The sorting will not detect this as a duplicate.

Organize the work papers for presentation to the contractor as a dispute.

Caution: Some invoices may be split to different budgets, departments, or work packages with accounting corrections appearing in subsequent months and they may not be duplicate billings.

Sample of Sorting Material Invoices from Supplier

A	B	C	D	E	F
Prime Contractor Invoice No.	Date	Vendor Name	Vendor Invoice No.	Amount	Same Invoice #
65053	11/5/2011	Acme Co.	42615049	$15,000.00	
65053	11/5/2011	Acme Co.	42615049	$15,000.00	True
65064	12/5/2011	Acme Co.	42615049	-$7,500.00	True
65064	12/5/2011	Acme Co.	42615049	-$7,500.00	True
65064	12/5/2011	Acme Co.	42615049	$15,000.00	True

In the above sample, the same invoice number 42615049 from the Acme Company appeared on contractor invoices 65053 and 65064 in two consecutive months. After reviewing the source documentation, it was determined that an accounting adjustment to different work orders was made by the contractor and no actual duplicate charges were billed. The total amount of the invoice was $30,000. This would not be an exception for disputing unless the owner has an issue with the accounting adjustment.

This method of detecting duplicate invoices can be used for subcontractor billings, third party equipment rental companies, duplicate contractor owned equipment numbers, or any labor billings where there is a potential overlap of pay periods on daily timesheets. It can easily sort through several months of invoices efficiently while eliminating unnecessary data to focus on only the exceptions.

The intent is obvious when duplicate invoices are submitted to the owner and these errors are found on a persistent basis. There is an intentional attempt to extort additional funds from the owner in the hopes the errors would not be detected. The evidence mounts when the billings that were duplicated are significantly larger than the smaller normal transactions. For example, there is a smaller chance of getting caught submitting a $25,000 invoice twice rather than a $5,000 invoice five different times. It only provides more evidence that other areas of the project may need more scrutiny and perhaps more auditors.

VENDOR JOB SITE TRAILERS

On large construction sites, a vendor may set up a material semi-trailer on the project to expedite issuing hard hats, gloves, safety glasses, and small dollar items that don't justify a lot of manpower to track. The material is "sold" at the time it is checked out of the trailer. A storeroom attendant from the vendor is on site and issues the material upon request. A monthly bill is prepared each month based on quantities issued and a price list. Sometimes the attendants' salary is split 50-50 with the project paying half.

The auditor should review these sign-out sheets to verify material is being signed for by the individual receiving the items. Sometime a general foreman may sign-out a large quantity based on new hires that started work. These sign-out sheets should be well documented and provided with the billing. Sign-out sheets with just hash marks or check marks and no indication of who obtained the material is a license to steal. Quantities billed each month should also be checked for reasonableness. Can a jobsite use 5,000 gloves in one month when there are only 200 craftsmen employed?

NON-CONSUMABLE ITEMS

Every project will need office furniture, computers, refrigerators, microwave ovens, overhead projectors, and other items that will not be consumed. These items will be left over at the end of the project and can be sold for salvage or used on the next project the owner has planned. There should be no confusion that the owner paid for and owns these items. Owner asset tag numbers should be permanently installed on these items.

Contractors may attempt to take these items with them when they demobilize, especially laptop computers. A running inventory list prepared in an Excel format should be created by the owner from the invoices submitted by the contractor and subcontractor(s) requesting reimbursement for these items. This list should have traceability back to the contractors invoice number, date, item description, and cost. Sub-tier contractors will also submit requests for payment for these items and those items should also be listed by subcontractor invoice number, date, item description, and cost with reference to the prime contractor's bill. An Excel format worksheet heading across the columns could be as follows:

NON-CONSUMABLE LOG
Contractor name/Subcontractor name
Invoice Number
Material Supplier
Vendor Invoice number
Vendor Invoice date
Description
Quantity
Unit Price
Total
Sales Tax %
Amount with Tax
Comments

Non-consumable items include:
Desks, chairs
Conference tables, folding chairs and tables
Planning tables and racks
Fire proof file cabinets
Book shelves
Supply cabinets
Copiers

Fax machines
Laptop computers, printers, and modems
Refrigerators, coffee machines
Clocks and radios
Radios, beepers, or pagers

Example of Field Office Equipment Log
Acme General Contractors

Invoice #	Date	Vendor	Vendor Inv.#	Description	Serial #	Total Amount
43665	1/20/11	Smith Furniture	29255A	8 - tables		$800.00
8788	4/30/11	Files R Us	36896	2 file cabinets	A45899, A45863	$80.00
129888	6/15/11	Miller Office Supplies	224533	1 HP Fax Machine	96358444	$750.00

Since these items are being used at a construction project, they will endure more abusive conditions than in a general office location. Therefore used furniture can be obtained at considerable savings rather than purchasing brand new items. A used furniture store can offer considerable quantity discounts just to make a sale.

If the owner is planning multiple projects, there should be a reasonable transfer price agreement for these items that benefits both projects where the completed project is credited for the fair value of the item and the new project is charged. A storage facility should be considered if there is a gap between projects of several months or years. This will avoid selling the items for scrap value and re-purchasing the same items later at higher prices.

SALES TAXES

Sales Taxes added on material purchases vary by state. Generally material purchased for a project may or may not be taxable while Labor is usually never taxable for Sales Tax Purposes. Some states may provide a Sales Tax Exemption for material used directly to expand the production of electricity or if the project is located within an Enterprise Zone. A Certificate of Exemption is normally issued by the owner to be furnished with the Purchase Order to inform the vendor not to bill sales taxes. These Exemptions should be used whenever available in order to save considerable construction costs. Exempt material becomes part of the new facility. It does not exempt other material used for temporary construction facilities or roads.

Sales taxes are usually imposed on the final sale to the end user for a product such as an automobile and not on each individual part from each parts supplier to the manufacturer. The owner has the responsibility to determine the taxability of material and pass that information to all contractors, subcontractors, and vendors. The owner will ultimately be held responsible for any Sales Tax Audit and pay any additional amount the state deems has not been paid.

The following table may provide some assistance as a general guidance for various items used in construction.

Contractor Purchase Category	Missouri Taxable or Non-Taxable	Comments
General building maintenance materials and supplies	Taxable	General cleaning supplies
Chemicals/Lubricants used for contractor equipment	Taxable	
Computer Hardware used for contractor operations	Taxable	
Engineering Services	Non-Taxable	Generally labor is not taxable
Furniture and Fixtures	Taxable	
Office/Administration Supplies	Taxable	
Lumber	Taxable	Temporary use lumber is taxable. Permanent structure lumber may qualify as exempt.
Professional Dues and Fees	Non-Taxable	
Rental Equipment - no operator	Taxable	Taxable, however the vendor may have embedded the sales tax in the rental price. If a registered vendor does not show a separately state sales tax on the invoice, the vendor paid tax at the time of purchase.
Rental Equipment with operator	Non-Taxable	Rentals with an operator are treated as a nontaxable service.
Safety Items	Taxable	
Tools and Maintenance Supplies	Taxable	

ROBERT LOUIS BECKER

CANADIAN SALES TAX

With more and more trade with Canada, it is becoming more common to have material shipped from Canada with Canadian sales tax added to the invoice. Most Americans are not familiar with this tax or the correct tax rate. On a recent project, due to the size and fast track schedule of the project, the contractor shipped sheet metal to Canada for fabrication into blower air ducts in order to utilize available capacity by an affiliated company. The invoice may be in Canadian dollars or U.S. dollars.

The Canadian sales tax may be referred to as PST or TPS with a rate of 7.5% applied to the material cost. PST is the initials for Provincial (State) sales tax and TPS is a Federal Tax, which in French means Taxe sur le Produit et Services (Tax on the product and services). It is like a value added tax, but it does not apply to goods sent out of the country. Both taxes replaced a manufacturer's tax. The TPS is also known as GST in English or Goods and Services Tax.

These taxes are intended to be collected on finished goods consumed in Canada. Any material exported from Canada should not have this tax added. Since the material was provided to their factory and only labor was used in Canada, there were no material costs incurred in Canada either. The contractor billed the project $6,692 for this tax. The project received a full refund only after this tax was disputed by the owner. The contractor was willing to pocket this tax as additional profit. What appeared to be a legitimate charge was not a project cost.

The Internet provides valuable information with one click away. I cannot emphasize enough how often this valuable tool including searches on Google saved considerable time and money for the owner. The owner should consider Internet access for their staff on major projects.

STOLEN TOOLS

At a construction site, auditors found brand new tools in their original boxes in the dumpster next to the warehouse. They could not understand why anyone would throw away brand new tools that have never been used rather than returning them to the vendor for credit. They later learned that the storeroom attendant on the back shift and the trash hauler were brother-in-laws. This Trojan horse method of stealing tools was almost foolproof since no one ever checks on trash leaving the project. Owner's representatives should periodically inspect trash prior to collection for inappropriate discording of valuable material, scrap, and/or inventory.

A painting contractor was at the project every day of the week. Some painting required spraying and it was best to perform some spraying when the construction site was less populated to avoid workers coming in contact with the paint spray or fresh paint. Painting was performed on backshifts and on weekends. The large construction site was experiencing heavy tool loses for rather expensive tools such as air powered rotary drills, air grinders, and compressors. How could these tools walk out the gate and not be detected? One rumor was that the stolen tools were removed in the empty 55 gallon paint drums the contractor shipped back to his home office. There was an opportunity to steal the tools by breaking into gang boxes on backshifts and fencing the tools later. Remember Rule Number One? Don't assume anything!

On a large construction project a contractor was using two different Cost Accounting codes for tools – one for new tools purchased and one for replacement tools. As a result, two different inventories were created for identical tools. This accounting for replacement tools was not an owner requirement. After all, who cares which tool is used to complete the job? This only duplicated the inventory and accounting, which served no purpose. Reviewers should be suspicious of any record keeping that is not mandated by Regulations or Generally Accepted Accounting Principles.

On the same project, workers were seen leaving the project with tools in their back pockets at quitting time. Anyone can unintentionally put a tool in their back pocket and forget about it so the owner was not trying to prove theft or accuse anyone of wrong doing. The owner organized a group of Union Stewards and Superintendents at quitting time near the exit and requested anyone with a tool to deposit it in a box until they returned to work the next day. There were no terminations or disciplinary action taken. The intent was to reduce the number of repetitive small tools walking out the gate. Large projects should consider random searches of lunchboxes by Security Personnel and metal detectors at construction gates.

WELDING RODS AND TIPS

A welding rod is inserted into a welding tip and is melted to fabricate the weld with the use of a welding machine. The welding rod becomes part of the finished steel that is bonded together. In some states, the welding rod is considered permanent plant and is tax exempt whereas the gases that burn the weld at high temperatures are consumed in the weld and are taxable.

Welding tips or nozzles are subject to wear and tear. These tips are not expensive and are replaced on a regular basis. Contractors may charge the project for these welding tips as they are welding supplies, in their opinion. However, if the project has a small tools adder based on labor hours worked, this item can be considered a small tool and compensated for in the small tools adder and not directly billable. The reviewer should review the terminology in the contract for the definition of a small tool and reimbursable welding supplies.

BULK ISSUES

Small disposable items such as grinding wheels, raincoats, or cotton work gloves are not worth the paperwork to track for each individual who was issued these items. These types of items may be bulk issued upon arrival and with one clean sweep of an accounting entry; there is no audit trail or traceability. This type of "Clearing House Accounting Method" should be reviewed periodically for abuse and whether the frequency of purchases and quantities purchased is reasonable based on the size of the workforce, the weather conditions, and the number of satellite storerooms. When the gloves are issued in bulk to the satellite storerooms, the reorder point has been hit and another maximum quantity is purchased. The owner's representative should perform unannounced spot inventory verifications on the date small disposable material is received at the warehouse and on the date material was transferred to satellite storerooms.

PAINT BRUSHES

Typically paint brushes are not very expensive but there is a tendency to clean the paint brushes after painting. This is a simple task for latex paint that cleans up with water. However with other paints the cleaning supplies, such as turpentine, may pose more hazardous environmental problems for disposal than the value of the brush. In those situations, the Owner may consider disposing of the paint brushes rather than cleaning them.

The following is an Audit Program for steps that could be followed performing project procurement reviews. The amount of resources needed to implement these audit programs is dependent on Project management but usually the amount of recovery as a result of this audit substantiates the effort.

AUDIT PROGRAM
Date 20XX

Project/Location:
Process: Project Procurement
Objective: Ensure material is procured efficiently, at lowest cost to meet construction requirements.

No.	Risks	Control Techniques	Audit Procedures	Workpaper Ref.
1	Proper segregation of duties does not exist.	Duties associated with purchasing, processing of accounts payable, and inventory management should be properly segregated.	Prepare a Segregation of Duties Matrix and test for completeness and accuracy. Test to determine if the following duties should be segregated: Create PO, Authorizing PO, Receiving goods, Prepare vouchers, Approve vouchers, Access to vendor master file, Counting inventory, Adjusting inventory. If these duties are segregated, it will be difficult for a single employee to commit a false-billing scheme.	
2	Lack of documentation for payment of invoices.	A 3 way match of Invoice, PO, and shipping documentation should support all disbursements.	Review invoicing process and ensure proper documentation exists for all disbursements. Examine contractor's job cost detail to determine where the contractor purchased a significant amount of material during a sample period (one to three months). Significant material purchased typically includes concrete, structural steel, reinforcing steel, (rebar & mesh), and/or lumber (for rough carpentry forms, etc.)	

No.	Risks	Control Techniques	Audit Procedures	Workpaper Ref.
3	Invoices are not properly cancelled.	All invoices should be stamped or properly marked to prevent reprocessing/ duplicate payments. Ideally voucher numbers should be included on the original invoice once processed. A process must be in place to detect and prevent duplicate payments. Supporting documents for the payments should be originals and must be effectively cancelled after payment to prevent accidental or intentional reuse. No payments should be based upon a verbal or written statement unless the vendor has been pre-approved for such.	Sample a selection of invoices and ensure invoices are clearly marked cancelled or have voucher numbers shown on invoice. Due to the high number of copies of original invoices used to substantiate project costs, all contractors should institute this control.	

No.	Risks	Control Techniques	Audit Procedures	Workpaper Ref.
4.	Price quotations from material suppliers are not itemized with unit prices for each specific item to be purchased.	"Lot pricing" quotations will not be considered sufficient substantiating detail.	Review competitive quotes obtained from material suppliers. Compare to purchase orders issued to suppliers. Compare to invoices received from suppliers for compliance with agreed prices, etc. Where cash discounts earned accrue to the Contractor rather than the Owner, be alert for quotes, which include excess cash discounts (i.e. more than 2% discount). Review invoices and related material delivery tickets for job description, delivery address, authorized invoice approvals, appropriate acknowledgement of receipt for use at the site, etc. Review contract for specific "basis" or "measurement method". Review for conversion factors (quoted in tons but billed in pounds).	

No.	Risks	Control Techniques	Audit Procedures	Workpaper Ref.
5	Returned material is not credited to project.	All credit memos should be approved by an authorized supervisor. Credit memos must be uniquely identifiable and traceable.	Select a sample of vendors based on materiality or risk profile and determine the frequency and dollar amount of credit memos. Ensure each memo is properly approved and explained. Be alert for indications of material being returned for credit to vendors with no corresponding credit to job cost. Be alert for material provided to Subcontractors with no corresponding back charge. Be alert for material provided to Subcontractors with lump sum firm prices and no credit is received for material provided by GC. Determine if Voids or material returns are approved by management. Determine if pre-numbered forms are used for material or equipment returns. Determine the reason for returning material such as poor vendor quality, contractor errors in estimating project needs, or material damaged in shipment.	

HOW TO DETECT CONSTRUCTION FRAUD

No.	Risks	Control Techniques	Audit Procedures	Workpaper Ref.
6.	Excess material is purchased and will not be used.	Contractor's original take-offs for material is compared to actual material purchased.	Purchases of material over and above reasonable amounts anticipated for scrap or waste should be the responsibility of the Contractor at no cost to Owner. Investigate any significant overages in quantities of material purchased. Compare the as-built quantity take-off to the actual quantities purchased and billed to the project.	
7	Contractor may bill for material from stock at "costs" higher than the actual cost or fair market value. Contractor may not issue fair credit for unused material or consumables which have been returned to his warehouse.	Items and quantities are "priced" from competitive sources.	Review list of items furnished during test period by GC from inventory or stock. Determine if quantity and prices are reasonable. Compare items charged with available third party sources using internet or manufacturer's catalogs. Summarize results. Determine if quantity furnished was actually installed, consumed, or still available on site.	

No.	Risks	Control Techniques	Audit Procedures	Workpaper Ref.
8	Contractor may purchase material from a non-competitive and/or related party supplier which could result in excessive costs, short shipments, or lower quality material.	Review of competitive bids to substantiate prices.	Review list of items procured from related party supplier, including freight costs compared to local supplier, and other justification for transacting business. List frequency of transactions. Determine if lowest overall cost was provided to the project, factoring in availability and project requirements.	
9.	Documents are not properly retained. Records may not be available for external parties, legal, tax, or audit purposes.	Ensure Record Retention Policies exist and are complied with.	Request a copy of the Records Retention Policy and select a sample of POs, invoices, and shipping documents and test for compliance. Most documents should be original; excessive photocopied documents should be scrutinized. Alterations, questionable handwriting, or illegible signatures are a red-flag.	

No.	Risks	Control Techniques	Audit Procedures	Workpaper Ref.
10.	Fraudulent vendors are set-up.	Vendor set-up requires proper approval and a due-diligence process to ensure vendor information is accurate and truthful.	Review vendor set-up and determine if vendors are approved and how existence of vendors is verified. Look for red-flags: PO Box Number No tax id Phone number – "answering service" or no phone number Vendor name is very similar to existing vendors Numerical fields that have all 9s, 0s, or 1s. Vendors with activity in only one given month. Compare vendor addresses to employee addresses. Also, look for residential addresses.	

CHAPTER 5 -
CONTRACTOR'S CONSTRUCTION EQUIPMENT

William "Willie" Sutton (June 30, 1901 – November 2, 1980) was a prolific bank robber stealing an estimated $2 million over his forty year career. Sutton is famously known for answering a reporter, who asked why he robbed banks, by saying "because that's where the money is." Sutton later denied ever having said this phrase.

The construction equipment owned by a contractor and rented to a project is "where the money is". Equipment rental is the one construction element that can generate more profit for contractors and subcontractors than any other cost element. Labor, material, and subcontractor costs are reimbursed to the contractors at actual cost and have limited fee markups (profits) defined by the contract. By comparison, construction equipment enables the contractor to generate cash flow every month just by parking their equipment on the project and keeping it on the project as long as possible even after it is needed. The owner and the reviewer should always be aware of how well the contractor manages his equipment as well as equipment rented from third-party vendors. Construction equipment audit plans that can be used for field verification can be found at the end of this chapter.

Equipment Definition – Bulldozers, cranes, tractors, pickups, frontend loaders, welders, and other major items that are not permanently installed but are needed to erect buildings and/or processes incorporated in the project.

This construction equipment can be owned by the Contractor(s) or rented from third-party equipment distributors with the intent it will be removed from the project after the anticipated use.

Contractor Equipment Managers

All major contractors will have experienced Equipment Managers that can generate considerable profits for their company by shipping as much equipment as they can from their warehouse in order to generate cash flow, whether or not the equipment has any intended use. This equipment will show up on the project as soon as the ink is dry on the contract. This would include office trailers, storage trailers, gang boxes, portable toilets, and tools. Remember these items are not billable while they are located at the contractor's home office and do not produce any income until they are relocated to the project.

One contractor delivered a motor grader to a project even though road maintenance was not in their scope of work. It would have been more prudent to hire a motor grader contractor/vendor on an as needed basis for snow removal or road repairs rather than provide a piece of equipment that was rarely used. The owner should have insisted that the motor grader be removed from the project or have the contractor provide justification why it was delivered.

THE PROJECT EQUIPMENT LOG

An Equipment Log should be established by the owner to include digital photographs taken by the owner's rep upon delivery and departure of each item that may provide evidence against later claims by the contractor/lessor. For example, who can contest a broken windshield repair when there is no way of disputing where or when the windshield was broken? It is presumed to have occurred on site when it could have occurred back at the contractor's yard and he is avoiding responsibility for his own repairs. Digital photos should be taken when the equipment is ready to leave to provide evidence of the existing condition to avoid potential repair claims. These photos should include date and time the photos were taken.

A Project Equipment Log can be prepared on an Excel Spreadsheet and maintained by an owner's representative for each Contractor/Subcontractor with the following information across the heading of each column:

> Column one: Arrival Date
> Column two: Contractor's Equipment Item Number and Equipment Type
> Column three: Description-Year-Make-Model-Gasoline or Diesel
> Column four: Third Party Rental Company Name (if any)
> Column five: Equipment license number (if any)/Odometer/hour meter reading
> Column six: Daily, Weekly, & Monthly Rental Rate
> Column seven: Expected Need

Column eight: Anticipated Departure Date
Column nine: Cost to pick up and deliver
Column ten: Date Picked up/Pickup number/Carrier
Column eleven: Comments

A physical inspection with photos taken upon arrival will dispel any attempts to bill pre-existing damage repairs to the new project. The hour meter/odometer reading will provide a starting point for monthly usage. The hour meters can be read on Sundays by owner reps once per month when the equipment is not in use to determine if the equipment is idle most of the month. The expected departure date puts the contractors on notice that these dates are expected to be met rather than provide extended revenues far beyond the need for the equipment.

It is not unusual to be billed by the third party vendor when the equipment is refurbished and inspected after it leaves the project. This appears to be billing for maintenance at the beginning, during, and at the end of rental regardless of the hour meter or usage. If one vendor seems to be abusing the normal contract terms, the owner can request the prime contractor to place future orders with other competitors.

BILLING PRACTICES

The following practices are used in the construction industry unless there are specific written contractual exceptions written in the lease contract.

Time Basis of Rates: It is a general practice in the industry to base rates on one shift of 8 hours per day, 40 hours per week or 176 hours per month (22 working days).
- Some lessors have monthly rental rates based on 160 hours per month (4 weeks at 40 hours per week) or 20 work days.

It is important to know the basis for the monthly rental rates to address potential claims for extra costs should the project change from a normal shift of 8 hours per day to extended shifts of 10 hours or more on a weekly basis. The project may also go to double shifts with two crews working 8 or 10 hour days per shift. The contractor may claim extra usage that was not quoted during the bidding process. The owner should review the contractor's claims for extra costs such as an additional 20-50% on all equipment. The project schedule in the original planning stages and pre-bid meetings should determine the established work week.

Cost of Repairs:
- Tractor Equipment and/or Rubber-tired Hauling Equipment:
  o Most lessors require lessees to bear all cost of repairs regardless of the cause.

- Many lessors measure tread wear to determine charges to lessees for tire wear.
- Non-Tractor Equipment:
  - Lessors usually bear the cost of repairs due to normal wear and tear.
  - Lessees bear the cost of other repairs.
- Cranes and Shovels:
  - Lessor usually bears the cost of repairs due to normal wear and tear.
  - Where equipment may be subjected to unusual abuse or wear and tear, lessors require lessee to bear the cost of all repairs regardless of cause.

The large amount of money invested for these items requires preventative maintenance on a scheduled periodic basis. The owner of the equipment, such as a third party company, will dispatch a qualified mechanic to the project and will bill for all travel time, parts, filters, working hours, motel, and meals associated with the visit. These costs can easily add up quickly to several thousand dollars per trip if the lessor's business office is several hundred miles from the project. The only recourse for the owner is to return the equipment as quickly as possible when it is no longer needed to minimize these costs.

Every piece of equipment should be in good working order prior to delivery. A scheduled preventative maintenance billed shortly after arrival at the project may not be the owner's responsibility because of usage or abuse at a prior project. If a scheduled preventative maintenance inspection after every 500 hours of usage requires a visit after only two weeks following delivery, the current project may be charged inappropriately. This may not avoid paying the scheduled maintenance but should set the tone for future rentals from that distributor if the owner or prime contractor disputes the charge. The owner has no way of validating the 500 hours of prior usage unless they request the maintenance records from the vendor, which may be altered or "not available". Usually the rental contract specifically states this provision that has been agreed to by the prime contractor. However, it should be a normal business practice to thoroughly inspect and repair any damage to large pieces of equipment caused by the previous project when it is returned. These repairs should be billed to the previous project.

There is also an element of safety. Should the major equipment item be involved in a catastrophic accident and OSHA determines the cause was failure to adequately maintain the item, the owner could ultimately be held responsible. Preventative maintenance records should be kept on each major piece of equipment to defend any liability claims for personal injury.

Operator Costs:
- Rental rates do not include the cost of an operator or oiler (if needed). Operators are normally furnished by the contractor and paid through his craft labor payroll.

Normal Wear and Tear:
- Normal wear and tear is expected to result from the use of equipment under normal circumstances provided the equipment is properly maintained and serviced.

It has been the author's experience that some labor disputes and grievances with the contractor can result in vandalizing equipment such as ripping up the seats. These repairs are costly since the replacements are factory brands manufactured only by Caterpillar, John Deere, etc. The contractor is responsible for the daily execution of the contract as well as the behavior of all personnel under his direction. The owner should contest these charges on the basis that those behaviors will not be tolerated. Those responsible for intentional vandalism should be removed from the project.

Fuel and Lubricants:
- Lessee is responsible for costs of fuels and lubricants.
- Lessee is also responsible for preventative maintenance such as oil changes and lubrication while renting the equipment.

Condition of Equipment:
- Equipment is to be delivered to the lessee in good operating condition and returned in the same condition less normal wear.

Freight Charges:
- Lessee pays for freight or drayage charges to and from destination. This includes additional labor charges for loading, unloading, dismantling, and assembly.

Rental Period:
- Normally, unless addressed specifically in the Purchase Order or Contract, the rental period starts when equipment leaves the lessor's warehouse and stops when returned to their warehouse.

Note: Some contracts specify that the rental period ends when the third party provider **is contacted** to pick up the item. This date can be crucial as many distributors may not be able to pick up the item for two or three weeks due to other priorities. It should be documented who was contacted, date, and time of the agreement. This could avoid several thousand dollars of additional rent for an item that is not needed and not being used.

Any reviewer should be aware of the contractor billing for rentals for a complete month even though the equipment left two or three weeks early. Without an auditor or owner's representative on the project, there is not much evidence to dispute the contractor's bill unless a third party carrier picks up the item and provides an invoice. That invoice will indicate the date of the service but does not always provide the equipment number or description of the item removed from the project. The Project Equipment Log, if maintained by the owner, should provide date of departure to resolve disputes. If the contractor uses his own trucks to remove equipment off the project, it is less obvious from the documentation what was removed. Another advantage of an Equipment Log is to establish when an item is no longer eligible for repairs that may be billed to the owner.

Payment and Taxes:
- Rentals are payable in advance of the month from the day of arrival or date shipped.
- No taxes are included in the rental rates.

The rental rate presumably recovers the sunk cost of the investment, depreciation, and obsolescence. Rarely is a discount provided to the owner for equipment items that are inoperable for repairs during the month. However, the owner has negotiated in good faith to have operable equipment that can perform in a safe manner. When the contractor or vendor provides poor performing out-of-date equipment that presents a safety hazard, the owner has the responsibility to take aggressive action to have the item(s) removed.

A valid dispute to consider is if a replacement rental item (a bulldozer) is needed to meet a critical path schedule while the original bulldozer is being repaired. The owner is then paying for two bulldozers instead of one and incurring twice the cost. While the contractor may not concede the point, it will be well worth bringing this to his attention. It is not always obvious by reviewing invoices that the second bulldozer is to replace the first bulldozer. To any reviewer not at the project, the assumption is that two bulldozers were needed to meet schedule.

Insurance:
- Industry practice requires the lessee to furnish the lessor a certificate of insurance prior to delivery of the equipment. This should be the responsibility of the contractor's Superintendent.

Sales Taxes on Rental Equipment

Depending on applicable local State Sales Tax Regulations, it is anticipated that the buyer of the equipment pays the sales tax at the time of purchase and therefore is no longer obligated to collect sales tax on the same item. Some states exempt the tax on the item if purchased for rental by a rental vendor so that tax can be collected on the rental rates each time the item is leased. The reviewer should consider the latest applicable state tax laws if sales taxes should be billed by vendors. Equipment provided by the contractor should not have additional sales tax billed, which should be clear from the bid documents. The contractor may collect for the sales tax but pocket the money as additional profit and not remit that tax to the state.

Knowing the components of the contractor equipment rental rates may reveal a hidden sales tax component within each equipment rate that is collected by the contractor and kept by him as additional profit. Contractors may be reluctant to provide this detailed information since it may also reveal hidden maintenance components, which may be billed separately, and fuel components, which are also billed separately. On a recent project where this information was requested, it was discovered that the contractor was including an 8% sales tax within each hourly rate plus a 20% profit adder. The sales tax rate should have been zero (non-taxable) and the 20% profit adder was not allowed per contract.

If equipment is rented from a leasing company in another state and delivered to the project by the vendor to a different state, there may be taxes due at the vendor's home state or where the sale was consummated. A Missouri vendor leasing equipment to a project in Illinois may not recognize the Illinois sales tax requirements but is obligated to collect and remit taxes to Missouri. The taxability can vary based on who picks up and delivers the equipment (the vendor or the contractor). Most contractors and subcontractors are not familiar with sales tax laws and will pass along any taxes as part of their project costs. The owner's staff on any large construction project should have access to their Tax Department staff familiar with sales taxes to resolve these issues.

RENTAL RATE COMPARISONS

Comparison of rental rates with outside equipment distributors or the Associated Equipment Distributors (AED) Green Book may indicate the contractor's rates are unreasonable. Competitive market rental rates are available from www.equipmentwatch.com, which includes access to the AED Green Book. Published since 1949, the AED Green Book provides average rental rates for construction equipment from hundreds of rental dealers nationwide. The AED Green Book also provides engine sizes, capacities, and manufacturers that are common in the industry. It is available for purchase on the web and well worth the investment. Electrical equipment rates, such as conduit pipe benders, can be found through the National Electrical Contractors Association or N.E.C.A.

The owner or reviewer should run a comparison of the contractor's Equipment List against the monthly rental invoice to determine if items are being charged to the project that have not been identified by contract and do not have a contractual rental rate. These discrepancies should be listed in an Audit Dispute for resolution. Likewise a comparison of the Contractor's Equipment rates with the actual billing rates should be made and listed as an Audit Dispute if discrepancies are found.

THIRD PARTY RENTAL RATES

You may remember Wile E. Coyote always obtaining equipment, such as rocket-powered roller skates, from the Acme Company so he could catch the Road Runner. These Acme Company items are an example of rental companies that lease items to contractors or individuals on a short term basis when ownership does not justify the capital to invest and keep on a permanent basis.

Daily, weekly, or monthly rental rates

Third party rental companies such as the Acme Company structure their rates for long term use rather than daily use as the following example shows:

Description	Daily	Weekly	Monthly
Rigid 300C Threading Machine	$150	$300	$675

This rate structure provides an incentive to the lessee to keep the machine longer or a full month compared to only a few days. The daily rate multiplied by 22 working days in a typical month would be $3,300 if rented on a daily basis or $2,625 more compared to the monthly rate. Likewise the weekly rate multiplied by 4 weeks per month would be $1,200 or $525 more compared to the monthly rate. The longer equipment can be rented out, the more cash flow is generated for the rental company. This rate structure is important when equipment is returned before the end of the month and the monthly rate is either prorated by a percentage or if the weekly and daily rate is used to account for each day on the project. Some rental companies wishing to maintain a good working relationship with the project will adjust the billing to the lowest beneficial cost in the hope of retaining more business in the future.

The rental rates from third party companies should be compared to rates provided by the contractor. The contractor's rates should always be lower since the equipment typically is rented for longer periods of time (maybe two or more years) and he is assured of recovering all costs plus collect fees. The third party equipment dealer has higher costs of overhead and idle time that has to be recovered on each piece of equipment. When third party rental rates are obtained for identical equipment, they provide an excellent bargaining tool for the owner to negotiate prices down to competitive "market rates".

Contractor Rental Rate Components

The owner should have the right to review the contractor's components that determine the rate structure for major pieces of equipment. The rates would include a depreciation factor, a preventative maintenance factor, fuel (if any), and perhaps a replacement factor when the item becomes obsolete. This breakdown should provide enough information to determine if a maintenance factor is included in the rates, say $1.25 per hour rented. The craft labor payroll should be checked for any employees billed to the project as mechanics or oilers to determine if the owner is being charged for a full time person that maintains the equipment while each rental rate includes a factor for this same cost. The contractor should not be entitled to collect for both. Also there should be some review of any equipment such as lube trucks being rented to the project that can be considered part of the maintenance factor. Hidden profit fees may also be a component included within each monthly rental rate that is also being billed on total monthly project costs.

Contractor Table of Equipment Rates

The contractor should submit prior to the bid award a list of his equipment rental rates including make, model, year, engine size, diesel versus gasoline, assignments, odometer readings, etc. This information is available but more than likely he may not want to share it with the owner. The more information that is provided can lead to more questions from the owner.

An Excel spreadsheet of all equipment provides an excellent audit tool to sort by item description and by rates. It may detect identical items listed twice in different sections of the contractor table of equipment rates. It could also disclose ambiguities in their rates as follows:

IDENTICAL TOOLS

Description	Daily Rate	Weekly Rate	Monthly Rate
Radial Arm Saw	$22.86	$114.30	$502.92
Saw Radial Arm 10"	$8.33	$41.65	$183.26
Skidmore Wilhelm	$34.09	$170.45	$750.00
Torque/Tension Tester - Skidmore	$10.00	$50.00	$219.98

Item descriptions that do not provide make or model or equipment codes will not provide enough information for field verification. The Skidmore Wilhelm, shown above, is a brand name tester used to verify calibration of torque wrenches. The last two items in the above table are presumed to be identical. Given the choice of rates on these identical items, which rate do you think the contractor will choose for billing?

Note: The contractor in the above table multiplies the daily rate by 22 working days in the month. The daily rate is also multiplied by 5 for a weekly rate. There was no price break provided for longer rental periods. The contractor can argue that his daily rate is lower than third party contractors but it also suggests none of his equipment has downtime or is not needed.

STANDBY

Standby time can be defined as the period during which equipment is assigned to a job and available for work but is not put into operation until needed. Only the fixed ownership costs of Depreciation and Overhead should be accrued for every hour the equipment is on standby. Variable operating costs are not accrued during standby time. Standby is normally limited to eight hours per 24-hour period.

Equipment rental rates should be provided by the Contractor for unforeseen standby due to:

a. Court order or order of other governmental authorities having jurisdiction.
b. The declaration of a national emergency or other governmental act.
c. Owner's failure to pay the Prime Contractor in accordance with the contract.
d. Labor disputes (strikes) and unforeseen project suspension due to funding limitations or other causes.

LEASE PURCHASE OPTIONS

Contractors and subcontractors should not enter into lease purchase options with equipment suppliers without the prior written consent of the owner. If purchase orders/rental agreements are not provided to the owner for review, the contractor could bill the owner for all rental costs of the item and obtain ownership at the end of the lease period. The owner should have ownership rights at the end of the lease for any equipment paid for by the owner.

When the contractor does not provide the Purchase Order revealing terms of the agreement, some invoices may indicate leasing terms, financing terms, the number of payments remaining, a percentage of the payment being applied to the purchase, sales tax, or other terminology not usually found on a pure leasing agreement.

WHAT IS A SMALL TOOL?

The contract should define a small tool as any hand tool with a purchase price less than $750 - $1,000 in value, for example. These are small inexpensive hand tools that do not retain much value, are more costly to track and inventory, and doesn't justify the manpower needed to account for them. Some contracts also incorporate a small tools list that defines types of small tools. A small tool should not be directly billed to the project if a small tools adder, say $4.00 per hour, is billed based on craft labor hours worked.

The definition of a small tool should specify that the unit price per each item does not include any contractor "handling charges", "warehousing charges", or "shipping charges". Some Contractors may buy a $950 tool and increase the price above this small tool threshold by adding unverifiable charges and thereby attempt to lease the item every month to the owner. They may also attempt to buy 4 items worth $250 each and claim the purchase was valued over $1,000 and therefore qualifies for monthly leasing to the owner.

The reviewer should be aware of extremely low daily rental rates which could red flag small consumable tools being billed as rentals and have been identified on the small tools list. None of the items listed in the following table have a value greater than $1,000, which defined them as small tools. The contractor should not directly bill for any of these items because they were being funded with a small tools adder based on every craft hour worked. Note that the lack of descriptions provided by the contractor contributes to this ambiguity.

Attempted Rental of Small Tools Valued Under $1,000

Description	Daily Rate	Weekly Rate	Monthly Rate
Fan 42"	$11.95	$59.75	$262.90
Grinder Bench	$1.00	$5.00	$22.00
Hammer Roto Bench 24Volt	$6.48	$32.40	$142.56
Hoist Chain 1/2Ton	$4.40	$22.00	$96.80
Vacuum - Upright	$5.71	$28.55	$125.62

The Internet provides easy access to prices from equipment suppliers to determine if a tool is valued under $1,000 and therefore qualifies as a small tool and therefore does not qualify as a leased tool. Some contractors may use the same tool list over several decades and are rarely challenged why rental was being billed. They will take offense when the reviewer challenges these rates.

The Small Tools List (Chapter 18) and the Contractor Equipment Rental Rates per the contract should be compared to determine if small tools are being directly charged to the project as rentals. The Small Tools List is only a starting point and does not reflect an all inclusive list of small tools.

There is one other note regarding the small tools adder worth mentioning. Small tools may be charged to the project based on craft labor hours worked, both for straight time and for overtime hours. These hours can compound to staggering large numbers over the course of just one year on large projects for both the contractor and all the subcontractors. The amount reimbursed to the contractor can be far above any actual needs for small tools. The owner can dispute the need to bill small tools based on labor hours worked by Superintendents and General Foremen. These individuals are in a management position by directing the work and not physically installing equipment requiring the use of small tools. The owner should consider exempting these hours for the purpose of calculating the small tools allowance.

GANG BOXES

A gang box is a large metal container that can be locked to store small tools overnight and on weekends. Some are designed as portable workstations for General Foremen with an overhead rain shelter so that drawings can be reviewed. Usually one gang box is assigned to each crew by craft for the prime contractor as well as each subcontractor. On large projects there could be well over 100 gang boxes.

Gang boxes can be owned for many years by the contractors and are moved from project to project. They can be new but more than likely they have suffered from wear and tear on several projects and may have been repainted since purchase. Gang boxes are available from manufacturers such as Greenlee and can cost over $850 each. The General Foreman's workstations are more expensive.

The following is the contractor's rental rates for their gang boxes.

Description	Daily	Weekly	Monthly
Gang Box	$8.78	$43.90	$193.16

Assuming a gang box has a replacement value of $850 and the monthly rental is $193.16, the gang box has paid for itself every 4.4 months. One gang box can collect rent of $2,317.92 every year it is on a project unless a cap has been established in the contract that rentals cannot exceed a percentage of its replacement cost. If 75% of the replacement cost or $637.50 is established as the stopping point on rentals, the owner can save $1,680.42 on every gang box per year. If a project has 200 gang boxes renting at $193.16 every month, the contractor collects $463,584 in rentals for boxes that cost him $170,000, assuming the boxes cost $850 each. Not a bad guaranteed return on your investment. Remember these are not new gang boxes but may be fully depreciated items paid for by previous projects. The contractor has no cost basis left anymore in these boxes and is motivated to deliver as many gang boxes as possible.

The gang box is only one item of several thousands of equipment rental items provided by the contractor. An owner with multiple projects being planned over several years should consider furnishing some common items such as gang boxes and sell them for scrap to avoid incurring these costs or negotiate maximum limit caps on rental costs.

PICKUP TRUCKS

Pickup trucks may be provided to Superintendents and General Foreman by the contractor as a means to transport materials or tools to and from the project. This is more common where a contractor moves from job to job each month. On longer term contracts where work is performed over several years the trucks become a fringe benefit for these employees and are only used for commuting to and from the job and home. More than likely, these trucks will be rented to the owner as a project cost even though they do not come on the project site but are parked in the employee parking lot. This may be viewed as an employee benefit negotiated between the contractor and his employees and could be absorbed by their overhead adder. This should be clearly agreed to in the contract.

Some projects allow for "Pool vehicles" on the project for short trips to deliver materials or expedite travel within the project. All of the contractor's employees have access to use these trucks. There may also be golf carts or John Deere Gators, which can be four wheel drive heavy duty transport vehicles. The reviewer should be aware of the contractor assigning golf carts or Gators for every General Foreman/ Foreman rather than sharing them under a "Pool" concept. There should be some agreement for having excessive vehicles on the project that create a safety issue when moving under cranes or loads being transported.

4 WHEEL DRIVE VERSUS 2 WHEEL DRIVE

Contractor rates may differentiate between four wheel drive and two wheel drive pickups with the four wheel drive costing more per month. The jobsite conditions may require a four wheel drive where mud, snow, or other poor road conditions exist. However many jobsites have established paved roads and would rarely require four wheel drive vehicles. These conditions should be considered when negotiating equipment rental rates for the project.

THREE QUARTER TON VERSUS ONE-HALF TON PICKUP

Pickup Trucks can vary by size and load carrying capacity. The three-quarter ton would be expected to have a higher rental rate than a one-half ton pickup. The only question is whether the larger size truck is needed and billable to the project if it is only used for commuting to and from the project.

Another type of pickup is the compact size pickup such as the Dodge Dakota, Ford Ranger, GMC Canyon, and the Chevrolet Colorado, which would not justify the same rental rate as the one-half ton pickup. If a full description vehicle list is not provided, there is no means of verifying what is being charged without field verification. Some contractors may argue that there is no established rental rate for a compact pickup so the higher priced one-half ton truck rate was used. How convenient for them! The owner should only pay for what is being provided and negotiate new rates for items not previously on the equipment list.

The following pickup truck monthly rental rates were billed at a project. The rates do not include fuel, minor repairs, or tires. The rates should allow replacement of the truck after 3 years of rental billings assuming the replacement cost is about $25,000. However most trucks are not replaced every three years and the contractor continues to collect this same rate regardless of age. The equipment rates are usually established at the beginning of the contract.

Sample Contractor Billing Rates:	
Truck, Gas Drive, Pickup, ½ ton	$700.00
Truck, Gas Drive, Pickup, Crew Cab	$990.00
Truck, Gas Drive, 1 Ton w/Hydraulic Gate	$1,100.00

Note that the above description lacks Make, Model, 2 wheel drive or 4 wheel drive descriptions. The presumption is these are full size pickup trucks and not compact pickups.

Note: When contractors fail to provide adequate documentation on equipment lists (or anything else that is requested), it sets the tone for the entire project that they are hiding something. This creates a lack of trust that pervades ongoing daily job progress but can be interpreted several ways. Perhaps they have never been asked for such detail so they ask, "Why do you need it?" "Because we are paying the bill!"

There should be total transparency with all transactions. No owner should accept an equipment rental list such as the above description for trucks without asking for more details. Just what am I paying for? A prompt response from the contractor is the only professional and ethical thing for them to do.

TRUCK ASSIGNMENTS

The contractor should provide a list of assigned vehicles that can be matched against payroll records. This comparison may reveal if excessive pickup trucks are being billed to the project. Pickup trucks should be provided to only certain job titles within their organization, and not to clerical staff or home office personnel. When an employee leaves the project for re-assignment and takes his truck with him, the assigned vehicle charges should cease as of the termination date. If the truck is billed to the project based on employee hours worked, there should be no billings for vacation hours or holiday hours.

TRUCK FUEL COMPONENT

Assigned pickups may have a billable fuel component related to hours worked or say, $7.00 per hour that reimburses the Contractor for gasoline and oil changes. Assuming the assigned pickup trucks are parked at the employee parking lot all day, this fuel component should be billed based on straight time hours only and not overtime. The contractor does not incur additional fuel costs whether the foreman works 8 hours or 10 hours each day. Likewise, if assigned vehicles such as pickups have a fuel component factor charge based on hours worked, obtaining fuel on-site from the gasoline/diesel fuel depot or submitting gas receipts from gas stations for reimbursement should be prohibited and disallowed.

DRAYAGE

A contractor's invoice may have different sections for vehicle reimbursement. Trucks used at the contractor's home office warehouse may be billed to the project as Drayage and have significantly higher hourly rates that include the driver. These drayage rates should be defined by the contract.

TRUCK WASH

Truck washes for assigned pickups to Superintendents or General Foremen may be billed to the project costing $10 or more without any written receipts submitted because the amount is nominal and does not require a receipt. The monthly rental rates should be adequate to compensate the contractor for occasional truck and car washes and should not be directly billed.

EQUIPMENT NOT NEEDED

Some portions of the project may be assigned to consulting companies that provide specific expertise in certain areas such as surveying. When these situations exist, the prime contractor may have brought their equipment to the project that they do not use on a routine basis. The consulting company may furnish their own equipment. In the example of site surveys, there may be no need for the prime contractor to have surveying equipment. The owner should always be aware when work is contracted to others and how it may impact equipment needs.

PAINTING AND HVAC

A contractor owned several office trailers that are brought to the project for his staff. There was some steps and decking required to connect the trailers for efficiency and to avoid mud from being tracked into the trailers. However the contractor authorized painting and new heating, ventilation, and air conditioning (HVAC) modifications because of the abuse these trailers received on the last project or because they were in storage for several years at their headquarters. These charges should be billed to the prior project or absorbed by the contractor's overhead adder. Ask yourself this question, "What did the owner do that requires a new air conditioner or paint for an equipment item that just arrived?"

COMPUTER PRINTERS

The contractor never seems to bring anything to the project that he provides free of charge to the owner including computers, computer printers, or fax machines. The following monthly rental rate was charged to the owner for a "High Speed Printer". What brand of high speed printer is worth $400 per month or $4,800 per year?

Printer, High Capacity	$410.00

Notice how this description lacks brand names such as Hewlett Packard or Dell, model number, or any other description that can be verified. Was this printer a combination printer and fax machine? Most printers are reasonably priced in order for the manufacturers to sell their printer cartridges, where the real money is made. The owner could provide a printer to the contractor for extended projects to avoid this charge

RENTAL OF CHAIN FALLS

Chain falls are available in various lifting capacities and in laymen's terms are like a block and tackle for lifting items such as pipe temporarily in place until the pipe can be welded, bolted, or installed. Chain falls can range in price depending upon their lifting capacity with the heavier chain falls costing more but generally are less than $1,000 each and can be considered a small tool and should not be directly billed as equipment rentals.

Pipe stands to permanently support pipe off the floor were delayed in fabrication causing the contractor to elevate pipe in place for welding using chain falls to support the pipe from overhead beams. A subcontractor attempted to bill rental for every hour in use, including overtime, while the pipe stands were being fabricated as follows:

Rental charges for Chain Falls

Weekending 8/2	Hours Used	Quantity	Hours	Hourly Rate	Billings per Week
Chain Fall (1-1-1/2 ton)	60	28	1,680	1.28	$2,150.40
Come-along Fall (1-1-1/2 ton)	60	24	1,440	1.28	$1843.20
Chain Fall 2 ton	60	23	1,380	1.54	$2,125.20
Weekending 8/9					
Chain Fall (1-1-1/2 ton)	50	33	1,650	1.28	$2,112.00
Come-along Fall (1-1-1/2 ton)	50	31	1,550	1.28	$1,984.00
Chain Fall 2 ton	50	22	1,100	1.54	$1,694.00
Weekending 8/16					
Chain Fall (1-1-1/2 ton)	50	28	1,400	1.28	$1,792.00
Come-along Fall (1-1-1/2 ton)	50	48	2,400	1.28	$3,072.00
Chain Fall 2 ton	550	32	1,600	1.54	$2,464.00
Weekending 8/23					
Chain Fall (1-1-1/2 ton)	650	31	1,860	1.28	$2,380.80
Come-along Fall (1-1-1/2 ton)	650	37	2,220	1.28	$2,841.60
Chain Fall 2 ton	650	28	1,680	1.54	$2,587.20
Total			19,960		$27,046.40
Billing after 6 months					$162,278.40
Average cost $700					
$700 x 108 chain falls					$75,600.00
Difference – (Overcharge)					$86,678.40

The subcontractor attempted to collect $162,278.40 for chain falls worth about $75,600 if purchased new. Although the contractor may have a claim that he would not normally own and stock 108 chain falls, his recourse could have been to purchase the chain falls and receive reimbursement by the project as a direct cost. The chain falls could be thrown in the dumpster at project completion and still save the owner substantial funds. The chain falls could have been rented from a vendor and returned at actual cost.

A third party rental company would not charge overtime for chain falls, so why is the subcontractor entitled to this exorbitant request? He could have argued that the chain falls were in place 24 hours a day for 7 days each week and was entitled to even more. Though the delay of pipe supports was not within the subcontractor's responsibility, he was responsible to complete his scope of work in a fiscally prudent manner without gouging the owner. The subcontractor did not incur additional costs for chain falls used on an overtime basis. A substantial credit was negotiated with the contractor.

DAMAGE TO CONTRACTOR EQUIPMENT

The contractor owns his equipment, delivers his equipment to the jobsite, operates the equipment with his personnel, and maintains the equipment with his personnel. Sometimes damage is intentional because of labor disputes. At no time does the owner touch any of this equipment. Equipment damaged beyond reasonable wear and tear is somehow the owner's fault. Rarely does the contractor take responsibility for damaged equipment or defend against claims by subcontractors. Usually the damage is less than their insurance deductible and therefore is billable to the owner.

Repairs and maintenance for reasonable wear and tear, such as oil changes, air filter changes, flat tires, hydraulic inspection, and lubrication are typically billed to the owner. However the owner should dispute any billings that improve the useful life of the equipment. For example engine replacements or overhauls, and transmission replacements could be argued are not normal wear and tear items and are therefore included in the rental rate. The owner has expectations that any equipment brought to the site is safe and in working order to perform the work and to meet the construction schedule. Just because it happened to break down upon arrival at the project is not the owner's responsibility. Seldom will the prime contractor dispute these charges from a subcontractor but pass them along to the owner plus his fees. It is up to the owner's representative to reject these charges.

Minor tire repair for flat tires can be expected on a construction site with nails and screws falling on the ground. However replacing tires on front end loaders and tractors are more expensive than fixing flats. If the tires are replaced due to normal wear, the reviewer should determine how long the item was on site and was the wear due to use on this project or some other project. If the tires need replacing due to damaged rims or abuse, an accident report should have been written. The operator may need some discipline and possible termination if safety was jeopardized.

The strongest defense is a good offense. These terms should be stated in the contract to avoid later conflicts:

> "Minor maintenance repairs shall be reimbursed at actual cost. Such costs include routine and preventative maintenance, minor repair and other incidental costs. Repairs and/or replacement of major components such as engines, transmissions, or air conditioning compressors that extend the useful life of the equipment are considered a capital investment qualifying for additional depreciation or tax credits. Expenditures that increase the resale value are considered to be reimbursed by the rental rates and are not directly reimbursable. Major repairs, engine replacements or overhauls, and new paint are not considered routine and ordinary. Any exceptions to these terms must have the owner's prior written approval".

WELDING CABLE

The following rental rate was billed for welding cable:

Cable, Welding, 2/0 $.49 per foot.

It could be argued that welding cable is part of the welding machines and welding machines are useless without the cable since that is the copper wire that facilitates the weld. Third party equipment distributors do not normally rent any welder without the cable and their rental rate includes both. What was unique about this rate is that several thousand feet of cable was charged each month that represented several miles or more than a reasonable amount needed to perform the welding task. The reviewer should divide the number of feet of welding cable by the number of welding machines to determine if total footage is reasonable since the welding has to take place within the vicinity of the welding machine. Be aware of unusual items that are rented that cannot be verified. How did the contractor know how many thousand feet was in the field? A reviewer always perturbs contractors by requesting actual documentation. Usually there isn't any documentation to substantiate the charge.

WELDING TANK RENTALS

A large project requiring substantial welding will require welding gases such as oxygen and acetylene. These gases are delivered from welding vendors in tanks and perhaps are stored in welding carts. These welding tanks and carts are rented to the project on a monthly basis at fairly low rates.

As the project progresses, these tanks are dispersed throughout the buildings, storerooms, and tool rooms. Rarely is there an adequate inventory method to retrieve the empty tanks and return them to the warehouse in order to return them to the vendor and have the rental charge stop. A tagging system that identifies empty tanks would facilitate removing empty tanks and carts on a routine basis.

FOUR PACK WELDERS AND WELDING INVERTERS

Four pack or six pack electric welders and welder inverters are separate items that perform welding but are bundled together in a metal rack that holds either four or six small welders for space efficiency. The following table shows the contractor's billing for four welders at $641.96 each compared to a third party rental company's rates for only $550 for all four or $137.50 each. In other words, the contractor should have billed the monthly rental rate of $641.96 divided by 4 to arrive at the correct rate. Instead he billed more than four times the going equivalent commercial monthly rate. He overcharged the owner $2,017.84 per month on only four welders!

Equip. #	Description	Daily Rate	Monthly Billings	Third Party Rental Cost	Credit
5646	Inverter 300A	$29.18	$641.96		
5647	Inverter 300A	$29.18	$641.96		
5648	Inverter 300A	$29.18	$641.96		
5649	Inverter 300A	$29.18	$641.96		
			$2,567.84	$550.00	$2,017.84

Notice the sequential equipment numbers used by the contractor. This indicates they were purchased new and assigned equipment numbers at the time they were placed in service. Since the welder numbers ran sequentially in series of four and knowing that these welders were rented in quantities of four led to further investigation of their rates. Comparison of the contractor rates with third party equipment company rates led to this audit finding.

This contractor used this rental rate sheet for many years at many projects and perhaps was never questioned by the owners about this overcharge. Perhaps the contractor was not aware of this mistake but more than likely the personnel that established the rental rate list were experienced enough to be familiar with all types of construction equipment. The owner recovered over $150,000 from the contractor for this "mistake".

HAND HELD THREADER

Electrical contractors use power threading machines and hand held threaders to fabricate electrical conduit. These tools create the end pipe threads on conduit in order to screw on elbows or other fittings to the conduit much like pipe fittings that are screwed onto water pipe. After cutting a piece of conduit to the needed length, the conduit needs to be joined to another conduit piece or fitting, and the threader cuts the grooves to allow this joining.

An electrical contractor used the following rates on his rental equipment list:

Description	Daily Rate	Weekly Rate	Monthly Rate
Hand Held Threader	$9.74	$48.70	$214.28

On the Small Tools List from the same contractor was shown "Threader, Pipe with handle". The hand held threaders are not very expensive and are far below the $1,000 threshold that defines a small tool. The contractor was essentially billing twice through the small tools adder for every labor hour worked and on their rental equipment list.

MISIDENTIFIED EQUIPMENT

The equipment rental list may not have exactly the same items that are on the project and an on-site spot inventory would verify these items. A bulldozer may have a different sized front end bucket than the equipment rate list shows. The contractor has substituted something of less value at a higher price. Their excuse may be that there was no equipment rate available that "fit" the item description so they billed whatever was the closest. Normally the closest is the higher cost alternative and not the lower priced rate. These rates need to be validated.

PNEUMATIC TOOLS NOT REPAIRED

Air operated or pneumatic tools use compressed air to operate rather than electricity. The familiar sound of a pneumatic torque wrench at a tire shop comes to mind. Also air operated tools can include air grinders and paint sprayers. It is my understanding that air or pneumatic tools have more industrial applications and can tolerate heavier use and abuse.

An outside Repair Vendor at a large construction site would pick up broken pneumatic tools weekly and take them to his shop. Each tool was inventoried based on specific engraved tool identification numbers. After repair, the warehouse would check in the tools based on tool I.D. numbers and issue them to the field through three satellite tool rooms. The craftsmen would check them out on a daily basis and return them to the tool room at the end of the day. If the tool broke, it would be tagged and returned to the warehouse to be picked up by the Repair Vendor.

A tool room attendant indicated he was experiencing a high volume of broken air tools after he issued them to the field. These tools were brought back after a few minutes as broken. It was easy to track a sample of newly repaired tools based on the I.D. numbers to the most recent invoices. A comparison of the tool to the invoice revealed the new parts billed were not installed on the tools such as pistol grips and chucks. In fact, there was no verification at the warehouse that the tool was operable when the tools were received from the vendor because there was no compressed air line that could be attached to the tool to verify the repair before it was issued to the field. The invoices were sent directly to Accounts Payable and no one was comparing the bill with the service provided. The vendor was collecting hundreds of dollars each week for doing nothing more than picking up and delivering broken tools.

While the warehouse felt they had good controls by tracking each tool by I.D. number, they assumed they were dealing with an ethical vendor. The vendor, when confronted, blamed the problem on employee grievances and acted as though he was unaware this was happening. The bottom line is that he was the main beneficiary of this deceit.

EVERYTHING IS NEGOTIABLE!

The owner always has the alternative to take exception with the contractor's business decisions and may order the contractor-owned equipment off site to be replaced with lower priced alternative equipment from third party vendors. Contractors are to execute their contracts with due diligence in the owner's best interest.

In Chapters 17 and 18, respectively, a Consumables Miscellaneous Items and a Suggested Small Tools List is available that can provide guidance for identifying items that may be erroneously directly billed to the owner but are reimbursed in a Small Tools Adder based on craft labor hours worked and thus double charged. These consumable items and small tools should never appear as a direct billing (on a Time and Material project) from the prime contractor or his subcontractors if they are provided for through a small tools/consumable adder.

AMERICAN INSTITUTE OF ARCHITECTS

The American Institute of Architects (AIA) has standard forms of agreements between owners and contractors that can provide contract formats including terminology for rental agreements. The website for this organization is WWW.AIA.Org. This website suggests the following terms for equipment rental charges that are chargeable to the project under Article 7 in AIA Document A111 dated 1997. It summarizes several topics discussed in this chapter.

ARTICLE 7. COSTS TO BE REIMBURSED.

1. Rental charges for temporary facilities, machinery, equipment, plus the cost of transportation, installation, minor repairs, dismantling, and removal that are provided by the contractor at the site, whether rented from the contractor or others.
2. Rental rates and related fair market values for "contractor owned" (i.e. affiliate owned, subsidiary owned, or related party owned) equipment shall be evaluated by contractor along with the projected usage. **Estimated total rentals shall be evaluated so that an appropriate rent versus buy decision can be made.**
3. Each piece of equipment to be rented shall have daily, weekly, and monthly rates and the lowest rate shall be used when monthly usage is billed.
4. For "contractor owned" equipment rented and charged to Cost of Work, the daily, weekly, and monthly equipment rental rates shall not exceed 75% of the published rates based on the latest edition of "Rental Rates and Specifications" published by the Associated Equipment Distributors (AED Green Book).
5. The total rentals chargeable for each piece of "contractor owned" tools and equipment shall not exceed 50% of the fair market value or original purchase price of such equipment.
6. Fair market value for used equipment as referred to in this contract shall mean the estimated price a reasonable purchaser would pay to purchase the used equipment.
7. Rental charges for equipment which is not "contractor owned" and is rented from third parties will be reimbursed at actual net rental

costs, as long as rental rates are consistent with those prevailing in the locality.

8. **All losses resulting from lost or stolen tools and equipment shall be the contractor's responsibility and the cost of such losses shall be considered to be covered by contractor fee.** If contractor carries insurance for such losses, it shall be the contractor's responsibility to pay any deductibles and to file for insurance recoveries.
9. All costs for minor maintenance and repairs shall be reimbursed at actual cost. Such costs include routine and preventative maintenance, minor repairs, and other incidental costs. **Repairs and/or replacement of a capital nature are considered to be covered by the rental rates.** Major repairs and overhauls are not considered routine and ordinary.

These terms and conditions may be too stringent for many contractors to accept because it severely restricts their upside profit potential. Most contracts do not define the specific equipment rental terms and rental rates. These terms should form the basis for negotiations.

OTHER PROJECT EXPENDITURES

The following list represents typical expenditures for office equipment, furniture, and miscellaneous items that are essential to complete the project.

1. Field Office Trailers
2. Safe, OSHA-approved stairs, handrails
3. Adequate heat, power, and air conditioning
4. Temporary electrical power distribution lines
5. Phone lines and switchboard equipment
6. Adequate lighting in the work areas, parking areas
7. Office furniture such as desks, chairs, conference tables, file cabinets, book shelves, supply cabinets, and folding chairs.
8. Office equipment and supplies to include copiers, fax machines, computers and printers, refrigerator, coffee machine, and supplies
9. Potable water
10. Pagers or portable radios
11. Copy, computer, and fax paper
12. Safety and security equipment including fire alarms and fire extinguishers, hard hats, safety glasses, First Aid kits, and emergency phone numbers
13. Trash removal

14. Sanitary facilities including use of existing facilities, trailer hookups, and portable units.
15. Owner Controlled Insurance Protection (OCIP)
16. Building Permits
17. Design Professionals such as Architects, Civil Engineers, and Electrical Engineers

The owner should realize that all of these items procured by the contractor will become part of his monthly rentals and be subject to markups and fees. Both the contractor's project office staff and owner's staff will avoid processing the repetitive monthly invoices for these items if the owner provides some of these items at the start of the project. When the owner provides these items, they are excludable from the project cost basis and are not included when computing any escalation formulas or bonuses.

WILLIE SUTTON RULE

"Go where the money is…and go there often."

The legend of Willie Sutton has resulted in the "Willie Sutton rule," used in activity-based costing (ABC) of management accounting. The rule stipulates that ABC should be applied "where the money is," meaning where the highest costs are incurred, and thus the highest potential of over-all cost reduction.

Interpreting this rule another way is when the owner has limited resources to review and audit project costs, the most beneficial use of time is to sample the areas with the largest potential for overcharges. The owner cannot expect significant audit findings (and recovery from the contractor) by spending a lot of time reviewing per diem expenses and travel costs when a significant portion of project costs are being incurred in areas such as equipment rentals. This is often referred to as "Getting the Most Bang for the Buck."

EQUIPMENT RENTAL CAPS

Under the discussion of Gang Boxes, it is apparent that contractor equipment rental rates can quickly recover the full cost of some items within a relatively short period so that the contractor can virtually replace his equipment inventory at the owner's expense with brand new items. Any payback period can be calculated by obtaining the new equipment price and divide by the monthly rental rate to obtain how fast the rental rate can fund a new piece of equipment.

The following table shows examples of equipment rented from a contractor without maximum rental caps on a three year project. The rental days are computed by multiplying total rental days by the number of units at the project.

Description	Approx. Current Retail Price	Approx. Rental Months Required to Purchase New Unit	Equivalent Quantity purchased to Date	Rental Days	Billed Total
Portable Building 8 x 16	$3,000	7.1	35.6	5,591	$106,732
Gator	$12,000	16.7	17	5,001	$204,600
Golf cart elec.	$4,000	8.7	13.3	2,222	$53,320
Come along 6T	$900	4.3	52.7	4,966	$47,425
Radio 6-pack plus charger	$1,400	2.3	152.4	7,819	$213,300
Weld Fusion Machine	$38,000	4.1	4.5	404	$171,700
Welder Propane 280A	$3,900	8.7	9.5	1,353	$36,896
Wire Feeder LN25	$2,000	5.4	74.6	8,829	$149,300

The third column in the table suggests the fast payback period of less than one year for the majority of these items. If the items had been purchased rather than rented from the contractor, the items could have been sold at project completion while saving substantial sums. The table also suggests an exorbitant number of items on the project that should have been better controlled. The contractor pocketed these amounts as extra profits.

This table format can be used for any purchase/lease option analysis on long term projects.

Replacement cost and useful life are obvious factors to consider when calculating monthly equipment rental rates. Any equipment dealer will have to eventually replace their inventory funded by the rental rates that also provide enough cushion for overheads and profits. Depending on the type of equipment and the amount of use, some equipment items may have a useful life of seven years, ten years, or longer before they need replacing. After a certain amount of time, the replacement parts become more difficult and expensive to obtain and the item may become obsolete or unsafe to operate.

The contractor's rental rates should be comparable to a third party rental company being in the same business and the recovery period for that equipment investment should be about the same. The contractor has less risk of recovery for his investment with each project since he has the discretion to deploy as much as possible whereas the rental company leases items on an as needed basis for shorter periods. Therefore you would think that contractor rental rates should be significantly lower, say 25%, than their competition.

When projects are scheduled to last for one or more years, the owner should negotiate a rental maximum cap on contractor equipment rentals to not exceed 50% of the fair market value of this equipment. The owner has compensated the contractor for the full value of his equipment when this limitation has been reached.

SUMMARY

Any owner of a large construction project is at a distinct disadvantage concerning equipment at his construction site. They rely on the contractor to have the expertise to complete the project with due diligence in the most economical manner. The contractor has the home field advantage. Owners are not familiar with the construction equipment being charged, whether it is the same items that agree with the rental rates, or if the items are actually being used.

Owners often fail to provide appropriate manpower for project oversight. Owners can take a pro-active approach by hiring consultants with construction equipment expertise. The investment is well worth it.

EQUIPMENT AUDIT PROGRAM
DATE

Project/Location:
Process: Equipment Rental
Objective: Ensure all costs associated with Equipment Rentals are reimbursable, have actually been incurred, and are billed at actual costs or in accordance with the contract. A secondary objective is to ensure that excessive equipment rental costs are not charged to the project.

No.	Risks	Control Techniques	Audit Procedures	Workpaper Ref.
1	Contractor-Owned equipment rental charges are not billed in accordance with contract.	Equipment rates for specific equipment items are established by contract.	Create or obtain an independent listing of Contractor equipment at each site during the audit test period. Obtain the invoice for the contractor's equipment rented to the project during the test period. Determine whether rental is being charged for inoperable equipment or items no longer on site. Analyze the basis for the contractor's rates and compare to the contract rates. Re-compute the contractor's invoice for equipment that arrived or departed during the test period to determine if charges are correct.	
2	Contractor owned equipment is rented when not on site.	An effective notification process is in place to report equipment arriving and leaving site at the end of rental period or for major repairs.	Review reporting process and ensure timely notification is available for all parties processing invoices. Ensure proper documentation exists showing equipment name, owner (if third party rental), date, and other notations such as obvious damage that may result in additional repair charges. Effective reporting process should also document receipt of rented equipment, date, owner, equipment number, and any obvious damage upon arrival that may result in additional repair charges.	

HOW TO DETECT CONSTRUCTION FRAUD

No.	Risks	Control Techniques	Audit Procedures	Workpaper Ref.
3.	Major repairs to contractor owned equipment is charged to the project.	General Contractor equipment and supply invoices are audited prior to reimbursement.	Review equipment supplier invoices for major repairs to large equipment items by equipment number and determine arrival date, cause for repairs, and if charges are prudent or necessary due to length of time on site. Determine if repairs are stated in rental agreement and should be part of normal maintenance included in rental rates.	
4	Contractor owned equipment is purchased for the project by Contractor and also rented at monthly rates.	An inventory equipment list exists for all major equipment purchased for the project.	Review purchases for major equipment items charged to determine whether contractor-owned equipment items might have been purchased and charged in their entirety to the job as well as being charged to owner as a rental. All project-owned equipment items will remain in the physical possession of owner.	

No.	Risks	Control Techniques	Audit Procedures	Workpaper Ref.
5.	Third-Party Equipment Rentals are overcharging owner projects monthly.	Third-party equipment rentals are audited prior to reimbursement.	Review invoices for proper calculation of partial weeks or months for returned items. Compare monthly rental charges with The Associated Equipment Distributors Green Book or other commercially available sources and determine that rates charged are consistent with those prevailing in the local area. Ensure that rates charged are the most economical to owner, such as monthly versus weekly or daily. Test sample third party equipment invoices for possible duplicate billing or overlapping billing during consecutive billing periods.	
6	Equipment is rented to the project for items not in use.	Owner site personnel verify monthly usage.	On a randomly selected week each month, perform an "unannounced" site visit to inventory equipment at each site, record the equipment number and hour meter usage or odometer, and determine if equipment is being used or should be shipped off site. Discuss projected usage with owner site personnel for items that appear to be out of use or disrepair for substantial periods.	

CHAPTER 6
CRAFT LABOR

BOGUS HOURS

Craft payroll time reporting all begins with the Craft Foreman's Daily Timecard. Each journeyman and apprentice craftsman is assigned to a specific Foreman for their daily work and supervision. The Foreman is responsible for reporting each man's daily hours and charging that time to a correct cost code. The Foreman may have a crew of two or more men for his specific trade such as laborers, boilermakers, carpenters, electricians, ironworkers, etc. The Foreman's Daily Timecard is entered into the payroll system for each man the next day by a payroll clerk and the hours are accumulated from the start of the shift on Wednesday to the following Tuesday until quitting time. The time reporting payroll system generates all labor cost reports, payroll W-2 earnings and tax withholding reports, as well as the payroll checks, which are distributed to the men each week on Friday. The Payroll Department has from the shift ending on Tuesday evening until Friday morning to have all payroll checks ready for distribution.

The project may have electronic key card access or time clocks that are punched upon entry and exit but the source of all paid hours is the Foreman's Daily Timecard. These Foreman's timecards may be reviewed and approved by a General Foreman or a Superintendent in the trade but chances are these supervisors are not as familiar with each person on the crew as the Foreman and wouldn't know their daily attendance. Their review may only be a rubber stamp of approval and not an attestation of attendance.

A Foreman may be protective of his crew and provide extra incentives such as paid time off, full pay for late arrivals or early leaves, and record a full eight hours as though the person worked. He may actually put down 10 hours worked so the individual is paid 2 hours overtime after he has left for the day if the project is working 10 hour days. When these Foremen's Daily timecards are compared with electronic gate logs and the Foreman is confronted with the evidence that the person was absent, their obvious defense is the gate log is not accurate or the key card malfunctioned and did not record the card swipe for that individual when he entered or left. A Foreman can only provide this excuse just so long. Unfortunately comparing Foremen's timecards with electronic gate logs is very time consuming and could require a dedicated person for this task. Thus the deception may never be detected. If the gate logs can be integrated electronically with daily time reporting, an exception report could be generated within minutes to identify these discrepancies.

On large projects, time clocks may be arranged under protective rain shelters in straight lanes or "cattle chutes" where the men walk straight through and clock in as they enter the project. Without anyone observing the process, the time clocks are only a symbol of timekeeping control if an individual can clock in multiple timecards or can clock in and turn around to leave the project. **The clock cards or employee badge swipes should be arranged to open a turnstile to admit only one person at a time and prevent the employee from leaving.** There should be a control in place that prevents clocking in for multiple individuals. Ideally the clock cards or electronic gate log should record the exact time each individual enters and leaves that could easily be compared to the reported payroll hours. Likewise the auditor should be aware of any exits on the project that allows individuals to leave the project with no detection. <u>These lanes for timekeeping should be locked at all times except for shift changes and the men should sign in for late arrivals or out for early quits in front of a payroll timekeeper.</u>

BOGUS CHARGES

Contractors may refuse to provide Certified Payroll Reports unless they are required by the contract or if the project is federally funded. A Certified Payroll Report provides a complete breakdown of hourly rates, fringes, payroll taxes, deductions from gross payroll, and net paid to the employee. Craft payrolls may be submitted to the owner by PDF files or hard copy summary of a payroll report generated from the contractor's payroll system. These hard copies are handy for visual review but they do not provide the powerful analysis that is available through knowledge of an Excel Format and the ability to sort and filter the data by name and pay period to detect duplicate hours charged to different work packages, etc. The Excel Format provides audit opportunities called Data Mining to perform numerous reviews expeditiously from payroll reports that contain hundreds of employees. Unfortunately most contractor software payroll programs are specific for reporting payroll and are not in an Excel format.

CRAFT PAYROLL AUDIT PLAN

The objective of this Audit Plan is to ensure that all costs associated with Craft Field Labor is reimbursable, have actually been incurred, and are billed at actual costs or in accordance with the contract. These audit steps are dependent upon the size and complexity of the project and the number of scope items that need to be completed. The larger the geographic area of a project and the tighter the completion schedule, the more craft and field supervision resources will be needed. If the owner does not have a security fence in place with electronic access (gate logs) that records entry and exist, what evidence does the owner have to contest the foremen's time cards that were approved by the Superintendent? Both men are attesting to the employee's presence. If the owner does not have enough personnel to review the gate logs, these excess billings will never be caught and the owner may be paying for time not worked. Craft labor payroll can be the largest cost element of the project.

GENERAL REVIEW OF MONTHLY CRAFT LABOR

These general review steps should be performed monthly to indicate if the contractor's payroll system is being over-ridden by manual intervention. A good payroll system should have built-in "red flags" that detect and prevent erroneous amounts being paid, such as $500 or more to an employee that exceeds his normal net take home pay. Someone has to override the "red flags" to allow the paycheck to be written. This general review should be performed for the prime contractor and all of his subcontractors.

1. Scan the hourly pay scale rates for Apprentices, Journeymen, Foremen, and General Foremen for compliance with prevailing hourly rates. The contractor should provide current union agreements in place that disclose all this information by craft. If not, this information is available from the unions.
2. Scan overtime pay scale rates for correct time and one-half and double time rates billed.
3. Spot check Apprentices every few months to verify they are not billed as Journeyman before they have completed their apprenticeship. An apprentice is paid significantly less than a journeyman and usually requires four years to complete an apprenticeship to become a Journeyman. Some payroll systems abbreviate craft pay rates as A - Apprentice, J - journeyman, F - Foreman, and GF - General Foreman. A contractor/subcontractor may bill the owner the Journeyman rate for all of his Apprentices and pocket the difference.

4. Review hours billed around Holidays and deer season for early quits, late arrivals, and extra days off.
5. Review hours billed for rain-outs or inclement weather. A union craft worker is entitled to two hours show-up pay if inclement weather cancels working outdoors. The craft can be held past the two hours if it appears the weather will clear but they must be paid while being held. The worker has to show up in order to be paid the two hours and cannot call in to qualify. The basic question is whether the employee was paid for a full day during a rain-out or did he leave after two hours? Craft employees are not salaried. Were payments rendered in compliance with the contract? As the job progresses and more buildings are completed, working outdoors in the rain becomes less of an issue.
6. Review total hours billed for the month to not exceed total straight time possible. In other words, with a four week month working 40 hours per person would be the equivalent of 160 straight time hours per man. With 300 men working that month, the expectation is that less than 48,000 straight time hours would be billed that month when considering illness, holidays, and early quits. This would be a quick validation before further investigation is needed.
7. Test for overlapping pay periods with the prior month's invoice. Were hours in the same week or partial week billed twice in two succeeding months?
8. Determine how new employees are added to or deleted from the payroll system. Does the owner require mandatory drug testing and orientation? Does each man have a picture badge for security purposes issued by the owner? Does each man sign withholding forms and personal contact information? Is the responsibility for adding new employees and terminations rotated periodically among payroll personnel?
9. Determine if per diem payments were paid to craft personnel. Typically union craft workers are not paid per diem.
10. Look for activity which may be inappropriate labor charges to the project. When the contractor charges craft hours to a subcontractor (in order to furnish a specific union trade skill) perhaps the hours reflect re-work that should be backcharged to the subcontractor and not billed to the owner. The contract should specify how re-work or repairs should be handled and credited to the owner. Contractors will hide their mistakes to avoid absorbing re-work costs.
11. Compare total craft headcount within a pay period with the number of payroll checks issued. Determine if extra checks were written that exceed the headcount. Perhaps someone in the Payroll Department is writing bogus checks.

12. Verify if the Payroll Department has segregation of duties between the time data entry and the writing of payroll checks. Does staff size justify rotating responsibilities for data entry so that individuals rotate data entry between crafts? Does a payroll clerk have a spouse or relative working in the crafts who could add overtime hours to the foreman's timecard for that relative without the foreman's knowledge? Look for any alterations to timecards.
13. Make "Exception Reports" on a periodic basis where someone only clocks in but does not clock out and is paid a full 8 hours. Why would an individual walk past the time clocks and forget to clock out? Spot check questionable items with gate logs to verify hours on site. The same individual(s) is usually a repeat offender and has never been caught on other projects billing for hours not worked.
14. Review new employee Social Security numbers for false number sequences. A list of proper Social Security groupings can be obtained from the Social Security Administration.
15. Verify the total charges by work package are tied to the summary and invoice recap sheets.

CRAFT ACCOUNTABILITY

1. Obtain a listing of all craft personnel assigned to the project during at least one full period of payroll charges to the contractor's accounting records.
    - Look for potential fictitious names and "ghosts" on the payroll.
- Perform an unannounced field face check on payday by observing foremen distributing paychecks to verify existence of craft employees. The one day workers will least likely to be absent will be payday.
    - Validate the security of the project for the possibility of individuals entering or exiting the project without detection.
    - Examine contractor procedures for adding and deleting craft to the project. Can one person in Payroll add or retain employees on their records without any oversight and approval?
    - Be alert for potential payroll fraud where the Foreman reports workers on the payroll after they have terminated their employment.
2. Determine if the payroll hours worked reflect actual payroll hours paid per the contractor's records. Review contractor records for payroll codes that reflect absences such as S for sick, V for vacation, LT for long term disability, or unexplained transfer of hours (from other projects or between line items), or other unusual postings.
3. Review details of payroll cost reports to verify if the contractor is in

compliance with contractual labor union rates and benefits. Look for unusual amounts paid outside of contract terms and seek explanation for items such as bonuses, back pay, and severance pay.

4. On a random basis each month, observe craft entering the project at the start of the shift and all time clocks being punched so that only one clock card per individual is punched. Immediately after the start of the shift and the time clocks are secure, prepare an exception report for all employees timecards not "clocked in". At the end of the shift, observe all craft exiting the project and all time clocks being punched. Prepare an Exception Report for all individuals not clocking out. If the project is working 10 hour days, observe the process at the end of 10 hours. The Exception Report should indicate all absentees or late arrivals for that day. Compare the Exception Report for late arrivals or early quits who have signed their names in the Payroll Department. Compare the Exception Report to the Foremen's daily timecards for that specific day and prepare work papers for presentation of the dispute to the contractor to seek reimbursement. The owner should emphasize that misreporting time is falsification of records, which could lead to termination for the fraudulent foremen submitting incorrect hours. It is up to the owner to bring these excess charges to the attention of the contractor. If the number of craft employees is too large to observe, perhaps only one craft such as electricians can be sampled.

5. Prepare a listing of craft personnel with names and job titles. Prepare a ratio of general foremen, foremen, journeymen, and apprentices. Is the number of supervisory craft personnel appropriate or is the project staffed with excessive field supervision such as personnel with the title "Assistant"?

6. Review for straight time and overtime hours reported. Does it appear overtime is scheduled and worked on weekends to compensate for non-productive hours during the week or as an incentive to crafts? Is overtime persistent or sporadic? Was overtime approved by owner?

7. Review foremen's timecards for reporting "working through lunch" as paid overtime. Determine why working through lunch (at overtime rates) is necessary on a consistent basis. Summarize the number of questionable instances where working through lunch was reported and tabulate amount to be disputed.

8. Select a test period for craft payroll during the summer months before or after a three day holiday weekend (Memorial Day, Fourth of July, and Labor Day). Review for paid vacations, holidays, sick leave, etc.
    - Was vacation used in conjunction with a three day holiday and vacation hours billed when the employee was absent? Craft

employees are paid vacations from their union and should not directly bill the project.
- Were sick days reported at the beginning or end of a long holiday? Craft employees are not paid for sick days.

Summarize the number of instances, hours, and costs billed for recovery from the contractor. All work papers should have enough detailed information to substantiate the dispute.

CRAFT STRAIGHT TIME AND OVERTIME

A union craft worker should report for work at the normal start time, say 8 A.M., get a one-half hour unpaid lunch, and leave at 4:30 P.M. to earn eight hours pay. Contract language should state that the men are "ready for work" at 8 A.M. and not arriving at the entrance. They should have their hard hats and safety glasses and receive their assignments at this time. Usually there is adequate time at the end of the day to secure their tools and retrieve their lunchboxes in order to exit at 4:30 p.m. There is usually an understanding that men can begin to put up their tools at 4:20 p.m. If they work through their lunch, they are entitled to one-half hour of overtime pay at time and one-half rates and eat their lunches as time permits "on the fly".

Any union craft labor work after 4:30 p.m. on weekdays and time worked on Saturdays is paid at time and one-half rates. Any union craft labor work performed on Sundays and Holidays is paid at double time their normal hourly rate.

If a union craft worker is paid $25 per hour for 40 hours of work, his gross pay will be $1,000 for that week. If he also works on Saturday at time and one half, his gross paycheck will be an additional $300 or $1,300 for the week. Let's say this same worker typically arrives late on Mondays or 5 hours every week. He loses $125 of straight time during the week but is rewarded $300 for working on Saturday. He is not out much money if he is assured overtime every Saturday. The point of this example is there could be many craft workers that game the system, which can ultimately impact productivity. If the worker happens to be a crane operator making lifts that are essential to the critical path schedule, the whole project can be delayed.

DRUG OR ALCOHOL ABUSE

Personnel that are habitually late, quit early, and usually find some excuse to go to their cars during lunch may be a safety concern. These individuals may have a substance abuse problem dealing with alcohol or drugs. Safety meetings and orientation should provide education for spotting signs of drug abuse such as disarrayed clothing, slurred speech, and demeanor. These personnel should not be retained on the project and random drug testing should be an expectation on any large project where lives could be at risk.

CRAFT LABOR RATE BUILD UP

The owner should request the following breakdown from every contractor and sub-contractor on the project in order to verify hourly billing rates. These breakdowns should be for every Union trade such as Laborers, Carpenters, Electricians, Pipefitters, Plumbers, Millwrights, Painters, Teamsters, etc. Additional breakdowns should be provided for First year Apprentices, Second Year Apprentices, Third Year Apprentices, Fourth Year Apprentices, Journeyman, Foreman, and General Foreman. These Union contract rates can easily be verified with each respective local Union. These breakdowns provide little room to hide additional markups or profits.

Boilermakers	ST	OT	DT
Journeyman hourly	31.50	47.25	63.00
Savings Plan	1.50	1.50	1.50
Subtotal	33.00	48.75	64.50
Payroll Taxes			
FICA - 7.65%	2.52	3.72	4.93
Federal Unemployment Ins. - .8%	0.26	0.39	0.52
State Unemployment Ins. - 5.20%	1.72	2.54	3.35
Subtotal	4.50	6.65	8.80
Fringe Benefits			
H & W	6.82	10.23	13.64
Pension	7.56	11.34	15.12
Annuity	3.87	5.81	7.74
Apprenticeship	0.35	0.35	0.35
Common ARC/Most	0.24	0.24	0.24
Training Funds	0.20	0.20	0.20
Subtotal	19.04	28.17	37.29
Insurance			
General Liability (3.87%)	1.28	1.89	2.50
Small Tools/Consumables	4.10	4.10	4.10
	61.92	89.56	117.19

Boilermaker Vacation Check-off	(1.50)	(1.50)	(1.50)
Subtotal	60.42	88.06	15.69
Overhead & Profit	5.50	5.50	5.50
Incentive	1.00	1.00	1.00
	66.92	94.56	122.19

These craft breakdowns are dependent on contract terminology. Some contracts may not have an Incentive Pay component of one dollar per hour or a Small Tools/Consumables adder of $4.10 per hour. The end result should provide an easily traceable and verifiable number of say $66.92 for straight time for each boilermaker journeyman billed. There should be very little variance from these rates until a union pay increase becomes effective.

PAYROLL TAXES

Social Security (F.I.C.A.), Federal Unemployment Insurance (F.U.I.), and State Unemployment Insurance (S.U.I.) apply to all employees. Social Security maximum limits to be withheld from the employee's earnings are as follows:

Year	Tax Base	Maximum Social Security Contribution	Maximum Total Contributions for Employer and Employee
2011	$106,800	$4,485.60	$11,107.20
2012	$110,100	$6,826.20	$13,652.40

The employer withholds 6.2% of the paycheck gross wages on the first $110,100 of earnings in 2012 plus 1.45% Medicare Tax, which has no maximum earnings cap limitations. The employer matches the 6.2% for a total of 12.4%. The contractor should not "round off" these percentages to 8% when billing the owner. Any cumulative billing to the owner that exceeds $6,826.20 per employee is an over-collection of the tax.

The Federal Unemployment Tax Act (F.U.T.A.) with state unemployment compensation provides unemployment compensations to workers who have lost their job. Only the employer pays the F.U.T.A. tax. It is not deducted from the employee's wages.

The effective Federal Unemployment Insurance rate is currently .8% of the first $7,000 of wages and the state's unemployment insurance rates, which can vary by state, can be 5.2% of the first $13,000 of wages for the State of Missouri, for example. When an employee reaches these statutory limits of $56 maximum for FUTA and $676 maximum for SUTA, respectively, the payroll tax billing should cease to the owner. With the current wage rates, it doesn't take but a few months to reach these statutory limits.

Some contractors/subcontractors will continue to invoice for the tax beyond the statutory limits and pocket the excess as profits. The extra amounts are not reported to either the Federal or State Governments. When a project begins and employees are transferred in from other projects during the year, typically the payroll taxes start being billed on the first dollar earned with no recognition of year-to-date compensation. Also when craft employees transfer to other projects during the year and transfer back, the payroll taxes may start being billed as though they are new employees. Thus the contractor invoices for costs they do not incur. To minimize this possibility, the following terminology should be included in Cost Plus contracts for both prime and sub-prime contractors:

> "For payroll taxes chargeable to the project when computing actual costs, the contractor/subcontractor shall compute the annual wage limits subject to certain payroll taxes. The contractor/subcontractor shall compute actual costs for payroll taxes when incurred up to the wage cut-off limit".

WORKER'S COMPENSATION INSURANCE

Contractors have different experience modifies that impact their insurance rates and they may not pass on their insurance discounts to the owner. The following terminology should be used in prime and sub-prime contracts:

> "Cost of the work shall include the actual net cost to the contractor for Worker's Compensation Insurance attributable to the Cost of Work wages".

PAID OVERTIME PREMIUM

Contractors should be held responsible for overtime worked caused by their own delays. The following should be incorporated into the contract language as follows:

> "Any overtime premium incurred by contractor for hourly workers shall require owner's advance written approval. If the contractor is required to work overtime as a result of an inexcusable delay caused by the contractor or anyone they are responsible for, the overtime premium portion of the payroll

and burden costs will be considered as a non-reimbursable cost".

Boilermaker Pay Rates and Fringes
1/1/2010-12/31/2010

	General Foreman	Foreman	Journeyman
Straight Time Wages	$35.38	$33.88	$31.38
Savings Plan	$1.00	$1.00	$1.00
Pension	$10.08	$10.08	$10.08
Annuity	$3.87	$3.87	$3.87
Health & Welfare	$7.07	$7.07	$7.07
Apprenticeship	$.35	$.35	$.35
Common ARC/Most	$.24	$.24	$.24
Local Training	$.20	$.20	$.20
Total ST Package	$58.19	$56.69	$54.19

The above table indicates that fringe benefits for this particular union are the same for all three positions. They are also identical for all levels of apprentices so there is no price break for benefits regardless of pay grade. There may be job titles known as Assistant Foreman. The owner should evaluate "Assistant" positions and their responsibilities for both craft and staff. Why does anyone need an assistant which may be a redundant position with little or no responsibilities?

APPRENTICESHIP SCHOOL

Apprenticeship wages are substantially less than a journeyman wages so the question is, "Why not staff the project with the maximum number of apprentices?" The problem is that apprentices cannot work alone. They are inexperienced and have to work in a crew where they receive on-the-job training (OJT).

Apprentices are required to attend classroom training in addition to their normal work duties. Classroom training is usually scheduled after hours similar to anyone attending night school to complete their college degree. Usually owners and contractors recognize the need to train new personnel in the building trades as older workers retire.

Apprenticeship schools may be scheduled during work hours and these men may be allowed to leave the project early to attend school. Normally the contract language states that apprentices shall not suffer a loss of pay and the expectation is they will be paid the full 8 hours for the day. Another interpretation is if the project is scheduled for 10 hour days, the apprentices are then paid a full 10 hours for the day with overtime rates when attending school.

These understandings should be in writing with prior approval from the owner. An owner may provide training for their own personnel during the normal business day because they have a vested interest in those employees that they expect will remain for many years on their payroll. However, the contractor employees do not provide a vested interest for the owner and will move on to the next employer or contractor as projects near completion. The owner has invested several thousand dollars for this training as well as providing the contractor's overhead fees and profit fees. The owner may never see a return on their money for this investment. The pre-bid conference should define the owner's financial responsibility for Apprenticeship Schools rather than relying on some verbal O.K. the contractor asserts was made later during the project.

OVERTIME ABUSE

When the gate logs are retrievable in an Excel format showing daily attendance, it quickly becomes evident that abuse may be occurring among craft personnel, especially those higher level employees who may have a reason to be at work for extended hours for Safety, Supervision, or Planning.

The following table shows one individual that reported hours worked when the gate logs indicate no work was performed at the project on those particular days. Perhaps the individual is claiming working from home, which is difficult to prove or disprove. There should be a clear understanding about time reporting and billable hours for working from home.

HOURS CHARGED – NO BADGED IN HOURS

Date	Daily Total			Badged In Hrs.	Comments
	ST	OT	Total		
4/18/08	8	0.0	8	0	< No Badged In Hours
5/26/08	8	0.0	8	0	< Memorial Day
6/20/08	8	0.0	8	0	< No Badged In Hours
7/3/08	8	0.0	8	0	< No Badged In Hours

7/4/08	8	0.0	8	0	Independence Day	
7/18/08	8	0.0	8	0	< No Badged In Hours	
8/5/08	8	0.0	8	0	< No Badged In Hours	
8/12/08	8	3.0	11	0	< No Badged In Hours	
9/9/08	8	3.0	11	0	< No Badged In Hours	
10/15/08	8	4.0	12	0	< No Badged In Hours	
10/20/08	8	0.0	8	0	< No Badged In Hours	
11/11/08	8	0.0	8	0	< Veterans Day	
11/26/08	8	2.0	10	0	< No Badged In Hours	
11/27/08	8	0.0	8	0	< Thanksgiving	
12/9/08	8	0.0	8	0	< No Badged In Hours	
12/17/08	8	0.0	8	0	< No Badged In Hours	
12/26/08	8	0.0	8	0	< No Badged In Hours	
12/30/08	8	0.0	8	0	< No Badged In Hours	
144.0	12.0	156.0				
$ 75	$ 75	$75				
$ 10,800	$ 900.00	$11,700				

The above table is proof that the contractor billed $11,700 for a Safety employee on the craft payroll that misreported hours as worked. This employee charged for Holidays as well as overtime on the day before Thanksgiving, which is not a Holiday. Another disappointment was the time span of misreporting hours for almost the entire year and overtime when the employee was absent for the entire day.

This table should serve as a format for reporting these disputes to the contractor. The owner should aggressively pursue these credits.

WORKING THROUGH LUNCH

Foremen's Daily Timecards should be visually scanned for working through lunch where the entire crew is paid one-half hour of overtime during the lunch hour. The type of craft and type of work being performed during this time period should be scrutinized. What work is being performed that is so essential that it cannot stop in order for the men to take a lunch? When none of the other crafts are required to work through lunch, the exceptions draw more attention to that particular craft or crew.

At a large project that had a rock crusher used to pulverize rock in order to produce concrete, an electrical crew reported working through lunch for the entire crew every day of the week for several months. Perhaps rock deliveries to the crusher by outside vendors may justify working through lunch in order to maintain the steady flow of rock deliveries, or a large concrete pour may be scheduled within the next week. However, there was an adequate supply of rock already stockpiled and the electricians were used more for troubleshooting in case of a breakdown.

Visiting the crew lunch trailer before the lunch hour provided evidence that the Foreman's Daily Timesheet had already been prepared before 11 o'clock and all individuals had one-half hour of overtime reported. Staying during the lunch period showed the crew arriving at the trailer and spreading out on the floor to catch a quick nap during the one-half hour period. This situation was reported to the owner's Project Manager that arranged for a similar visit the following day to witness the same situation.

Where it appears that consistent paid overtime for working through lunch is not required or reasonable, the reviewer should witness what the crew is doing during this time and request a refund for paid overtime.

The other question is dealing with the Foreman who misreported time worked. If an individual cannot be trusted with documentation, should he be left on the project to perpetuate other mistakes which could be more serious such as misreporting accidents or critical safety inspections?

DUPLICATE TIMESHEETS

Just like material invoices that are submitted to the owner twice for reimbursement, daily timesheets from the contractor or subcontractors can be submitted twice over several months. These daily timesheets indicate the names, hours, and what tasks were performed on time and material contracts. These duplicates are hard to detect from a cursory review of the stacks of paperwork submitted and the limited time period to audit the monthly invoice bundle on large projects.

There is an assumption that with advances in computer programing and software, such "mistakes" like duplicate timesheets could never occur. Many daily timesheets are nothing more than an Excel spreadsheet listing days and hours worked. Since the computer listing is a manual operation of inputting data by the subcontractor personnel, there are no red flags built in that locks up the data entry and asks, "Are you sure you want to enter the same information again?"

The same technique for finding duplicate material invoices is used to find duplicate daily timesheets by sorting by the date worked or by duplicate amounts. If crew sizes are the same and the same hours are worked by the

HOW TO DETECT CONSTRUCTION FRAUD

same crew each day, there should be many identical dollar amounts billed on different days, assuming billing rates remain the same for everyone on the crew. However, overlapping time periods of the same workdays on the contractor's summary billing may be an indication of double billing as follows:

Invoice #	Invoice Date	Time period
A	6/8/XX	5/1/xx-5/30/XX
B	7/6/XX	5/15/xx-7/2/XX

Duplicate timesheets may have been submitted for the overlapping period of 5/15 and later that could have been included in both Invoice A and B. The time periods from two different (and sequential) monthly invoices need to be compared. The question is why would the contractor arbitrarily have these unusual cutoffs in their billing cycle?

To determine if duplicate daily timesheets were billed, transfer all data to an Excel spreadsheet and sort in ascending order all data by actual date worked or pre-numbered timesheet number. We use the same formula comparing timesheet dates by each row to the previous row in the table to determine if any duplicates occurred.

Original Data

	A	B	C	D	E	F
	Prime Inv. #	Sub Inv. #	Date	Timesheet Date	Amount	Formula
1	4423	A	1/5/2012	12/5/2011	$1,500	
2	4423	A	1/5/2012	12/8/2011	$2,750	=IF (D2=D1,"TRUE")
3	4423	A	1/5/2012	12/12/2011	$3,200	=IF (D3=D2,"TRUE")
4	4423	A	1/5/2012	12/20/2011	$15,000	=IF (D4=D3,"TRUE")
5	4459	B	2/8/2012	1/9/2012	$2,235	=IF (D5=D4,"TRUE")
6	4459	B	2/8/2012	12/20/2011	$15,000	=IF (D6=D5,"TRUE")
7	4459	B	2/8/2012	1/18/2012	$1,625	=IF (D7=D6,"TRUE")
8	4459	B	2/8/2012	1/24/2012	$6,650	=IF (D8=D7,"TRUE")
9	5325	C	3/2/2012	2/8/2012	$9,000	=IF (D9=D8,"TRUE")
10	5325	C	3/2/2012	1/24/2012	$6,650	=IF D10=D9,"TRUE")
11	5325	C	3/2/2012	2/15/2012	$1,375	=IF (D11=D10,"TRUE")
12	5325	C	3/2/2012	2/8/2012	$9,000	=IF (D12=D11,"TRUE")

The above table is the raw data before any sorting.

Sorted Data by Timesheet Date (Column D)

	A	B	C	D	E	F
	Prime Inv. #	Sub Inv. #	Date	Timesheet Date	Amount	Formula
1	4423	A	1/5/2012	12/5/2011	$1,500	
2	4423	A	1/5/2012	12/8/2011	$2,750	FALSE
3	4423	A	1/5/2012	12/12/2011	$3,200	FALSE
4	4423	A	1/5/2012	**12/20/2011**	**$15,000**	FALSE
5	4459	B	2/8/2012	**12/20/2011**	**$15,000**	TRUE
6	4459	B	2/8/2012	1/9/2012	$2,235	FALSE
7	4459	B	2/8/2012	1/18/2012	$1,625	FALSE
8	4459	B	2/8/2012	**1/24/2012**	**$6,650**	FALSE
9	5325	C	3/2/2012	**1/24/2012**	**$6,650**	TRUE
10	5325	C	3/2/2012	2/8/2012	**$9,000**	FALSE
11	5325	C	3/2/2012	2/8/2012	**$9,000**	TRUE
12	5325	C	3/2/2012	2/15/2012	$1,375	FALSE

The three TRUE exception statements in the above table reveals three duplicate timesheets were invoiced worth $15,000, $6,650, and $9,000, which totals $30,650. Therefore $30,650 more is being billed to the owner for subcontractor labor costs that were never incurred. In other words, if the Subcontractor can sneak in duplicate timesheets, he is rewarded with very little effort. What is more egregious is that the amount of the duplicates indicates an intentional fraud. None of the usual smaller timesheets were duplicated. So if I wanted to intentionally profit from this scheme, I would choose the larger timesheet amounts because submitting a higher number of timesheets with small amounts would run a better chance of being caught through casual inspection.

Most sophisticated computer accounting systems would not allow for these types of mistakes. If I were a contractor, I would tabulate my monthly expenditures and compare that total with the amount of the monthly billing to the owner. Total costs incurred for material purchases or subcontractor payments could be compared to how much I will be receiving from the owner. If there is a disparity of $30,650 more being billed than my costs, there should be a reason.

This technique of finding duplicate submission of timesheets can be used for an entire year of project costs by subcontractors. The effort can take very little time and be very rewarding.

CRAFT LABOR TERMINATIONS

Employment in the building craft trades is temporary in nature depending upon the weather, the economy, and job progress. When the project is complete, the craft sizes are reduced based on project needs. This is commonly referred to as a Reduction in Force.

A craft person that is terminated is usually paid for a full 8 hours for his last day since it is unknown how long he will clear through payroll, return his tools, and return safety equipment. He is to have his last check in hand on the last day of work before he leaves for the day. This last paycheck pays him for all workdays during his last week through his last day.

A notification system should be in place to cancel his right to access the project after he leaves. His electronic badge should be surrendered to Payroll when he receives his last check. His electronic badge should be voided to disallow the turnstile to open and prevent him from re-entering the project. This eliminates any hostile confrontations if the individual feels he was wrongly terminated and protects the owner's property from potential and willful vandalism.

GATE LOGS AND ATTENDANCE RECORDS

Every large construction site should have adequate security with perimeter fencing and controlled access through contractor gates. In the case of large power plants, factories, or commercial sites, the access roads should be separated between contractor employees and owner employees in case of a labor dispute so that any picket lines set up by the contractor's employees or sub-tier contractors would not interfere with the plant's daily operations. This would also avoid the owner's personnel from crossing a picket line. Two separate turnstiles for owner personnel and contractor personnel should also be established. Usually there are two separate distinct parking areas for contractor personnel and owner employees.

The gate logs are permanent records generated by electronic card readers that record entry and departure times, usually in military time, each hour of every day when the employee's badge is swiped through a card reader. This card reader is similar to a credit card transaction. This card reader also opens a turnstile that allows only one person to enter or exit at a time to prevent any tailgating.

Why are turnstiles and badge readers important? Suppose a crew decides to commit fraud and they hand over their badges to the last person to leave at the end of the shift. The majority of the crew leaves site after 8 hours of work where there is no turnstile. The last person leaves after 2 hours of overtime and badges out for everyone. As a result, everyone in the crew is paid 2 hours overtime because the foreman's timecard agrees with the gate log. The next morning, the last person to leave still has all the badges and "clocks in" for everyone, who report for work one hour later. This person hands over their badges to them at the lunch trailer and no one is the wiser. Who can argue with their payroll records unless they witness this process or someone spills the beans?

A gate log record of all entries and departures that is retained beyond the life of the project can save the owner thousands of dollars for time that was paid in error. On a recent project, a crew of 3 doing subcontractor work arrived and departed at the same time. Everyone over-reported their time on site by one or two hours per day. The overpayment isn't a matter of only one person being wrong but the error is multiplied by 3 employees each day. When confronted, they claimed they should be paid portal to portal or from the time they left their motel to the jobsite and from the jobsite to the motel. There was nothing in the contract stipulating this payment. In addition, it did not require more than 15 minutes to travel between those locations.

If the gate log is available in an Excel format, each daily arrival and departure at the project may be stated in military time in rows by employee. A simple formula subtracting departure time by entry time will provide total hours on site. Within a matter of minutes an entire week, month, or year can be compared to hours billed by individual and by employer. The gate log data should be retrievable with searches by employee name, employee number, and employer name.

A few audits of the gate logs pointing out reporting discrepancies will act as a deterrent for the entire project. If the contractors know they are being monitored and will have to answer for these disputes week after week and have to pay for these errors from their own profits, the word gets out that these errors will not be tolerated. Since it is difficult to have employees return payments made in error, their employer will have to absorb these costs. A credit memo from the contractor to the owner is expected in the next invoice.

AUDIT ENHANCEMENT

Unfortunately any comparison with gate log attendance records and payroll reporting is a time consuming manual effort that requires at least one dedicated person. The security badge numbers for accessing the plant will not be the same number as the contractor's employee payroll number. Therefore sorting by employer name, employee name, or Social Security Number may be necessary. Different employees could also have similar names such as John Smith. The same employee can also work for multiple subcontractors as a carpenter for the ABC Company from January to March and then the CBS Company for the rest of the year.

While the gate logs are available on a daily basis, the foremen's timecards and payroll records are not available each day for comparison. The weekly payroll reporting for craft starts on Wednesday at 8 a.m. and ends on Tuesday at 4:30 p.m. of the following week. The monthly payroll for Staff is accumulated and billed to the owner once per month so there is always a lag of several weeks for Staff before a reconciliation can occur. By the time a discrepancy becomes apparent, it is difficult and time consuming for both the owner and the contractor to resurrect the facts from memories. Perhaps the employee had to leave the project early to buy or pick up material for the project. He should not be docked for that excused time away from the Project.

With the advances in computer programming, the gate logs and the employee payroll system could be linked by employee name to "Red Flag" exceptions by day. Any time reporting of 8 hours per day could be compared to the difference between arrival time and departure time to verify a match. Exceptions should be reported to the contractor(s) as soon as possible. These discrepancies may also bring attention to specific Foremen or General Foremen that falsify their timesheets.

Unfortunately many gate log reporting systems are designed for security and are not in the same computer language as payroll systems. These two incompatible systems were never intended by their manufacturers to be linked and therefore they are stand-alone products.

Owners of large construction projects that will consume thousands of man-hours and span several years should consider the gate log reporting system as verification of the contractor payroll. Owners want daily cost reporting rather than weekly or monthly results for cash forecasting and budgeting, which provides a stimulus for real time cost accounting and reporting. Perhaps this will push the development of merging both the payroll system and a gate log reporting system. Since labor costs and overtime are among the highest percentage of the project's overall cost, the payback should justify the investment.

CRAFT PAYROLL CHECKS AND DIRECT DEPOSIT

Craft union employees working on construction projects will travel all over the country to any project that provides stable working hours as well as substantial overtime. They may be away from their primary residence for a significant portion of the year. Most craft unions want to be paid with a physical paper check each Friday rather than having the check wire transferred as a direct deposit. The men need their checks cashed in order to pay their living costs while they are away from home. In addition, many of the construction workers do not want their spouses knowing how much they earn either because of divorce or child support reasons.

Using direct deposit for payroll checks eliminates the possibility of lost checks, stop payment costs for lost checks, and replacements. Direct deposits also eliminates the non-productive time of distributing the checks every week. Direct deposit of payroll checks should be used whenever possible however the unions have historically resisted this payment method.

A local bank may offer to cash the payroll checks for a fee without requiring the men to open a checking account at their bank. This check cashing fee is usually a project cost and billable to the owner.

CRANE OVERTIME – EQUIPMENT HOURS VERSUS OPERATOR'S HOURS

A crane company provides a crane, an operator, and an oiler to a project. The crane is rented for $90,000 per month based on 160 hours in a typical month and the operator and oiler are paid for hours reported on daily timesheets. In an attempt to speed up their cash flow, the crane company bills the crane hours in advance of each month on a separate invoice. The payroll for both men end on Tuesday of every week and are billed after the month ends.

The crane rental of $90,000 per month is based on monthly usage estimated at 160 hours per month or 40 hours per week straight time for four weeks. After the project started, the schedule was accelerated 2 hours of overtime per day. The overtime billing rate for the crane is $562.50 per hour ($90,000/160 hours). Total scheduled hours to be worked per month changed to 200 hours or 50 hours per week (4 weeks at 10 hours per day for 5 days per week). The crane overtime is billed for the 40 extra hours (200 revised hours minus 160 hours quoted) at $562.50 per hour or $22,500 in addition to the base rent of $90,000.

Many reviewers would not consider the two separate invoices together (for the rental and the labor to operate it) but the hours worked by the operator and the oiler has to be considered before paying for crane overtime. Rain out days, Holidays, and Fridays when both employees leave early to drive back home (which can be several hundred miles) can impact total crane hours. How can the crane hours billed exceed total operator hours billed since the crane cannot run by itself?

Let's say there is inclement weather for 8 days during the month. Instead of working 200 hours during the month, only 12- ten hour days are worked due to rain. The total hours worked is 120 hours, which is less than the 160 hours agreed to in the original contract. The base rental is still billed at $90,000 as agreed, but there is no overtime due on the crane. The crane rental company's home office will bill the scheduled hours every month. In this case, $22,500 could potentially be overbilled to the project for crane rental overtime not worked.

While this potential overbilling may be caused by inattention to detail, poor communications, or intentional fraud, the result is the same – the owner is stuck with the bill. The crane company wants to bill the maximum possible while the crane is deployed. The prime contractor does not perform due diligence when reviewing these invoices. No one compared the rental invoice to actual labor hours worked. The owner is ultimately responsible for protecting his assets. This extra review effort should be considered when a rental company furnishes both equipment and labor to operate the equipment. In this particular example a substantial credit was received from the crane company.

THE NATIONAL MAINTENANCE AGREEMENT TERMS

The National Maintenance Agreement establishes mutual understandings for working conditions such as hours of pay, holidays, and overtime on union projects. The purpose is to avoid conflicts between various Building Trade Union contracts and differences that may occur in terminology. In order for the project to progress with minimal interruptions and grievances, the National Maintenance Agreement provides guidance for common work rules at most construction sites.

The following terminology is from the National Maintenance Agreement regarding Holidays, Reporting Time, and Overtime. It is used here for illustrative purposes, with notes, to provide examples of administering craft payroll reporting and pay. While not all projects fall under the National Maintenance Agreement, it is discussed here to provide a better understanding for readers who are not familiar with craft union labor agreements.

Article XI – Holiday

1. For purposes of uniformity, the following holidays shall be observed and, if worked, shall be at the rate applicable in the appropriate local agreement not to exceed double time:

    New Year's Day   President's Day (Federal)
    Memorial Day   Independence Day
    Labor Day   Thanksgiving Day
    Christmas Day

    Note: There are seven recognized holidays for craft union personnel to have a day off without pay. Certain top ranked foremen and/or General foremen within each building trade are guaranteed 40 hours pay (Article XIII below) and will receive the holiday pay of 8 hours straight time.

2. If any of these listed holidays falls on Sunday, the following Monday shall be observed as the holiday. If any of the listed holidays falls on Saturday, the preceding Friday shall be observed as the holiday.

3. "President's Day" may be considered a floating holiday and may be celebrated on an alternate day, if the affected participants to this Agreement within a specific Building Trades Council's geographical jurisdiction mutually agree to celebrate said holiday on another work day. Authorization must be obtained in writing from the NMAPC administrative office.

   Note: Some projects may recognize the day after Thanksgiving as the floating holiday due to poor attendance on that particular Friday.

Article XII – Minimum Pay/Reporting Time and Call-Ins.

1. An employee who reports for work at the regular starting time and for whom no work is provided shall receive pay equivalent to two (2) hours at the applicable hourly rate, provided the employee at the Employer's discretion remains available for work. Any employee who reports for work and for whom work is provided shall be paid for actual time worked but not less than two (2) hours. It will not be a violation of this Agreement when the Employer considers it necessary to shut down to avoid the possible loss of human life because of an emergency situation that could endanger the life and safety of an employee. In such cases, employees will be compensated only for the actual time worked. In the case of a situation described above where the Employer request employees to remain available for work, the employees will be compensated for such time. If a project is shut down because of weather, employees who report for work shall be paid actual time worked but not less than two (2) hours. Procedures for prior notification of work cancellation shall be determined at the pre-job conference. The provisions of this Section are not applicable where the employee voluntarily quits or lays off or is out due to a strike.

   Example 1: An employee reports to work and it is raining. He waits 2 hours while it continues to rain and the day is considered a "rain out". He does not work that day but receives 2 hours straight time pay for "showing up". He has to "show up" and not just call in.

   Example 2: An employee reports to work and it is raining but it stops. He is paid 8 hours straight time for being at work for the full day even though he was prevented from working while it was raining. He may actually work 6 hours but was delayed because of the rain.

   Example 3: An employee reports to work and it rains for 1 hour. He starts to work at 9 a.m. and works until noon when it rains the

rest of the day. He goes home at noon and is paid 4 hours straight time even though he worked less than 4 hours.

Example 4: An employer has the option of stopping work if rain and lightning create hazardous conditions for employees working outside. The employee is paid for actual time worked.

2. A Call-In prior to and continuous with an employee's normally scheduled shift shall be paid for, on the basis of hours actually worked prior to the scheduled shift, at the applicable overtime rate. **A Call-In is an employer's request to start work before the normal shift.**
   A. When an employee is called in to work at or after the established starting time on Saturday, Sunday, scheduled day off or holiday, the employee shall be paid not less than four (4) hours at the applicable overtime rate for that day, except when his/her call-in is prior to and continuous with the normal work hours.
   B. Any call-in not continuous with the employee's regulator work shift, will be a minimum of four (4) hours pay at the applicable overtime rate.

   Note: An employee required to report on Monday morning before his scheduled shift is paid double time because these hours are considered Sunday work if they occur before 8 a.m. Monday morning. An employee required to report on Tuesday through Friday before his scheduled shift is paid time and one half before 8 a.m. A call-in or call back to work outside of his regular shift is compensated for at four hours minimum to compensate him for travel to and from work at odd hours.

   Craft foremen and general foremen may be paid overtime every morning to organize and lay out assignments for men before their arrival in order to expedite progress. Any Safety Meetings or "Plan of the Day" meetings before the normal starting time is paid at overtime rates.

Article XIII –Supervision

1. The designation, appointment, and determination of the number of foremen and/or general foremen shall be the sole responsibility of the Employer. There is a requirement for initial supervision. However, the Employer shall not be unwarrantedly burdened with additional demands for supervision.

2. When established for a craft, one (1) top hourly craft supervisor (foreman and\or general foreman) shall be guaranteed forty (40) straight time

hours per week. The forty (40) straight time hour guarantee applies to straight time hours, and the accumulation of overtime hours may not be considered for the purpose of applying those overtime hours to the "guaranteed forty (40) hours" provision. The forty (40) hour guarantee provision shall apply on a per employer, per craft, per shift basis. It is understood that the individuals receiving such guarantee may, at the discretion of the employer, be required to remain on the job.

Note: The prime contractor and each subcontractor may have a top hourly craft supervisor guaranteed 40 hours straight time pay per week. If the subcontractor has multiple crafts, there may be a top craft supervisor for each craft.

3. Such guarantee shall not apply when the first or commencing week of a job is less than forty (40) hours, or when the top hourly craft supervisor is terminated due to reduction in-force or job completion.

Article XIV – Travel and Subsistence

1. No subsistence, travel allowance, mileage or pay for travel time will be paid to any employee covered by the terms of this Agreement.

2. If the Employer of his subcontractor voluntarily agrees to pay travel or subsistence monies to any craft working in the plant on maintenance, repair, or renovation work, the Craft Named employees will automatically be entitled to receive the applicable travel and subsistence provisions contained in their Local Labor Agreement.

Article XV – Work Hours per Day

1. Eight (8) hours per day shall constitute a day's work and forty (40) hours per week, Monday to Friday, inclusive, shall constitutes a week's work. The regular starting time shall be eight (8) o'clock A.M. and the regular quitting time shall be four-thirty (4:30) o'clock P.M.; lunch time shall be twelve (12) o'clock noon to twelve-thirty (12:30) o'clock P.M.

Note: When crafts are required to "Work through Lunch", they are paid one-half hour of overtime and eat lunch "on the fly" or when it is convenient. Management should provide prior approval for working through lunch and this paid overtime. The decision to work through lunch for a concrete pour is understandable since the process cannot be stopped or the concrete will dry and it is desirable to have one continuous concrete pour. Other processes such as delivering rock for a road improvement are not essential to

require working through the lunch period. Overtime should not be decided by the truck drivers.

2. When shifts are required, the first shift shall work eight (8) hours at the regular straight-time rate. The second shift shall work seven and one-half (7 ½) hours and receive the equivalent of eight hours pay at the employee's regular straight time hourly rate plus $.25. The third shift shall work seven (7) hours and receive the equivalent of eight (8) hours pay at the employee's regular straight time hourly rate plus $.50. A thirty (30) minute lunch period shall be mutually agreed upon by the Job Superintendent and the Union Representative and shall not be considered as time worked.

   Note: These provisions may vary concerning the incentive rates of $.25 and $.50 for back shifts.

3. All time worked before and after the established work day of eight (8) hours, Monday through Friday, shall be paid at the appropriate overtime rate. All work commencing with the beginning of the established workday on Saturday shall be paid at the rate of time and one-half. All work commencing with the beginning of the established work day on Sundays and/or holidays shall be paid at the rate applicable in the appropriate local agreement not to exceed double-time.

4. By mutual consent of the Employer and the Union, the starting and quitting times of any shift, including day of work, may be changed for all or any portion of a participating job. For the purpose of this Article, the standard work day of eight (8) hours for the job or portion thereof to which any such change of starting time applies shall begin with such agreed starting time.

   Note: Some projects may start before 8 a.m. during the summer to take advantage of daylight savings time and more daylight as well as avoiding the hotter weather. The normal starting time then becomes 7 a.m. and normal quitting time is 3:30 p.m.

5. Employees shall be at their posts prepared to start work at the regular starting time.

   Note: This normally means the craft are at their respective gang boxes receiving their assignments for the day and obtaining their tools and materials. It does not mean they are leaving their respective change shacks and walking to the work area.

CHAPTER 7 –
STAFF SALARIES

SALARIED OVERTIME

When do salaried staff earn overtime? Is it after the first 8 hours in a day or after casual overtime is worked such as more than 50 hours in six consecutive days? This may be a contractual agreement with the owner or based on the contractor's employee policies. A component of the hourly salary rate may allow for some expected overtime to meet unexpected project requirements and therefore there is no additional cost billable to the owner until the staff employee exceeds 50 hours. Any salaried overtime at the jobsite should be defined in writing so the owner is aware of what is reimbursable.

When the contract is silent and there is no casual overtime, the Federal government defines overtime as hours worked that exceed 40 hours in a work week for non-union white collar administrative and clerical staff. A workweek for non-union personnel is normally hours worked Monday through Sunday. These workers are normally paid twice per month and billed to the owner once per month.

EXAMPLES OF ABUSE

Let's follow some examples regarding paid overtime for staff assuming there is no casual overtime component. If a staff person works 4 days in one week for 8 hours per day, he has earned 32 hours of straight time pay. If he takes Friday off for personal business (which is non-billable) and then returns to work on Saturday, he may consider the Saturday as overtime pay since it is above and beyond the normal workweek of Monday through Friday. But he has to satisfy the 40 hours per week requirement to get paid overtime. Therefore if he works a total of 40 hours in six days with one day off, he is only entitled to straight time pay unless there is some other prevailing agreement. Wouldn't it be nice to work only 4 days per week, take every Friday off, and get premium pay to make up for the missed day?

This same Federal Law applies to subcontractors/consultants wanting overtime pay before meeting their 40 hour minimum. Some non-union management or staff workers travel to the jobsite several hundred miles from their home and want to leave early on Fridays in order to have a longer weekend. So they work 4 days at 9 hours each day. The total is 36 hours of straight time, not 32 hours straight time plus 4 hours overtime. Auditors should be aware of this Federal law to avoid this simple way of overbilling the project for both staff employees and non-union consultants/service providers.

Union craft workers do get paid for every hour worked and would get paid overtime each day for all time exceeding 8 hours per day.

SALARIED STAFF ON MULTIPLE PROJECTS

Some major projects may have more than one Work Order, Purchase Order, or contract with the same contractor on the same construction site. There may be ongoing maintenance work, a remodeling job, and a new installation job awarded to the same contractor during the same year. It would be easy to bill the same hours for the same staff person on multiple projects. The contractor may submit separate billings by Purchase Order, Work Order, or Contract number. No one considers if a duplication of hours could occur since each invoice may be reviewed independently by different departments or personnel such as the Accounts Payable Department, Project Controls Department, and Construction Audit Department.

The owner's auditors can summarize the monthly payrolls by project on an Excel spreadsheet with the heading of each job at the top of the worksheet and the employee name and badge number listing by pay period along the left side of the page. All straight time hours and overtime hours worked by individuals should be posted to this spreadsheet to determine if the same hours were duplicated. The same is true when there is an overtime exemption for the first 10 hours worked that is considered casual overtime and not directly billable. When the staff billing rate was established, an allowance may have been provided for some overtime each week that was anticipated to be worked. These "professionals" are paid to get the job done and their staff billing rates normally includes some component for this overtime without billing for the first hour of overtime worked.

By totaling all hours billed by project by person by pay period, the straight time hours may exceed 40 hours per week or perhaps the 10 hour overtime allowance is being billed for all hours worked. This can result in significant savings to the project over several years if the owner would make the effort to track these hours on an Excel spreadsheet every month. No salaried staff employee should be billed for more than 40 hours of straight time per week, i.e. 45 hours of straight time. In this example, the five extra hours billed is profit to the contractor because he did not actually incur additional costs.

OVERHEAD FEE - BONUSES

Most contractors bill an overhead fee to cover their home office costs and other "indirect" costs such as executive salaries, home office building maintenance, home office clerical staff, training, bonuses, etc. This fee could be 15% added for every direct dollar spent and is often forgotten when disputes arise as to what is billable or non-billable. Since bonuses for contractor staff working at the project are discretionary in nature, bonuses should be predefined as billable or non-billable and the owner should provide prior approval before the payment is made to the employee and billed to the owner.

If a contractor staff employee is paid a $3,000 annual performance bonus, the contractor bills that amount to the owner plus his overhead fee and profit fee. So why not be generous with the owner's money since more paid bonuses will enhance the contractor's bottom line? The monthly overhead fee of 15% added to every invoice should be adequate to compensate the contractor for most staff bonuses.

Bonuses can create animosity if the owner's employees do not receive comparable bonuses for similar work and the payments become known through the monthly invoice payment process. After all, these dollars ultimately come from the owner who may not be as generous with their own employees. The owner may be under tight budget constraints because of the project so the owner's employees may have experienced minimal raises and little or no performance bonuses. Preferably, since bonuses are discretionary and determined by the contractor, they should not be a direct billable cost.

Some contractors want to pay a retainer bonus to keep "key" employees as the project nears completion to prevent employees from leaving early in order to go to another project. These payments may represent several weeks pay in a lump sum. These bonuses, if paid, should have the prior written approval of the owner. The owner may decide that the employee, based on his past performance, isn't worth retaining on the project after all and isn't worth a retainer bonus.

Seldom will a construction contract provide details regarding bonuses. The bonuses may be included in the contractor's existing employee compensation policies and they routinely pass these costs on to the owner as a cost of the project. Contractors will rarely seek prior approval from the owner if they will be denied but instead will spend the money first and then ask for forgiveness later.

SALARIED RATES

Most owners should have the right to know the components of contractor staff rates. Each component such as the hourly rate, benefits, insurance, cell phones, and car allowance that is included in the billing rate can reveal if these same items are billed separately in other sections of the invoice. These would include vacations, holidays, sick leave, funeral leave, and auto reimbursement. It may also reveal hidden mark-ups on such obligations as workmen's comp and other insurance. If the salary rates fully compensate the contractor for his staff, there may not be any additional overhead and fee adders charged on staff salaries.

TOTAL STAFF HOURS BILLED - HOLIDAYS

There can be 10 or more paid holidays for staff employees including New Year's Day, Dr. Martin Luther King's Birthday, President's Day, Memorial Day, July 4th, Labor Day, Thanksgiving and the day after Thanksgiving, Christmas Eve, and Christmas Day. There is a possibility that holidays can be directly billed for each staff employee on the project while the hourly staff rates include a component for this time off. Here is another example of a "double dip".

The total work hours in a year is 2,080 hours based on 40 hours per week times 52 weeks. If the 10 holidays are deducted from the total hours available, the maximum hours available to be worked is only 2,000 hours (not including paid vacations and sick leave). Deducting 3 weeks of vacation allowance plus one week of sick leave leaves 1,840 work hours in one year.

If the owner can recap the entire year that straight time hours were billed, he may find these holidays and vacations were directly billed to the project. If an employee is billed for 2,100 hours straight time and the contractor provides no transparency for allowed time off, the contractor billed more than the annual $50,000 salary for that employee and over-recovered his cost. There is no other explanation. It is imperative that staff payroll hours are summarized in an Excel format so these tabulations can be performed for the entire year.

To take this example one step further, staff labor rates (both hourly and salaried) are based upon an assumption that the employee will work 1,840 straight time hours in a year (considering 3 weeks of vacation, 10 holidays, plus one week sick leave). To calculate the per hour cost of an employee's total compensation, the estimated total annual cost was divided by 1,840 hours. For example, if an employee's salary and benefits is $50,000 per year, then the straight time hourly billing rate would be $27.17 ($50,000/1,840 hours = $27.17 per hour). If the excused absences are not included in the billing rate and were directly billable based on 2,080 hours per year, the hourly billing rate would be only $24.04 per hour ($50,000/2,080).

The easiest method for a contractor to pay his staff employees is through the project's payroll system because he cannot write a payroll check from his home office payroll system for an employee not assigned to the home office. So both the time worked and the allowed time off is paid to the employee on his bi-weekly payroll check and billed to the owner. It is up to the owner to dispute this excess billing and request a refund from the contractor.

Some contractor's code their paid time off on the payroll register to indicate V for vacation pay, H for holiday pay, S for sick pay, and O for other pay. This provides an easier audit trail for a small project staff to determine total allowed time off. Not every payroll register has this transparency. If "H" appears on the payroll register with billable costs and the salary component includes paid holidays, the contractor is obviously billing for holidays.

Most owners, due to time constraints, do not compile total hours billed for the entire year as well as for multiple work orders per employee to realize how much extra was charged for staff. Is the contractor intentionally billing extra profits or was this an oversight? This one audit finding can justify staffing a construction site with an auditor representing the owner's best interests.

WORKING THROUGH LUNCH (PAID OVERTIME) FOR CONTRACTOR AND SUBCONTRACTOR STAFF

The contractor or subcontractor staff may report working through lunch at time and one half overtime rates. Sometimes staff positions are filled with a service company or vendor that provides bodies and these individuals are not direct employees of the contractor. These individuals soon realize their positions are temporary and will last only for the duration of the project.

These staff individuals may start reporting their time as working through lunch every day regardless of what they are working on. Their immediate supervisor may or may not hold them responsible to correctly report their time worked. A check with the gate logs during the lunch hour may indicate they leave the project to eat at a local restaurant. When challenged why they reported overtime, they will respond that they had to run an errand such as going to the Post Office, picking up office supplies, etc.

The owner's staff has to decide how much time they want to devote to these games. They could ask for copies of cancelled checks made payable to the Post Office or a copy of the invoice or receipt for the transactions that occurred on these trips or just disallow overtime during these trips that could be better scheduled. The bottom line is that some supervisor allows these abuses to continue and approved their timecards for overtime. Falsification of project documents including timecards could lead to termination and should be emphasized to all project personnel. These supervisors are risking their own jobs by knowingly recording overtime as hours worked when the employee is eating their lunch. It only takes one incident such as a termination to notify all project staff that time reporting "mistakes" will not be tolerated. The owner's staff should have strong evidence that abuse did occur over an extended period of time to defend against any wrongful discrimination case that may be filed.

STAFF LABOR RATE INCREASES

Contractors update their staff labor rates on an annual basis. During this revision process, rates are increased and some employees are promoted to higher positions. Usually the owner does not formally review and approve the updated staff labor rates or the impact on project costs due to employee promotions. These rate changes are not published but will show up on the next payroll where the new effective rates take place. Usually the invoice reviewer is the only one aware that changes were billed. The percentage rate changes should be reasonable to reflect the general rise in inflation and the job market. Also job title promotions may reflect a higher salary entitlement but is the employee actually assuming that higher position and more responsibilities?

Contractor staff labor rates may be part of the contract as an Addendum or Appendix to the contract. Therefore any changes to the contract, such as new staff rates, should require a formal written Change Order that is approved in advance by the owner with the effective date of acceptance. This Change Order proposal should be submitted to the owner for approval prior to the inception date of the new rates along with internal cost support. The owner should review the internal cost support and the individual's qualifications to determine the appropriateness of all adjustments. The contractor should not bill the new rates until the owner has approved the rate changes.

ALLOWANCE FOR VEHICLE EXPENSE

Some staff labor rates may include a rate per hour for contractor provided vehicles for certain job titles. However, the contractor may also directly bill the owner for pick-up trucks, gas, and maintenance, which represent potential duplicate charges for vehicle expenses. The contractor should provide a list of assigned vehicles so the owner can determine if a staff member's billing rate includes this charge. The reviewer should also determine if gasoline, maintenance, and repairs are being charged directly to the project for vehicles that should not be directly charged.

Pick-up trucks can be leased for a fixed amount each month from third party companies. In other words, the rental company does not increase the monthly rental rate when the driver works overtime. The owner may unknowingly be billed higher vehicle costs when the staff bills for overtime. There is no correlation between the pick-ups costing more per month when overtime is worked because the vehicles are parked in the employee parking lot longer each day. The employee may have the use of a pool vehicle such as a truck, golf cart, or gator while on the project. The owner should be cognizant of any potential overcharges and request a refund of the total amount.

CELL PHONES

Cell phones have become a business necessity for contacting personnel after hours and on weekends. Cell phones may be reimbursed to the contractor in the salary rates for certain key personnel based on hours worked. The monthly cell phone costs are normally fixed each month and do not increase when the employee works overtime. The reviewer should determine, within the terms of the contract, how cell phone costs are reimbursed.

As a side note, some cell phone bills that are provided for review will detail hours and dates used as well as the amount of time used for texting. Since texting is not the normal business means of communications but typically for personal use, the bill can reveal personnel that are not performing their job duties and are spending an unreasonable amount of time on personal business. This could represent a safety hazard on a construction site and should be brought to the attention of the contractor.

CERTIFIED PAYROLL REPORTS

On any Federal project where the use of public monies is used, the project will likely require the payment of prevailing wages under the provisions of the Davis-Bacon Act or other minimum-wage payment requirements.

Confirmation of the payment of subcontractors of such prevailing wages will be done by way of Certified Payroll Reports. These are reporting forms on which the respective employer certifies to the owner the actual amount of wages, taxes, and fringe benefits paid to the individual employees for hours worked on particular dates.

Staff salary rates may be exempt under the prevailing wages for union workers but all employers still have to pay at least the Federal Minimum Wage amounts to their administrative staff. Contractors are reluctant to provide

Certified Payroll Reports for their staff employees and may totally refuse to provide them.

EMPLOYEE BENEFITS

A contractor may bill the project for staff fringe benefits such as pension profit sharing, 401K matching funds, medical and dental insurance, and employee life and accident insurance. The calculation of the bill may be based on head count, gross payroll, or some other percentage factor.

The reviewer should bear in mind that perhaps not all staff members may qualify for participation in these programs without several years of service with their company. At many remote project locations, the contractor will hire local residents for the duration of the project with no intent to offer them future employment after the project ends. These personnel may never qualify to participate in dental plans or pension profit sharing without being vested with the company. The contractor may invoice for these "costs" that are retained as profits.

PER DIEM POLICY

Per diem policies were discussed in Chapter 2 under Corporate Policies. Per diem amounts are an IRS determined average (based on locality) for reimbursement of meals and incidentals other than lodging and travel expenses. Actual receipts are required for lodging. The following discussion provides guidance for managing per diem expenses.

Employers in the construction, aerospace, defense contracting, nuclear power generation, and other similar industries fill many of their technical positions with "temporary" employees provided by technical services firms also known as job shops. The job shops are employment agencies specializing in locating highly skilled technical employees, including engineers, designers, architects, programmers, and toolmakers. The duration of the employee's job may vary from a few days to several years, depending on the length of the contract between the employer and the employment agency.

An employer gives the employee a daily allowance of up to $XXX to cover travel expenses associated with the job assignment even though, in many cases, the employee resides in the vicinity of the job assignment. The employer makes no attempt to verify that the employee qualifies for travel status (being away from home overnight) and there is no requirement that the employee account back to the employer for funds expended. The employer does not include the daily allowance in the employee's income, does not report it on Form W-2, and does not classify it as wages for employment tax purposes.

Per diem can be paid for temporary assignments of up to one year and after one year the term and the amount may change to "Subsistence".

The difficulty of auditing per diem payments is that the amounts may vary based on job title and there is no written contractual basis to identify abuses and seek refunds for the owner. The following per diem and subsistence format may help set the rules for both owner and contractor for administration if the contract is silent regarding per diem and subsistence payments.

Employee Name	Position or Title	Days on Site per Week	Home Location	Duration on Project	Per Diem or Subsistence Rate

Rules:
1. Cannot have per diem/subsistence and out of pocket reimbursement in the same period, unless traveling off-site.
2. Reimbursable relocation expenses are limited to _____.
3. Weekend travel is limited to _____.
4. Subsistence is provided only if on-site _____ days per week.
5. The rates shown above must be effective through January 1, 20xx.
6. Job assignments less than ___ months must be per diem or out-of-pocket reimbursement (not subsistence).
7. Job assignments greater than ___ months must be subsistence based.
8. The maximum per diem is $_____ per week.
9. The maximum subsistence is $_____ per month.
10. No per diems may be charged when the employee is not on-site, including weekends.

TRAVEL TIME

What is travel time? Travel time allows for compensating an employee for his salary or hours "on-the-clock" while he is traveling to or from the project. Many technical consultants, service technicians/vendors providing mechanical repairs to construction equipment, and "Subject Matter Experts" will expect to be paid for their time for the full day regardless of how many hours are actually spent on the project. Their contracts and purchase orders should define travel time.

A large project held a monthly progress meeting which required the attendance of the contractor's Vice President to be in attendance. He flew from South Carolina to Missouri and returned to South Carolina the same day. The monthly progress meeting usually ran about 6 hours and discussed project milestones, safety issues, critical path items, and projected target dates. All of his expenses were paid by the owner to include air fare, car rental, airport parking in South Carolina, and gasoline for the rental car. This project was built before video conferencing was established.

The total hours reported by the Vice President was usually 15 hours including travel time, after considering airport delays and driving home from the airport. The contractor billed overtime for the Vice President to attend these meetings. The owner objected since the Vice President was salaried and the contractor did not actually pay overtime to the Vice President and therefore did not incur any overtime costs. These charges were pure profits for the contractor. Since the contract was actual cost plus, the amount was refunded. Without a thorough review of the billing, this refund would never have been disputed.

Some technical consultants travel to their personal residence on weekends several hundred miles from the project and in order to be available for work on Monday mornings, they drive back to the project on Sunday. This driving time on Sunday is charged at double time rates even though the trip was for personal reasons and not required by the project or owner. Contract terminology should be very specific that travel time will only be reimbursed with the prior approval of the owner, especially when double time is incurred.

CHAPTER 8 -
CONTRACTOR INSURANCE

All contractors and subcontractors performing work at the project site must be covered by all insurances required in the contract. This applies to all individuals working as contractors, sub-tier contractors, or consultants in any capacity. The prime contractor's Superintendent is responsible to confirm the presence of all such insurances and secure the correct Certification of Insurance from each company before allowing any work to proceed on the site. There should be no exceptions.

The owner should designate a responsible department to document receipt of all insurance certificates and request updated Certificates of Insurance upon expiration of the old certificate. The Certificates of Insurance are usually issued for one year terms by the insurance carrier and names the owner as a secondary beneficiary.

Every company has to carry Worker's Compensation, Employer's Liability, Commercial General Liability Insurance, Business Automobile Liability, Owner's Protective Liability, and Builder's Risk. These insurance policies, with their limits of liability, should be defined by contract. The contract should also define the method of reimbursement by the owner to the contractor. These policies are mandatory as a cost of doing business regardless of how many contracts or which contracts the contractor is working on. So the question becomes "How does the owner know he is only paying for insurance applicable to his project?" Additional insurance required by the contract, such as flood insurance or umbrella insurance, can be billed as a direct billable expense if the owner is named as an insured.

The contractor may attempt to invoice other home office insurance indirectly and discreetly through craft payroll adders for every hour worked. There may also be components in equipment rental rates or staff salary components to "pocket" more of these indirect costs and pass them on to the owner. The intent of many contracts is to have the overhead adder fee, say 15% of all direct costs, as the means to reimburse the contractor for overhead insurance costs not related to the project. If insurance is also directly billed, we have a case of the "double dip". Craft and Staff payroll rates and benefits should have full transparency with each element described as a union obligation or contractual commitment. There should be no unexplained adders or percentage factors that add to a staff or craft billing rate.

Insurance companies provide discounts in their premiums for experience modifiers, premium discounts, policy dividends, retrospective rating plan premium adjustments, assigned risk pool rebates, and refunds. Contract terminology should specify that all premiums for any insurance required for the project should reflect the net actual cost to the contractor.

Some contractors carry "self-insurance". The problem with self-insurance is there is no way to verify the actual cost incurred since there is no invoice from a third party insurance carrier. These charges can carry hidden profits for the contractor. Also self-insurance does not explain the mechanics of the owner being reimbursed for any claims.

As a contract condition for a "Time and Material" project the following terms should be stated: "No charges for self-insurance will be considered as a reimbursable cost under the term of this agreement. The cost of any self-insurance shall be considered to be covered by the contractor's Fee."

If self-insurance is accepted by terms of the contract, the costs for self-insurance should not exceed the comparable cost of purchasing conventional insurance from third parties.

OWNER COORDINATED INSURANCE PROGRAM (OCIP)

The owner of the project may secure specific insurance coverage for itself, enrolled contractors, subcontractors, and consultants who perform on-site labor or whose contract requires on-site labor at the project site only. This coverage is during the construction or renovation of the property only. The OCIP does not provide coverage for the operations of contractors while working at any other locations such as at their fabrication shops. The OCIP is intended to offer broad coverage with relatively high limits. The OCIP does not normally include Automobile Liability, Property, or contractor's equipment insurance.

OCIP advantages to Owners over Traditional Insuring Methods:
- Lower costs to the property owner as bulk purchase of insurance lowers total cost.
- Owner controlled insurance broker requires more stringent safety and loss control procedures.

- Reduction in time required for contractors to obtain insurance certificates.
- Improved risk control and claim handling.

OCIP disadvantages to Owners over Traditional Insuring Methods:
- Increased administrator burden.
- Increased accounting effort required to isolate contractor and subcontractor costs and insurance burden.
- Potential for contractors insured under the OCIP to claim for non-project injuries.

OCIP advantages to Contractors over Traditional Insuring Methods:
- Potential greater insurance limits than contractor could otherwise obtain.
- Potential for contractor to work on projects that contractor could not otherwise obtain.

OCIP disadvantages to Contractors over Traditional Insuring Methods:
- Potential gaps in insurance coverage.
- Potential losses in prepaid insurance premiums.
- Uncompensated administrative costs of the contractor.

Owner Controlled Insurance Programs (OCIPs) are becoming a standard feature in the construction industry. The owner buys insurance for all the participants on a construction project and requires the participants to reduce their price by eliminating all of their insurance costs in exchange for owner-provided coverage. The coverage can include General Liability, Builder's Risk, Worker's Compensation, design errors, and omissions as well as excess, umbrella, and other special coverage. An "OCIP Administrator", usually a third party insurance company, administers the OCIP program. The OCIP Administrator acts as an agent of the owner and usually is supplied by the broker that sets up the OCIP program.

Cost saving is the primary advantage of an OCIP. The owner-developer always indirectly bears the cost of insurance on a construction project. The design consultants, contractor, subcontractors, and other parties involved in the project, in pricing their work, pass through the cost of insurance plus a markup. Insurers and brokers assert that an owner can save from 0.5 to 2 percent of total construction costs by using an OCIP. The savings come from the elimination of contractor markup on insurance costs and the ability to obtain insurance at a lower cost than contractors, subcontractors and others can obtain it individually.

OCIP coverage will be tailored specifically to the project. Contractors and subcontractors must be required to provide proof of insurance by their own carriers for non-covered activities. Warranty work and call-backs are not covered after completion of the project by OCIP.

WORKER'S COMPENSATION

Worker's compensation is a form of insurance that provides wage replacement and medical benefits for employees who are injured in the course of employment in exchange for mandatory relinquishment of the employee's right to sue his or her employer for the tort of negligence. Weekly payments in place of wages, compensation for economic loss, reimbursement or payment of medical and like expenses, and benefits payable to the dependents of workers killed during employment (functioning in this case as a form of life insurance) are provided through worker's comp. General damages for pain and suffering and punitive damages for employer negligence are generally not available in worker's compensation plans.

Worker's compensation is administered on a state-by-state basis with a state governing board overseeing varying public/private combinations of workers compensation systems.

It is illegal in most states for an employer to terminate or refuse to hire an employee for having reported a workplace injury or who have filed a workers' compensation claim. However, it is often not easy to prove discrimination on the basis of the employee's claims history.

Statistics show that many workplace accidents occur on Mondays, when workers are not focused on their jobs and may still be reliving the weekend. Accidents also increase with overtime with fatigue becoming a factor. Some employees are notoriously accident prone and experience repetitive minor injuries due to carelessness, not following directions, or inattention to detail. These individuals, after considerable coaching, may persistently have accidents and pose a hazard to other workers. Accident reports must be kept for OSHA requirements and the frequency and severity of injuries.

As the project nears completion and workers are faced with job layoffs, an employee may consider intentionally being injured in order to draw worker's comp if future job prospects look daunting. Though difficult to prove, the owner and contractor have an obligation to sustain a safe workplace and perform a thorough investigation and review of all accidents, their causes, trends, and prevention.

BUILDER'S RISK INSURANCE

Builder's risk insurance is a special type of property insurance which indemnifies against damage to buildings while they are under construction. Builder's risk insurance is coverage that protects a person's or an organization's insurance interest in materials, fixtures, and/or equipment being used in the construction or renovation of a building or structure should those sustain physical loss or damage from a covered cause.

Builder's risk insurance usually indemnifies against losses due to fire, vandalism, lightning, wind, and similar forces. It usually does not cover earthquake, flood, acts of war, or intentional acts of the owner. Coverage is typically during the construction period only and is intended to terminate when the work has been completed and the property is ready for use or occupancy.

Usually the owner of the building buys this insurance but the general contractor constructing the building may buy it if it is required as a condition of the contract. It may be necessary to show proof of insurance to comply with local city, county, and state building codes.

NON-BILLABLE INSURANCE

There are several types of coverage that companies carry as an ongoing business that are not directly related to any specific project. This insurance may be obtained regardless if the contractor has one or fifty projects. The reviewer should scrutinize the billing and the contract for terms requiring the owner to reimburse the contractor for specific coverage that is not related to the project.

Kidnap and Ransom Insurance - This insurance covers the perils of kidnap, extortion, wrongful detention, and hijacking in high risk areas around the world. The policies do not directly pay ransoms. Criminal gangs are believed to make $500 million a year from kidnap and ransom payments. The contractor on a project in Illinois actually billed this insurance as a component of their equipment rental rates to recover this cost. This was denied by the owner because it was compensated for in their overhead fee percentage.

Directors and Officers Liability Insurance – This liability insurance is payable to the directors and officers of a company, or to the organization itself, to cover damages or defense costs in the event they suffer such losses as a result of a lawsuit for alleged wrongful acts while acting in their capacity as directors and officers for the organization. Such coverage can extend to defense costs arising out of criminal and regulatory investigations.

STAFF LABOR RATES

Some contractors may develop staff labor rates based on job titles and employee responsibilities regardless of the project or the owner. These rates are used on multiple projects and adjusted annually. There is a possibility that an OCIP project is billed the same staff labor rates as a non-OCIP project. A component of the staff labor rates is Worker's Compensation Insurance, which is a component paid for by the owner on an OCIP project. Thus the owner of an OCIP project may be overbilled for this component of staff labor rates if he is providing this coverage.

SUMMARY

Many years can be devoted to become an expert regarding Insurance. The point of discussing contractor insurance is to provide some knowledge as to what insurance costs are directly billable and not billable. Be aware that contractors/subcontractors may attempt to bill:

1. For the cost of insurance that is already provided by the owner in an OCIP Policy and which exceeds the allowable amounts.
2. For an insurance policy but the contractor does not obtain the insurance policy.
3. For overhead fees and profit fees on insurance costs when those costs may be "pass through" costs (not subject to any additional fees) based on the contract terms.
4. For adders to craft payroll hourly rates, staff labor rates, or equipment rates that are disguised as insurance components that are not directly billable.

CHAPTER 9 -
LIEN WAIVERS

A **Lien** is a security interest in the particular real estate that has been improved. A Lien is placed by a contractor, subcontractor, an equipment rental company, or a material supplier to secure payment for labor, material, or equipment used in the property's improvement. A Lien provides for the right to sell the property (against the owner's wishes) to which the Lien attaches if the debt is not paid. The threat of a Lien being placed on real property motivates prime contractors to pay their bills for goods and services provided by others.

A **Lien Waiver** is executed to waive an individual's or a company's right to assert a Lien. Owners and prime contractors should obtain Lien Waivers from the subcontractors, rental companies, and material suppliers that exceed a threshold of business activity. Lien laws exist in every state and vary greatly in their terms.

Where an owner requires Lien Waivers from all significant parties doing business on a project, the prime contractor has the requirement to pay those companies in exchange for their Lien Waiver, which indicates they acknowledge payment and are giving up their right to place a Lien for that time period or that payment, however the terms are structured. Those Lien Waivers are provided to the owner, who should diligently track both those Lien Waivers that have and have not been received. Once a valid Lien Waiver has been received in the terminology that is acceptable to the owner and supplier, the supplier no longer has the right to file a Lien on that portion of the payment or time period.

A WORST CASE SCENARIO

A contractor was hired to rebuild a coal fired furnace at an existing utility coal plant for a lump sum amount. He negotiated and contracted for all labor, materials, rental equipment, and subcontractors. As the job progressed things went from bad to worse. The existing building had more obstructions than anticipated, which caused more problems and delays in tearing out the old furnace and installing the new furnace while dealing with existing piping, electrical conduit, overhead beams, walls, etc. The vendors and contractors were not getting paid on time but they knew the full faith and credit of the utility and knew their money would be paid in the end. The contractor ran out of money as he reached the maximum contract price to bill the owner. Eventually the subcontractors and suppliers filed Liens in order to be paid. The owner was unaware of any problems but ultimately had to settle each Lien by paying out of pocket. At the end of the project, the utility had to pay thousands in unpaid bills in order to clear all the Liens and had to file suit against the prime contractor.

FULL VERSUS PARTIAL WAIVERS OF LIEN

Since Lien rights are created by statute and not of common law, they can be waived. The Waivers themselves are necessary both as a protection of the owner and as an inducement to the owner to release additional payment.

Many owner payment procedures will require the delivery of appropriate Lien Waivers for all payments in prior periods as a condition of releasing the current payment. If a single sub-sub-vendor is delinquent in the delivery of a single Waiver, it can have the effect of locking up the entire general payment. Attention must be continually and persistently focused on maintaining all required Waivers on an absolute current basis.

PARTIAL WAIVERS OF LIEN

A partial waiver of Lien is a document issued by the payee to waive its rights to assert a Lien for an amount equal to the respective payment. This is usually a straightforward procedure accepted by most without much objection. If a subcontractor bills $150,000 during the month of August, the Waiver may identify the amount of $150,000 being waived, or for all work performed during the month of August, or by specific invoice number. The Waiver is not all inclusive for prior or later months, future invoices, or future claims that are in dispute but have not been billed.

FULL WAIVERS OF LIEN

This Waiver generally releases all rights to every Lien on the property that is the subject of the agreement for work completed or yet to be completed. If the general contractor provides the owner with a 100 percent payment bond, and the subcontract agreement provides for arbitration after a certain dispute resolution procedure is followed, payment rights of the subcontractor have been substantially protected. Requiring the subcontractor to execute a full Waiver puts the problem resolution back into the subcontractor procedure and not onto the property.

FINAL WAIVERS OF LIEN

A final release of Lien usually accompanies the final release of all retention at project completion and acknowledges that there are no other disputes, claims, or counterclaims, and all bills to vendors, suppliers, rental agencies, and sub-tier contractors have been made. The release indicates no future Liens will be filed.

LIEN WAIVER EXAMPLE

Several years ago, we hired a Plumber to install a bathtub in our basement bathroom as well as ceramic tile surrounding the tub. For some unknown reason the home builder installed a bathroom with sink and toilet and left the rest of the room empty but allowed enough space for a tub. We thought having a full bath would add to the resale value of the house.

Since I did not know much about this Plumber or his reputation, he asked me if I wanted Lien Waivers and I said yes. He seemed rather perturbed about getting them but I didn't think it should be a big deal. Lien Waivers are a common practice in the construction industry.

If a material supplier (a tub salesman) does not get paid for furnishing the tub, he has no other recourse but to file a Lien on the property where it was installed (my house). As a homeowner, I pay the Plumber and he pays the tub salesman. The homeowner assumes all obligations are satisfied and usually does not pursue a Lien Waiver from the Plumber. A Plumber's Lien Waiver does not stop other vendors from filing a Lien if they know the final consumer of their product. This tub salesmen's Lien may not be discovered until several years or decades later when the house is listed for sale and there is a title search for a clear title. A Lien filed on any property "clouds" the title and needs to be cleared before title to the house can be transferred.

Some deceptive contractors skip town with all the money without paying their suppliers (more profit), leaving the owner with the obligation to pay for the tub again even though it was included in the installed price. The same thing happens on large construction projects when the owner pays the prime contractor acting in good faith and finds out later that his suppliers and subcontractors did not get paid.

The owner should seek competent legal advice to confirm the specific requirements and details of local law. The owner should determine the frequency of transactions with suppliers in a quarter (say over 25 transactions for small consumables) or capital spending cut off limits (say over $25,000) that require Lien Waivers. Obtaining Lien Waivers from all suppliers is a very time consuming and labor intensive process for everyone. Many small vendors may refuse to provide Waivers. A final Lien Waiver from the prime contractor and subcontractors should be stated in the contract.

WAIVER FORMS

Because the terminology can differ between what the owner's attorneys require and the material or subcontractor's attorney require, there should be a resolution in the early stages of the contract negotiations. Each party wants to protect their respective rights. Some Waivers are time specific to include all material and labor performed through a period such as June 30. Some Waivers are dollar specific to include identifiable invoice numbers and amounts. These match ups can be very time consuming when deductions have been taken, disputes are unresolved, and Credit Memos are pending and have not been issued. The owner's attorneys should provide guidance based on the location of the project and applicable state laws.

LIEN WAIVER LOG -TRACKING LIENS

Tracking Lien Waivers on large projects may require a full time staff person. Lien Waivers may be rejected by the owner if the forms are unacceptable or if they are not signed by a Company's Officer. A Lien Waiver Log is provided in Chapter 16 using the contractor's monthly workbook (Chapter 14) for submission of invoices. The idea is to copy and paste invoice details directly from the material, third party rentals, and subcontract sections of the workbook (to include invoice numbers, dates, and amounts) to the Lien Waiver Log. This eliminates the repetitive manual typing of each invoice number, invoice date, and invoice amount that can easily consume hundreds of man hours. It would be faster and easier to copy and paste hundreds of lines of data and can be performed in minutes and results in fewer typo mistakes as well as better employee morale for the individual responsible for this arduous task. More attention can be placed on pursuing open Liens than typing the information.

This clerical individual should be familiar with Excel and the copy and paste functions. The columns with invoice numbers, dates, and amounts are highlighted, and copied from the Invoice Workbook directly to the Lien Waiver Log. With each monthly submission of invoices, this individual updates the Lien Waiver log and thus has a list of Liens that should be submitted the following month for closure. As can be seen on the Invoice Workbook, the same invoices are listed in the Material tab as the Lien Waiver Log.

The Lien Waiver Log also draws attention to the Lien Waivers that are past due by comparing the current date with the Invoice date. This should expedite attention to the vendors, subcontractors, and equipment rental companies who are delinquent in providing Lien Waivers.

This simplification of administering Lien Waivers is a reason to adapt an Invoice Workbook Format instead of working with hard copy invoices, PDF files, or data that cannot be organized or sorted.

CHAPTER 10 - CONSTRUCTION PROJECT CONTROLS

An ounce of prevention is worth a pound of cure. Why hire attorneys and auditors to recover excessive fraud and waste at the end of the project if an adequate owner's **Project Controls Group** had been established at project inception? Why not have a dedicated owner's staff that can define project scope, review and approve bidders, is knowledgeable of claims by contractors for change orders, and can identify risks that can be avoided. Heading off problems that may impact designs, scope changes, and project delays will avoid spending significantly more funds than trying to recoup money after it has been spent. Having competent and experienced personnel familiar with contracts and contract terminology and who can have defined authority will pay big dividends at project completion.

ORGANIZATION OF A PROJECT CONTROLS GROUP

At some projects, Project Controls Groups are virtually non-existent. There are no formal processes, procedures, or policies evident. Some actions were accomplished but the results were not in keeping with the best industry practices or Corporate Policy requirements.

The following outline indicates the Key Objectives of a Project Controls Group.

MISSION STATEMENT:

The Mission of any Project Controls Group is to provide oversight responsibilities and management planning, execution and close-out, the audit process, the company's process for monitoring compliance with laws and regulations, and the company's code of conduct.

Key Functions and Activities:
Operate as a Focal Point for:

Project Process Monitoring
Audits and Assessments
Process Monitoring and Quality Control
Risk Management
Contract Administration
Document Control

Cost Monitoring & Reporting
Budget Control
Change Management
Invoice Management
Schedule Monitoring

Audits and Assessments
Key Objective:
Provide guidance on audit and compliance activities and processes. The Project Controls group is responsible for ensuring the development and documentation of procedures to include safety, engineering, procurement, construction management, administration and documentation. These activities include Internal and External Audit Support, and reporting both external and internal audits and reviews at the project level. Provide tracking of findings and corrective action until closure.

Process Monitoring and Quality Control
Key Objective:
Maintain, communicate, and administer quality assurance monitoring practices to confirm contractors are complying with Quality Assurance/ Quality Control and technical requirements of contracts including environmental, health and safety compliance and reporting.

Risk Management
Key Objective:
Administer development and updating of project risk to improve project performance by avoiding unanticipated events and thereby reduce the frequency of deviations from schedule, cost, and completion.

Contract Administration
Key Objective:
Develop and implement contract administration practices that effectively

meet company obligations under its various contracts and ensure contractor/vendors are meeting requirements of the contract.

Document Control
Key Objective:

Develop, maintain, and administer document control practices with sufficient storage of critical documentation to meet business, regulatory and legal requirements. This includes ensuring that documentation meets retention policy criteria as well as disposal of documentation.

Budget Control
Key Objective:

Ensure Budget/Cost management processes are implemented to include cost control functions, cost reporting, and contingency management, cost analysis, and forecasting. Ensure project teams are providing timely and accurate information on project cost performance.

Change Management
Key Objective:

Ensure project teams are providing timely and accurate change order information and are complying with contractual requirements and other applicable policies and procedures.

Invoice Management
Key Objective:

Develop, implement, and administer invoice review, approval, and processing practices that effectively meet the company's obligations under its various contracts and ensure contractor/vendors are meeting contract requirements. Determine that payment is only made to vendors/contractors who perform in accordance with applicable contract terms and conditions. This includes an in-depth audit of all supporting documentation and administering effective collection of Lien Waivers.

Schedule Monitoring
Key Objective:

Develop, maintain, and communicate schedule monitoring to include schedule analysis and early identification of potential schedule conflicts/delays.

DISPUTE RESOLUTION

Inevitably there will be disputes that arise during construction. The contract should have a clause to resolve disputes with an adequate descriptive process that outlines the steps and what levels of project management are necessary to resolve the dispute. The auditor reviewing invoices may be the first person to identify questionable billing amounts that will evolve into a dispute requiring resolution by management.

As stated elsewhere in this book, it is imperative that the owner's management fully supports the audit effort and not side with the contractor to infer the audits are a waste of time for the project. The owner's management should be knowledgeable of the contractual terms and can provide invaluable guidance from an experienced construction viewpoint. This experience may enlighten the auditor concerning common business practices or construction methods that may be misunderstood by the auditor and may mitigate a dispute.

The auditor should be familiar with the construction contract and construction practices before making incorrect assertions to upper management concerning audit findings. All assertions should be supported with detailed work papers to document any audit findings that management can follow and come to the same conclusion as the auditor. An inexperienced auditor will quickly lose management support as well as his credibility when the owner's management devotes an exorbitant amount of their valuable time providing an inexperienced auditor with training.

The Dispute Form

The dispute has to be concisely described in one or two sentences with reference to the source document where the dispute originated. Any contractor needs to know where this question originated so he can review the same document. The dispute description, amount of the dispute, the profit fees, and the total amount of the dispute can be shown on an Excel format Dispute Form with the subsequent row provided for the contractor's response. The third row of the dispute form will provide for either acceptance of the response or further details of why the response was not acceptable as follows:

Dispute Description	Resolved?	Amount	Fees	Total
Acme Invoice 45699 dated December 9, 20xx includes sales tax for material that is tax exempt.	Yes	$1,000	$90	$1,090
Credit will be issued on our Credit Memo A12390 next month.				
Credit was received on Credit Memo A12390 dated February 3, 20xx. Resolved.				

The second column provides an easy reference for dispute status resolution and avoids having to read through each dispute description to determine if there are any hanging issues. The three rows on the above table can be merged in a far left hand column to number each dispute so that these three rows represent only one dispute. An example of an Audit Dispute Form is provided in Chapter 15.

The cleanest audit trail for assuring disputes are resolved is to have the contractor provide a Credit Memo rather than burying the amount in the following month's invoice. If the dispute concerns labor, the credit may appear as a one line item at the bottom of a payroll ledger, which could take considerable effort to locate. The Audit Dispute Form can list the Credit Memo Number and date. Some disputes can take several months to close out but they must be tracked for closure. These Audit Dispute Forms can be transmitted electronically to the contractor via email with all supporting work papers attached. The contractor can also respond electronically with their response.

The most effective method to expeditiously resolve disputes is through a face to face meeting after both parties have an opportunity to review the issues and provide supporting documentation to mitigate the dispute. Otherwise these disputes can drag on for months with electronic emails being traded with no progress.

One tactic the contractor may use is to delay any response for 60 or more days. The contractor may delay all outstanding issues until near project completion and agree to settle for 50% of all claims. By the end of the project everyone is ready to move on and this negotiated settlement may seem to be a good deal. However the owner may be giving up a considerable amount of money if each dispute is a valid claim for funds the contractor was not entitled to. With this tactic the contractor gets additional funds that were overcharged just by patiently waiting out the owner.

CHAPTER 11 -
FREIGHT AND FUEL SURCHARGES

Among the material and equipment invoices will be the freight costs to deliver material to the jobsite. The terminology deserves some understanding.

F.O.B. Jobsite or Destination – This term indicates the freight costs are included in the cost of the item and no extra shipping costs will be billed. It also means the shipping company is liable for any damage to the item while in transit. The buyer is not responsible for any additional freight or damages to the items.

F.O.B. Shipping Point – this term is more common as the project is responsible for both the shipping costs plus any damages while in transit. Usually the manufacturer bears no responsibility for the shipping of the item.

These shipping terms are important to determine if additional freight costs are billed to the owner and also when any damage claims that can be mitigated because of shipping damage.

DIESEL FUEL SURCHARGES

In addition to the normal freight costs of the truck and driver, the shipping company wants to recover the cost of fuel when diesel prices increase above the national average. Freight costs may be regulated by a State Public Service Commission based on distance and tonnage.

A fuel surcharge is a separate additional charge made to shippers of freight above and beyond standard published contract rates to move freight. A fuel surcharge is put in place when fuel costs exceed a certain defined level, often $1.20 per gallon. The fuel surcharge collected by the carrier is typically passed on to the leased operator hauling the freight.

Fuel Surcharges are typically based on a national average fuel price. The national average most widely used is created by the Department of Energy (DOE) on a weekly basis. The DOE surveys a group of truck stops around the

U.S. to determine the national average fuel price and regional price averages. There is no Federal regulation of fuel surcharges. Companies that apply surcharges use their own formula for calculating their surcharge.

Every Monday, the U.S. Energy Information Administration (EIA) conducts a survey of retail on-highway diesel fuel prices from a sample of approximately 350 truck stops and retail service stations around the country. The survey results are published by 5:00 p.m. Monday or on Tuesday when there is a Federal Holiday on Monday. The results are compiled into a U.S. average price and average prices for eight regions of the country and California as follows:

Weekly Retail On-Highway Diesel Prices

Region	8/15/11	8/22/11
East Coast	3.871	3.844
New England	4.001	3.899
Central Atlantic	3.983	3.944
Lower Atlantic	3.811	3.788
Midwest	3.815	3.789
Golf Coast	3.806	3.772
Rocky Mountain	3.826	3.815
West Coast	3.863	3.855
California	3.957	3.928

Source: http://www.eia.gov/oog/info/wohdp/diesel.asp

The most accurate way to calculate fuel surcharges is to incorporate the vehicle's fuel efficiency into the formula:

Per Mile Fuel Surcharge = (Current Fuel Price − Base Fuel Cost)/ MPG
Total Fuel Surcharge = Per Mile Fuel Surcharge x Estimated Mileage
Fuel Efficiency = 5.5 mpg
Current Fuel Cost = $4.30 per gallon
Base Fuel Cost = $2.50 per gallon
Total Miles = 1,800
Per Mile Fuel Surcharge = ($4.30 - $2.50)/5.5 mpg = $.33 cents per mile.
Total Fuel Surcharge $33 x 1,800 = $594.00

If you want to calculate the total per mile fuel cost for a trip, you would just take the Current Fuel Price and divided it by the MPG.

$4.30/5.5 MPG = $.78 per mile multiplied by total miles of 1,800 and the result is $1,407.27 total fuel cost.

There is no standard formula for a fuel surcharge for every segment of the industry or for every carrier. Freight brokers may not pay a fuel surcharge. Regional carriers will often pay a fuel surcharge based on the regional average of the country where they operate. Some carriers pay only on loaded miles and some carriers pay on all miles. Some carriers calculate their fuel surcharge monthly and update it monthly and some calculate it weekly and update it weekly. Because the nature of their business is different and their fuel economy is different, a fuel surcharge will be different for dry van carriers, flat bed carriers, reefer carriers, specialized carriers, etc.

Diesel prices on the West Coast, especially in California, are relatively higher than other regions of the country, partly because of taxes, but mainly because of supply issues.

The State of California assesses a combine state and local sales and use tax of 7.25 percent on top of the 24.4 cents/gallon Federal excise tax and an 18 cents/gallon State tax. Washington's tax of 34 cents/gallon is one of the highest in the country. Besides taxes, West Coast retail prices are more variable than others because there are relatively few supply sources – 21 of the 36 refineries located in West Coast states are in California.

California refineries need to be running at near full capacity just to meet in-state demand. If more than one refinery in the region experiences operating difficulties at the same time, the diesel supply may become very tight and prices may spike. The West Coast's substantial distance from Gulf coast and foreign refineries is such that any unusual increase in demand or reduction in supply results in a large price response in the market before relief supplies can be delivered. The farther away the necessary relief supplies are, the higher and longer the price spike will be.

Fuel Surcharge Index.org represents the collaboration between the shipping and trucking community by providing shippers and carriers with fuel prices on over 5,500 truck stops that are updated every 24 hours. It allows the user to accurately calculate the fuel surcharge rate for a load based on the daily fuel prices along a route. Gone are the days of basing a fuel surcharge rate on a regional or national fuel price average calculated weekly. By using a weekly calculation, if fuel prices increase during the week, the shipper wins and the carrier loses. If fuel prices fall during the week, the carrier wins and the shipper is the loser. More information for this subscription service can be found at http://www.fuelsurchargeindex.org/.

Additional information is available from the web by doing web searches as well as the American Truck Business Services at the web site: http://www.attrucktax.com/fuelsurcharge.htm.

ROBERT LOUIS BECKER

When auditing the reasonableness of the diesel fuel surcharge, the trip distance for the material that was shipped can be verified through Mapquest or Tripquest websites. A reviewer may never be able to verify to the penny the exact amount calculated by the shipper. This information can always be requested for verification.

CHAPTER 12 -
FUEL TAXES FOR NON-HIGHWAY USE

Gasoline and Diesel fuel contain fuel taxes levied by both the Federal and State where the fuel is delivered or consumed. A federal excise tax is imposed on gasoline ($.184 per gallon), clear diesel fuel ($.244 per gallon), and clear kerosene ($.244 per gallon).

Is there a federal excise tax on diesel fuel?

There is a federal excise tax on un-dyed (clear) diesel fuel. Clear diesel is designated for use in highway vehicles; however diesel is a product that can be used in many ways. It can be either clear or dyed red. Red diesel is for off-road use only and is not taxed. It powers off-highway equipment such as cranes, bulldozers, generators, stationary equipment, and heats homes, offices, and shops.

Clear diesel is taxed and it powers highway vehicles but it is also used for many of the same off-road uses as red diesel. Because the tax on diesel was initiated to help cover the cost of building our federal highway system the tax is considered to be a "road" tax. Therefore, any use of clear diesel fuel in a manner that is not connected to use in a licensed highway vehicle, can be non-taxable and subject to refund.

How do I recover diesel fuel taxes paid for my non-highway equipment?

If you purchased un-dyed fuel and paid federal fuel tax for non-highway equipment, you have the option to either:
- Claim an annual federal fuel tax credit using Form 4136, Credit for Federal Tax Paid on Fuels when you file your Federal Income Tax return, or
- If you paid more than $750 of federal fuel tax per quarter for fuel used

off-highway, you may claim a refund by filing Form 8849, Claim for Refund of Excise Taxes.

A credit or refund is not allowable for the following:
- Any use in the propulsion engine of a registered highway vehicle, even if the vehicle is used off the highway.
- Any fuel that is lost or destroyed through fire, spillage, or evaporation.
- Any use of dyed diesel fuel or dyed kerosene. In fact, you may be subject to a substantial penalty if you use dyed fuel as a fuel in a registered diesel-powered highway vehicle.

You must have records to support your claim and they should clearly establish the number of gallons used during the period covered by the claim, the dates of purchase, the names and addresses of suppliers, and amounts bought from each in the period covered by the claim, the purposes for which you used the fuel, and the number of gallons used for each purpose.

How do I get more information about credits and refunds of fuel taxes?

You can either call 1-800-829-1040 or see Publication 378, Fuel Tax Credits and Refunds.

Taxes assessed by states can be obtained on the Web at www.illinoisgasprices.com.

The point of this discussion is that the contractor may file a claim for refund of Federal Excise Tax on all his projects annually and not pass on the credit to the owner for fuel consumed on his project. A fuel distributor/vendor may exclude the fuel tax in each billing when diesel is delivered to the project fuel depot. The owner should be aware of these potential overcharges.

CHAPTER 13 -
TRAVEL AIRLINE TICKETS, BOOKING CLASS AND ABBREVIATIONS

When auditing airline travel, the industry uses abbreviations that are not easily understood. The cancelled ticket is often included as documentation for the trip but without knowing the booking class and abbreviations, most auditors would glance over the receipt without questioning the contents. The following codes may be helpful as a reference for air travel costs.

Booking Class

The following codes are used on airline tickets to identify the class of service and the associated fare structure.

First Class Examples: A, F
Business Class Examples: C, D, J
Economy Class Examples: H, K, L, M, O, N, S, V, Q, & Others

There should be a well-established policy in the contract that First Class Airfare is not reimbursable, only Economy Class unless there has been prior approval.

Detailed Booking Class:

A – First Class Discounted
B – Coach Economy Discounted
C – Business Class
D – Business Class Discounted
F – First Class
H – Coach Economy Discounted
J – Business Class Premium

K – Thrift
L – Thrift Discounted
M – Coach Economy Discounted
P – First Class Premium
Q – Coach Economy
R – Supersonic
S – Standard Class
T – Coach Economy Discounted
V – Thrift Discounted
W – Coach Economy Premium
Y – Coach Economy

There are significant discounts if airfare is booked at least two weeks in advance. Staff employees returning to their principle residence once every month should take advantage of every discount available since these trips are usually predetermined. This should be a stated policy for the contractor.

CHAPTER 14 -
INVOICE WORKBOOKS

When a project is started some consideration should be made concerning the massive amount of information that will be generated and how that information can be assembled, summarized, and easily retrieved for permanent archives. The following Excel format should be used by the prime contractor when submitting monthly invoices for reimbursement. This format provides the advantages of expediting any audit review, sorting data by vendors or subcontractors for analysis and providing the listing of suppliers, rental companies, and sub-tier contractors that will require lien waivers.

The prime contractor has to summarize all vendor invoices, subcontractor invoices, and third party rental invoices on his monthly invoice. Using a standardized invoice format in Excel simplifies the process. An entire year of invoices from the contractor can be summarized and sorted without having to work with pdf files and hard copy invoices when drilling down to a specific vendor spending or subcontractor payments. Needed information can be available within minutes instead of hours.

The information needed for the Lien Waiver Log can be copied and pasted without having to manually enter this same information which could lead to typo mistakes and transpositions. The data to update the Lien Waiver Log can be entered within a few minutes and will avoid a tedious task where personnel can be better utilized pursuing the waivers and contacting suppliers for those who have not complied.

Each separate tab within the same workbook is linked to other tabs by formulas. In order for the formulas to work, the tabs on the Excel workbook must have the names inserted on the tabs such as "Lead Sheet" for tab one, "Recap" for tab two, etc. Formulas will carry forward the needed data to the Lead sheet and Recap sheet, thus eliminating manual mistakes carrying totals forward.

Each tab is labeled
(1) Tab one is "Lead Sheet"
(2) Tab two is "Recap"
(3) Tab three is "Craft Labor". The formula on the Invoice Recap sheet to pull data from tab three cells is "=Craft Labor!B24", or the last cell summarizing craft labor.
(4) Small Tools is "Craft Labor!B28" or the last cell summarizing small tools. Small tools are billed based on craft labor hours worked multiplied by $3.80 found on Tab three.
(5) Tab four is "Materials". The formula on the Invoice Recap sheet to pull data from tab four cells is "=Materials!C52" or the last cell summarizing materials.
(6) Tab five is "Equipment". The formula on the Invoice Recap sheet to pull data from tab five cells is "=Equipment!E33" or the last cell summarizing equipment.
(7) Equipment Third Party (also on tab five) is found at "=Equipment!E27"
(8) Tab six is "Misc Expenses". The formula on the Invoice Recap sheet to pull data from tab six cells is "=Misc Expenses!C33" or the last cell summarizing miscellaneous expenses.
(9) Tab seven is "Subcontractors". The formula on the Invoice Recap sheet to pull data from tab seven is "=Subcontractors!C27" or the last cell summarizing Subcontractor expenses.
(10) Tab eight is "Staff Labor". The formula on the Invoice Recap sheet to pull data from tab eight is "Staff Labor!k32".

There are no additional markups on Staff labor or Staff travel expenses in this particular contract. The Overhead Fee of 6% and the Profit Fee of 3% are calculated based on the total cell value listed in each column Subtotal with the formula =round(c15*0.06,2) and =round(c15*0.03,2), respectively. The subcontractor fee of 3% and 1.5% is multiplied by the Subcontractor values in cell 16, columns C, D, and E, respectively. Additional information concerning Excel workbooks is available from any Excel publication.

Craft Labor postings were pulled from their internal payroll reports summarizing the monthly charges to different work packages. These internal payroll reports were available for inspection at the contractor's Home Office.

The twelve workbooks from 12 consecutive months can be assembled into a new file so that all material, all subcontractors, and all staff labor billings can be arranged for review. The staff labor hours can be summarized for the entire year as well as the total payroll cost. Most of the work has already been done by the prime contractor by arranging this data when he prepared his monthly billing. If this information was only provided in hard copy files, it would add substantial effort for the owner to recreate this same information into Excel.

There may be some resistance by contractors to use these worksheets for billing purposes. However, after they became accustomed to inserting information into a standard format each month, they found some clerical errors were eliminated and the process reduced their time to assemble the invoice. The use of formulas for overhead and profit fees reduced mistakes made performing these calculations manually. The invoice copies submitted with each monthly billing should be in the same order as the summary listing to facilitate the invoice audit review process and the time to "Tick and Tie" each invoice.

Tab 1. Lead Sheet

Bill To:	XYZ Company (Owner)		**Remit To:**	(Prime Contractor)
	Accounts Payable			PO Box
	P.O. Box			St. Louis, MO 63179
	St. Louis, MO			Checking Acct #
	accountspayable@yyy.com			ACH Routing #

Attention:			
Project Number:		**Invoice Date:**	1/21/20xx
Project Name:		**Invoice Number:**	1234
Due Date:	2/21/20xx	**PO Number:**	
Period Covering:	12/01/xx - 12/31/xx		

Pay Item	Work Package No.	Amount	
913	WP-G913	$ 46,698.97	"=Recap!C33"
921	WP-G921	$ 341,580.16	"=Recap!D33"
902	WP-C902	$ 405,577.66	"=Recap!E33"
Due This Invoice		**$ 793,856.79**	"=Sum(e25:e27)"

Tab 2. Recap

Invoice Recap				
"='Lead Sheet'!E18"				
"=+'LeadSheet'!B21"				
Work Package Code	WP-G913	WP-G921	WP-C902	Total
Description	General Conditions	Startup Assistance	Final Site Work	
Contractor Pay Items	913	921	902	
Status	In Progress	In Progress	In Progress	

#	Item	WP-G913	WP-G921	WP-C902	Total	Formula
1	Craft Labor	16,573.14	9,434.82	38,006.32	64,014.28	"=sum (c9:e9)"
2	Small Tools	1,232.15	665.00	2,546.95	4,444.10	"=sum (c10:e10)"
4	Materials	43,264.90	9,575.69	17,033.70	69,874.29	"=sum (c11:e11)"
5	Equipment (Contractor Owned)	325,000.00			325,000.00	"=sum (c12:e12)"
6	Equipment (3rd Party Rental)	43,667.87			43,667.87	"=sum (c13:e13)"
7	Misc. Expenses	58,053.21	9,515.11	142.34	67,710.66	"=sum (c14:e14)"
8	**Subtotal**	487,791.27	29,190.62	57,729.31	574,711.20	"=sum (c15:e15)"
3	Subcontractors	189,239.85	472,671.94	375,744.22	1,037,656.01	"=sum (c16:e16)"
9		-	-	-		"=sum (c17:e17)"
10	Staff Labor	106,920.00			106,920.00	"=sum (c18:e18)"
11	Staff Travel & Per Diem	10,330.83	820.20		11,151.03	"=sum (c19:e19)"
12	Overhead 6%	29,267.48	1,751.44	3,463.76	34,482.68	"=sum (c20:e20)"
13	Fee 3%	14,633.74	875.72	1,731.88	17,241.34	"=sum (c21:e21)"
	Subcontractors Overhead 3%	5,677.20	14,180.16	11,272.33	31,129.69	"=sum (c22:e22)"
	Subcontractors Fee 1.5%	2,838.60	7,090.08	5,636.16	15,564.84	"=sum (c23:e23)"
14	**Grand Total**	846,698.97	526,580.16	455,577.66	1,828,856.79	"=sum (c24:e24)"
15	Direct Pay to MBE					"=sum (c25:e25)"
	Credit Items - Fee Only				$ -	"=sum (c26:e26)"
16	**Amount Due - Current Mo**	846,698.97	526,580.16	455,577.66	1,828,856.79	"=sum (c27:e27)"
						"=sum (c28:e28)"

HOW TO DETECT CONSTRUCTION FRAUD

17	Less: Adv. Pmt	800,000.00	185,000.00	50,000.00	1,035,000.00	"=sum (c29:e29)"
						"=sum (c30:e30)"
18	Net Due This Period	46,698.97	341,580.16	405,577.66	793,856.79	"=sum (c31:e31)"
						"=sum (c32:e32)"
19	Total Due	46,698.97	341,580.16	405,577.66	**793,856.79**	"=sum (c33:e33)"
	Work Package Recap					"=sum (c34:e34)"
	Work Package Code	WP-G913	WP-G921	WP-C902	Total	
	Description	General Conditions	Startup Assistance	Final Site Work		
1	Total of Previous Invoices				Total -	
2	Total Due This Period				-	
	Plus: Adv. Pmt				-	
3	Total Invoiced To Date				-	
4	PO Authorized Amount				-	
5	Remaining Authorization				-	

Tab 3 – Craft Labor

Craft Labor					
"=+'Lead Sheet'!E18"	Cost				
"=+'Lead Sheet'!B21"	$64,014.28				
Work Package Code	WP-G913	WP-G921	WP-C902	Total	
Description	ACI GC	Startup Assistance	Final SiteWork		
Contractor Pay Items	913	921	902		
Laborers	5,926.16		9,669.50	15,595.66	"SUM(B8:D8)"
Operators	9,464.44		566.96	10,031.40	"SUM(B9:D9)"
Carpenters	984.08	1,274.96	298.13	2,557.17	"SUM(B10:D10)"
Millwrights				-	"SUM(B11:D11)"
Boilermakers			15,904.29	15,904.29	"SUM(B12:D12)"
Iron Workers	198.46	8,159.86	11,567.44	19,925.76	"SUM(B13:D13)"
Pipefitters				$ -	"SUM(B14:D14)"
Teamsters				$ -	"SUM(B15:D15)"
Pile drivers				$ -	"SUM(B16:D16)"
Cement Masons				$ -	"SUM(B17:D17)"
Mechanics					"SUM(B18:D18)"
Clerk					"SUM(B19:D19)"
QA/QC					"SUM(B20:D20)"
					"SUM(B21:D21)"
					"SUM(B22:D22)"
					"SUM(B23:D23)"
Total Hrs., Wages & Burden	16,573.14	9,434.82	38,006.32	64,014.28	"SUM(B24:D24)"
				-	
Small Tools Allowance Summary					
Total Craft Hours This Period	324.25	175.00	670.25	1,169.50	"SUM(B27:E27)"
Total Small Tools ($3.80 Per Hr.)	1,232.15	665.00	2,546.95	4,444.10	"SUM(B28:E28)"

"=ROUND(B27*3.80,2)"

HOW TO DETECT CONSTRUCTION FRAUD

Tab 4.- Subcontractors

Subcontractors						
"=+'Lead Sheet'!E18"		Grand Total				
"=+'Lead Sheet'!B21"		Cost	$1,037,656.01	"=+$F$27"		
Work Package Code		WP-G913	WP-G921	WP-C902		
Description		General Conditions	Startup Assistance	Final Site work	Total	
Contractor Pay Items		913	921	902		
Vendor Name	Invoice No					
MID AMERICA				16,266.00	16,266.00	"=SUM(C10:E10)"
DOVER PIPE FABRICATION				4,800.00	4,800.00	"=SUM(C11:E11)"
ACE PAINTING CO.				41,695.00	41,695.00	"=SUM(C12:E12)"
MILLER		9,065.00	42,980.00		52,045.00	"=SUM(C13:E13)"
MANVIEW			136,184.02		136,184.02	"=SUM(C14:E14)"
NATIONAL INSULATION			37,000.00	7,380.00	44,380.00	"=SUM(C15:E15)"
ROCKY TAYLOR		82,900.00			82,900.00	"=SUM(C16:E16)"
TRIANGLE			84,730.00		84,730.00	"=SUM(C17:E17)"
UNITED HVAC				192,000.00	192,000.00	"=SUM(C18:E18)"
UNITED HVAC				5,849.81	5,849.81	"=SUM(C19:E19)"
UNITED HVAC				32,753.41	32,753.41	"=SUM(C20:E20)"
UNITED HVAC			65,500.00		65,500.00	"=SUM(C21:E21)"
VALLEY BUILDERS			70,685.80		70,685.80	"=SUM(C22:E22)"
VENUS CONCRETE			(27,000.88)		(27,000.88)	"=SUM(C23:E23)"
YELLOW CONSULTING		102,293.55	62,593.00		164,886.55	"=SUM(C24:E24)"
VH BUILDERS		(5,018.70)			(5,018.70)	"=SUM(C25:E25)"
UNITED HVAC				75,000.00	75,000.00	"=SUM(C26:E26)"
Grand Total		189,239.85	472,671.94	375,744.22	1,037,656.01	"=SUM(C27:E27)"

Tab 5. - Materials

Source		Total Cost				
Materials		3rd Party Materials	63,153.41	"=+$F$43"		
"=+'Lead Sheet'!E18"			6,720.88	"=+$F$50"		
"=+'Lead Sheet'!B21"		Grand Total	69,874.29	"=SUM(C2:C3)"		
Work Package Code			G-913	G-921	C-902	
Description			General Conditions	Startup	Final Site work	Total
Contractor Pay Items			913	921	902	
Vendor Name		Invoice No				
3rd Party Materials						
HANDY MATERIAL CO.			138.00			138.00	"=SUM(C10:E10)"
HANDY MATERIAL CO.			341.95			341.95	"=SUM(C11:E11)"
HARVEY WATERWORKS			7,920.00			7,920.00	"=SUM(C12:E12)"
THE GATE CO			2,078.00			2,078.00	"=SUM(C13:E13)"
MASTER COMPANY			(123.59)			(123.59)	"=SUM(C14:E14)"
SOUTHWESTERN SUPPLY			229.11			229.11	"=SUM(C15:E15)"
SOUTHWESTERN SUPPLY			280.95			280.95	"=SUM(C16:E16)"
SEALY CERTAIN			302.36			302.36	"=SUM(C17:E17)"
SEALY CERTAIN			275.36			275.36	"=SUM(C18:E18)"
CIRCLE R SHEETMETAL				6,978.00		6,978.00	"=SUM(C19:E19)"
MASTER CARR				41.69		41.69	"=SUM(C20:E20)"
ATLAS ROCK					544.00	544.00	"=SUM(C21:E21)"
THE GATEWAY CO					3,553.00	3,553.00	"=SUM(C22:E22)"
CIRCLE R STEELMETAL					216.20	216.20	"=SUM(C23:E23)"
BLACKS SANITATION					1,314.50	1,314.50	"=SUM(C24:E24)"
TRI COUNTY PETROLEUM					2,786.00	2,786.00	"=SUM(C25:E25)"

HOW TO DETECT CONSTRUCTION FRAUD

MASTER	898.17			898.17	"=SUM(C26:E26)"
FOSTER	232.08			232.08	"=SUM(C27:E27)"
ENGINEERED SALES	805.27			805.27	"=SUM(C28:E28)"
MASTER	70.77			70.77	"=SUM(C29:E29)"
PHILLIPS	180.14			180.14	"=SUM(C30:E30)"
APPLIED SERVICES	1,322.20			1,322.20	"=SUM(C31:E31)"
MIRACLE CO	39.96			39.96	"=SUM(C32:E32)"
BLACKS SANITATION	962.61			962.61	"=SUM(C33:E33)"
FOSTER	619.68			619.68	"=SUM(C34:E34)"
ROLLINS LUMBER		621.00		621.00	"=SUM(C35:E35)"
COLLINS TRUCKING	17,291.00			17,291.00	"=SUM(C36:E36)"
THE BAXTER GATE CO			4,723.00	4,723.00	"=SUM(C37:E37)"
THE BAXTER GATE CO			3,442.00	3,442.00	"=SUM(C38:E38)"
THE BAXTER GATE CO	865.00			865.00	"=SUM(C39:E39)"
THE BAXTER GATE CO		1,935.00		1,935.00	"=SUM(C40:E40)"
THE BAXTER GATE CO	1,815.00			1,815.00	"=SUM(C41:E41)"
THE BAXTER GATE CO			455.00	455.00	"=SUM(C42:E42)"
Total Third Party Materials	36,544.02	9,575.69	17,033.70	63,153.41	"=SUM(C43:E43)"
Contractor Materials					
Fuel	39.89			39.89	"=SUM(C43:E46)"
Welding Supplies	1,676.51			1,676.51	"=SUM(C47:E47)"
Drayage	5,004.48			5,004.48	"=SUM(C48:E48)"
TRUCK PERMITS					"=SUM(C49:E49)"
Total Contractor Materials	6,720.88		-	6,720.88	"=SUM(C50:E50)"
Work Package Totals	43,264.90	9,575.69	17,033.70	69,874.29	"=F43+F50"
	"=+C43+C50"				

Tab 6. - Equipment

		Source	Total Cost	
Equipment		3rd Party Rentals	43,667.87	"=+E27"
1234		Contractor Rentals	325,000.00	"=+E32"
12/01/10 - 12/31/10		Grand Total	368,667.87	"=SUM(D2:D3)"
Work Package Code		G913		
Description		General Conditions	Total	
Contractor Pay Items		9		
Vendor Name	Invoice No			
3rd Party Rentals				
FARM SUPPLY		6,900.00	6,900.00	"=SUM(C10:D10)"
FARM SUPPLY		6,900.00	6,900.00	"=SUM(C11:D11)"
LILLIAN RENTALS		374.99	374.99	"=SUM(C12:D12)"
LILLIAN RENTALS		650.00	650.00	"=SUM(C13:D13)"
OFFICE TRAILERS INC.		1,600.00	1,600.00	"=SUM(C14:D14)"
OFFICE TRAILERS INC.		4,639.28	4,639.28	"=SUM(C15:D15)"
OFFICE TRAILERS INC.		385.00	385.00	"=SUM(C16:D16)"
PEMBROOK TOOL		11.76	11.76	"=SUM(C17:D17)"
SADY EQUIPMENT		424.02	424.02	"=SUM(C18:D18)"
S & X ASSOCIATES		450.00	450.00	"=SUM(C19:D19)"
TILLEY RENTALS		340.00	340.00	"=SUM(C20:D20)"
TILLEY RENTALS		285.00	285.00	"=SUM(C21:D21)"
UNITED		(121.76)	(121.76)	"=SUM(C22:D22)"
MILNER RENTALS		15,000.00	15,000.00	"=SUM(C23:D23)"
STEVES CRANES		1,696.44	1,696.44	"=SUM(C24:D24)"
ARC WELDERS INC.		576.40	576.40	"=SUM(C25:D25)"
HERB EQUUIPMENT		3,556.74	3,556.74	"=SUM(C26:D26)"
Total Third Party Rentals		43,667.87	43,667.87	"=SUM(C27:D27)"

Contractor Rentals					
Constructors	Concrete Forms				
Constructors	Equipment	325,000.00		325,000.00	"=SUM(C31:D31)"
Total Contractor Rentals		325,000.00		325,000.00	"=SUM(C32:D32)"
Work Package Totals		368,667.87		368,667.87	"=SUM(C33:D33)"
The formula under Equipment is =+'Lead Sheet'!E18 for the invoice number to appear.					
The second formula under Equipment is =+'Lead Sheet'!B21 for the time period to appear.					"=E27+E33"

Tab 7. – Misc. Expenses

Misc. Expenses		Misc. Expenses	67,710.66	"=+$F$33"		
"=+'Lead Sheet'!E18"		Staff Expenses	11,151.03	"=+$F$60"		
"=+'Lead Sheet'!B21"		Grand Total	78,861.69	"=SUM(E2:E3)"		
Work Package Code		G-913	G-921	C-902		
Description		General Conditions	Startup Assistance	Final SiteWork	Total	
Contractor Pay Items		913	921	902		
Vendor Name	Inv. No					
Misc. Expenses (Incl Insurance, Training, Sanitation, Craft Labor Subsistence and Other Misc. Costs)						
SECURITY NATIONAL BANK		525.00			525.00	"=SUM (c11:e11)"
WHITES SANITATION		24,508.69			24,508.69	"=SUM (c12:e12)"
FTS DELIVERY		366.60			366.60	"=SUM (c13:e13)"
UPS		38.75			38.75	"=SUM (c14:e14)"
ACCESS COURIER		25.58			25.58	=SUM(c15:e15)"
UPS		27.29			27.29	"=SUM (c16:e16)"
UPS		43.51			43.51	"=SUM (c17:e17)"
COMMERCIAL DOCUMENT SOLUTIONS		963.72			963.72	"=SUM (c18:e18)"
MINOLTA		41.57			41.57	"=SUM (c19:e19)"
BB LOGISTICS		332.55			332.55	"=SUM (c20:e20)"
ARROW		128.06			128.06	"=SUM (c21:e21)"
CENTRAL BILLINGS		298.77			298.77	"=SUM (c22:e22)"
WASTE MANAGEMENT		11,632.36			11,632.36	"=SUM (c23:e23)"

OFFICE CONSULTANTS	14,042.75			14,042.75	"=SUM (c24:e24)"
PRO-GUARD		8,861.50		8,861.50	"=SUM (c25:e25)"
CONSTRUCTORS SUBGUARD INS		92.75		92.75	"=SUM (c26:e26)"
SS HANSEN	1,526.88			1,526.88	"=SUM (c27:e27)"
XYZ CONSTRUCTORS - SAFETY SUPPLIES	88.89			88.89	"=SUM (c28:e28)"
XYZ CONSTRUCTORS - UNION DUES	220.00			220.00	"=SUM (c29:e29)"
XYZ CONSTRUCTORS - INSURANCE	1,266.92	560.86	142.34	1,970.12	"=SUM (c30:e30)"
XYZ CONSTRUCTORS UNION BENEFIT ADJ	1,975.32			1,975.32	"=SUM (c31:e31)"
					"=SUM (c32:e32)"
Total Misc. Expenses	58,053.21	9,515.11	142.34	67,710.66	"=SUM (c33:e33)"
Staff Expenses					
MOBILE - FUEL CHARGES	3,003.12			3,003.12	"=SUM(C36:E36)"
CASEYS - FUEL	161.42			161.42	"=SUM (C37:E37)"
CASEYS - FUEL	43.75			43.75	"=SUM (C38:E38)"
EXPENSE REPORT - CHUCK STONE	541.20			541.20	"=SUM (C39:E39)"
EXPENSE REPORT - JIM BELLWEATHER	146.35			146.35	"=SUM (C40:E40)"
EXPENSE REPORT - BILL MILNER	616.00			616.00	"=SUM (C41:E41)"
EXPENSE REPORT - JESSIE JAMES	1,214.40			1,214.40	"=SUM (C42:E42)"
EXPENSE REPORT - KATHY WRIGHT	649.00			649.00	"=SUM (C43:E43)"
EXPENSE REPORT - RICK MILNER	211.20			211.20	"=SUM (C44:E44)"
EXPENSE REPORT - RICK MILNER	211.20			211.20	"=SUM (C45:E45)"

EXPENSE REPORT - KIM TAYLOR	149.65			149.65	"=SUM (C46:E46)"
COMPUTER CHARGES NOVEMBER -		550.00		550.00	"=SUM (C47:E47)"
CELL PHONE - ED CAMDENTON	82.18			82.18	"=SUM (C48:E48)"
CELL PHONE - TROY BAILEY	78.95			78.95	"=SUM (C49:E49)"
CELL PHONE - JACK BRANCH	46.07			46.07	"=SUM (C50:E50)"
CELL PHONE - JIM HAMILTON	79.10			79.10	"=SUM (C51:E51)"
CELL PHONE - BILLY KIDD	78.93			78.93	"=SUM (C52:E52)"
CELL PHONE - BILL CARSON	47.31			47.31	"=SUM (C53:E53)"
AIRFARE CHARGES	1,441.00	270.20		1,711.20	"=SUM (C54:E54)"
SUBSISTENCE W/E 111011 - TROY BAILEY	510.00			510.00	"=SUM (C55:E55)"
SUBSISTENCE W/E 111011 - ROBERT SMITH	510.00			510.00	"=SUM (C56:E56)"
SUBSISTENCE W/E 111011 - PAUL SCALES	510.00			510.00	"=SUM (C57:E57)"
TAX ON SUBSISTENCE -					"=SUM (C58:E58)"
					"=SUM (C59:E59)"
Total Staff Expenses	10,330.83	820.20		11,151.03	"=SUM (C60:E60)"
Work Package Totals	68,384.04	10,335.31	142.34	78,861.69	"SUM(C62:E62)"

Tab 8. Staff Labor

Staff Labor											
"=+'Lead Sheet'!E18"	Cost										
"=+'Lead Sheet'!B21"	106,920.00	"=+K32"									
Work Package Code											
Description											
Pay Items											

Emp No	Name	Title	Hours Billed			Rate Billed		Amount Billed			
			ST	OT	Total	ST	OT	ST	OT	Total	
·	G. Washington	Project Director	120.0		120.0	95.0	95.0	11,400.00	-	11,400.00	"=sum (I10+J10)"
	J. Madison	Project Manager	120.0		120.0	55.0	55.0	6,600.00	-	6,600.00	"=sum (I11+J11)"
	T. Jefferson	Project Manager	120.0		120.0	45.0	45.0	5,400.00	-	5,400.00	"=sum (I12+J12)"
	B. Franklin	Project Engineer	120.0		120.0	40.0	40.0	4,800.00	-	4,800.00	"=sum (I13+J13)"
	W. Fillmore	Senior Estimator	120.0		120.0	50.0	50.0	6,000.00	-	6,000.00	"=sum (I14+J14)"
	A. Lincoln	Senior Estimator	120.0		120.0	55.0	55.0	6,600.00	-	6,600.00	"=sum (I15+J15)"
	C. Coolidge	Senior Estimator	120.0		120.0	50.0	50.0	6,000.00	-	6,000.00	"=sum (I16+J16)"
	J. Cash	Estimator	120.0		120.0	55.0	55.0	6,600.00	-		"=sum (I17+J17)"
	F.D. Roosevelt	Project Engineer	120.0		120.0	40.0	40.0	4,800.00	-		"=sum (I18+J18)"
	R. Nixon	Procurement	120.0		120.0	30.0	30.0	3,600.00	-	3,600.00	
	R. Kennedy	QA/QC Manger	120.0		120.0	24.0	35.0	2,880.00		2,880.00	
	J.F Kennedy	Safety Manager	120.0		120.0	24.0	75.0	2,880.00		2,880.00	

J. Carter	Safety Engineer	120.0	120.0	40.0	40.0	4,800.00	4,800.00	
R. Paul	Safety Engineer	120.0	120.0	40.0	40.0	4,800.00	4,800.00	
M.L. King	Safety Engineer	120.0	120.0	60.0	60.0	7,200.00	7,200.00	
J. James	Project Engineer	120.0	120.0	55.0	55.0	6,600.00	6,600.00	
J. Hancock	Financial Coordinator	120.0	120.0	45.0	45.0	5,400.00	5,400.00	
M. Romney	Office Manager	120.0	120.0	35.0	35.0	4,200.00	4,200.00	
K. James	Document Control	120.0	120.0	25.0	25.0	3,000.00	3,000.00	
B. Obama	Project Admin/ Payroll	120.0	120.0	28.0	28.0	3,360.00	3,360.00	
Work Package Totals		2,400.	2,400.			106,920.00	106,920.00	

"=sum (I28+J28)"
"=sum (I29+J29)"
"=sum (K10:K31)"

CHAPTER 15 –
INVOICE AUDIT DISPUTE SHEET SAMPLE

ROBERT LOUIS BECKER

INVOICE AUDIT SHEET

Company:		Invoice Date:	9/12/11	Invoice Total:	1,437,473.10	Audit Due Date:	10/12/11
Project:		PO No.:		Amount in Dispute:	11,866.38	Approved By Date:	10/17/11
Invoice No.:	3524	Items in Dispute:	4	Amount Approved:	1,425,606.72	Payment Due Date:	
Invoice Received:	9/16/11	Detail Received:	9/18/11	Disputed Amt Resolved:		Released for Approval:	
		Review Complete		Net Amt Deducted:	11,866.38	Payment Date:	10/18/11
Construct.Audit:	9/20/11	Cost Analyst:	9/21/11	Applied Credits:		Amount Paid:	
Tax Department:	9/20/11	Plant Review:	9/22/11	Approved for Payment:	1,425,606.72	Variance:	$0.00
Submitted to AP:	10/1/11					(Paid vs. Approved)	

Disputed Types:	Craft Labor = CL	Materials = ML	Equipment = EQ	Small Tools = ST	Missing Backup = BK	Re-Calculation Error = RC		Fee Not Applicable = NF
	Staff Labor = SL	Rentals = RT	SC = Subcontractor	Tax = TX	Miscellaneous = MS	Other = OT		
	NF					$ -	$ -	$ -
CREDITS	NF					$ -	$ -	$ -
	NF					$ -	$ -	$ -

HOW TO DETECT CONSTRUCTION FRAUD

Item No.	Type	Comments By: INSERT NAME	Description / Comments	Resolved?	Disputed Amount	With OH & Fee Adder	Total
1	CL	Owner	Total craft labor billing is $437,637.58. Supporting documentation is $436,206.29. Please explain difference of $1,161.51.		1,161.51	1,266.05	1,266.05
2	SC	Owner	Bailey & Sons Invoice 7200 dated 8/22/2011. Retention was not billed by subcontractor but Prime Contractor is billing retention to Owner. Please provide credit.		4,959.00	5,405.31	5,405.31
3	ML	Owner	Tools R Us Invoices 7287, 7339 and 7288 was for material delivered to Contractor's home office in Chicago, Illinois rather than at the jobsite with other material from this vendor delivered directly to the jobsite during the month. Why was this material not delivered directly to the jobsite?		4,531.75	4,939.61	4,939.61
4	ML	Owner	Acme Supply Invoice 5431 is for 4 Bridge Reamers, which are small tools and not directly billable.	Yes	234.33	255.42	255.42
		Contr.	Credit provided on next month's invoice.				
		Owner	Resolved.				
				TOTAL DISPUTED	10,886.59	11,866.38 -	11,866.38

THE PRIME CONTRACTOR'S NAME, PROJECT NAME, INVOICE NUMBER AND INVOICE DATE ARE POSTED TO THE TOP LEFT OF THE INVOICE AUDIT SHEET.
THE NUMBER OF ITEMS IN DISPUTE IS THE RESULT OF THE FORMULA = COUNT A23:A40. THIS FORMULA AUTOMATICALLY COUNTS THE NUMBER OF DISPUTES.
THE INVOICE DATE RECEIVED AND THE DATE THE DETAIL WAS RECEIVED IS IMPORTANT TO START THE CLOCK TICKING ON COMPLETING THE AUDIT.
THE AUDIT DUE DATE IS THE FORMULA =IF(F9="","",F9+24). THE AUDIT SHOULD BE COMPLETED WITHIN 24 DAYS OF RECEIPT OF INVOICE.
THE PAYMENT DUE DATE IS THE FORMULA =IF(F9="","",F9+30). THE INVOICE IS DUE FOR PAYMENT 30 DAYS FROM THE INVOICE DATE.
THE RELEASE FOR APPROVAL DATE, THE PAYMENT DATE, AND THE AMOUNT PAID DATE ARE ENTERED LATER WHEN INFORMATION IS AVAILABLE FROM ACCOUNTS PAYABLE. THESE ARE ACTUAL DATES.
THE VARIANCE FORMULA IS =IF(M3="",0,IF(I3<0,M13-I15,I15-M13)). THIS COMPARES THE AMOUNT PAID TO THE AMOUNT APPROVED FOR PAYMENT. THIS VARIANCE IS TRACKED FOR LATER RESOLUTION..
THE REVIEW COMPLETION DATES ARE ENTERED BY THE VARIOUS DEPARTMENTS PERFORMING REVIEWS. THESE DATE PROVIDE A TRACKING OF THE INVOICE.
THE INVOICE TOTAL IS ENTERED FROM THE INVOICE. THE AMOUNT IN DISPUTE IS THE FORMULA =SUM(L42). THIS IS THE TOTAL OF DISPUTES WITH OH&FEES INCLUDED OR THE 7TH COLUMN.
THE AMOUNT APPROVED IS THE FORMULA = IF(I3>0,I3-I5,SUM(0-I5)+I3).
THIS FORMULA DEDUCTS THE DISPUTES FROM THE INVOICE TOTAL.
THE FORMULA FOR DISPUTED AMOUNT RESOLVED IS =N42.
THE FORMULA FOR NET AMOUNT DEDUCTED IS =O42.
THE FORMULA FOR APPROVED FOR PAYMENT IS = I3-I11+I13.
THE DISPUTES ARE ENTERED WITH A FULL DESCRIPTION OF THE DISPUTE AND THE AMOUNT BEING DISPUTED. THE OVERHEAD AND FEE ADJUSTMENT ADDS THE FEES FOR A FULL RECOVERY OF THE $.
THE RECONCILED AMOUNT IS ENTERED AFTER RESOLUTION OF THE DISPUTE.
THE CONTRACTORS ENTER THEIR RESPONSE TO EACH DISPUTE WITHIN THE SAME BLOCK OF TEXT AND TRANSMIT ELECTRONICALLY BACK TO AUDITOR. SEE RESOLUTION TO DISPUTE #4.
THE DISPUTE TYPES ARE ENTERED IN THE SECOND COLUMN BASED ON THE ABBREVIATED EXAMPLES PROVIDED.
THE AUDIT SHEETS CAN BE MERGED BY DISPUTE TYPE FOR THE ENTIRE PROJECT. THE AUDIT SHEETS CAN ALSO BE "AGED" TO DETERMINE THE RESPONSIVENESS OF THE CONTRACTOR.
CREDIT MEMOS CAN BE TRACKED IN THE AREA FOR CREDITS TO PROVIDE OTHERS WITH AN AUDIT TRAIL.

Tracking Disputes

On large projects that span several years and that develop a significant number of disputes, it is beneficial to track disputes and their resolution so than repetitive claims are not revisited or have to be renegotiated once they have been settled. A Resolution Log should be established that summarizes the Invoice Dispute Sheets after claims are no longer contested. The following columns would be suggested with brief descriptions under each heading on an Excel Spreadsheet.

Repetitive Invoice Audit Issues - Tracking Dispute Log
Dispute Log Header

Type of Dispute – Staff Labor, Craft Labor, Small Tools, Material, Equipment, Subcontractors, Fees, etc.

Month/Year – When dispute originated.
Invoice Number – First Contractor's invoice where dispute originated.
Description – Brief description of the dispute and why there is a conflict.

Resolution Log Header
Month/Year – When dispute was resolved.
Description of Resolution
Owner's Favor – (Yes or No) If Yes, are credits due retroactively?

CHAPTER 16 -
LIEN WAIVER RECORD LOG

Project Name	Invoice Number	Inv Date	Inv Period	Cost Summary	Vend. Inv No	Vendor Name	Amount	Lien Waiver Status	Date Signed	Partial or Final	Amt Waived
Our Project	3524	12/1/11	Oct-11	Mat		HANDY MATERIAL CO.	138.00	Waived	1/2/12	F	138.00
Our Project	3524	12/1/11	Oct-11	Mat		HANDY MATERIAL CO.	341.95	Waived	1/2/12	F	341.95
Our Project	3524	12/1/11	Oct-11	Mat		HARVEY WATERWORKS	7,920.00	Open	1/2/12	no waiver	
Our Project	3524	12/1/11	Oct-11	Mat		THE GATE CO	2,078.00	Waived	1/2/12	F	2,078.00
Our Project	3524	12/1/11	Oct-11	Mat		MASTER COMPANY	(123.59)	Waived	1/2/12	F	(123.59)
Our Project	3524	12/1/11	Oct-11	Mat		Southwestern Supply	229.11	Waived	1/2/12	F	229.11
Our Project	3524	12/1/11	Oct-11	Mat		Southwestern Supply	280.95	Waived	1/2/12	F	280.95
Our Project	3524	12/1/11	Oct-11	Mat		SEALY CERTAIN	302.36	Waived	1/2/12	F	302.36
Our Project	3524	12/1/11	Oct-11	Mat		SEALY CERTAIN	275.36	Waived	1/2/12	F	275.36
Our Project	3524	12/1/11	Oct-11	Mat		CIRCLE R SHEETMETAL	6,978.00	Waived	1/2/12	F	6,978.00
Our Project	5524	12/1/11	Oct-11	Mat		MASTER CARD	41.69	Waived	1/2/12	F	41.69
Our Project	3524	12/1/11	Oct-11	Mat		ATLAS ROCK	544.00	Waived	1/2/12	F	544.00
Our Project	3524	12/1/11	Oct-11	Mat		THE GATEWAY CO	3,553.00	Waived	1/2/12	F	3,553.00
Our Project	3524	12/1/11	Oct-11	Mat		CIRCLE R STEELMETAL	216.20	Waived	1/2/12	F	216.20
Our Project	3524	12/1/11	Oct-11	Mat		BLACKS SANITATION	1,314.50	Waived	1/2/12	F	1,314.50
Our Project	3524	12/1/11	Oct-11	Mat		TRI COUNTY PETROL.	2,786.00	Waived	1/2/12	F	2,786.00
Our Project	3524	12/1/11	Oct-11	Mat		MASTER	898.17	Waived	1/2/12	F	898.17
Our Project	3524	12/1/11	Oct-11	Mat		FOSTER	232.08	Waived	1/2/12	F	232.08
Our Project	3524	12/1/11	Oct-11	Mat		ENGINEERED SALES	805.27	Waived	1/2/12	F	805.27

Our Project	3524	12/1/11	Oct-11	Mat	MASTER	70.77	Waived	1/2/12	F	70.77
Our Project	3524	12/1/11	Oct-11	Mat	PHILLIPS	180.14	Waived	1/2/12	F	180.14
Our Project	3524	12/1/11	Oct-11	Mat	APPLIED SERVICES	1,322.20	Waived	1/2/12	F	1,322.20
Our Project	3524	12/1/11	Oct-11	Mat	MIRACLE CO	39.96	Waived	1/2/12	F	39.96
Our Project	3524	12/1/11	Oct-11	Mat	BLACKS SANITATION	962.61	Waived	1/2/12	F	962.61
Our Project	3524	12/1/11	Oct-11	Mat	FOSTER	619.68	Waived	1/2/12	F	619.68
Our Project	3524	12/1/11	Oct-11	Mat	ROLLINS LUMBER	621.00	Waived	1/2/12	F	621.00
Our Project	3524	12/1/11	Oct-11	Mat	COLLINS TRUCKING	17,291.00	Waived	1/2/12	F	17,291.00
Our Project	3524	12/1/11	Oct-11	Mat	THE BAXTER GATE CO	4,723.00	Open	1/2/12	no waiver	
Our Project	3524	12/1/11	Oct-11	Mat	THE BAXTER GATE CO	3,442.00	Waived	1/2/12	F	3,442.00
Our Project	3524	12/1/11	Oct-11	Mat	THE BAXTER GATE CO	865.00	Waived	1/2/12	F	865.00
Our Project	3524	12/1/11	Oct-11	Mat	THE BAXTER GATE CO	1,935.00	Waived	1/2/12	F	1,935.00
Our Project	3524	12/1/11	Oct-11	Mat	THE BAXTER GATE CO	1,815.00	Waived	1/2/12	F	1,815.00
Our Project	3524	12/1/11	Oct-11	Mat	THE BAXTER GATE CO	455.00	Waived	1/2/12	F	455.00
Our Project	3524	12/1/11	Oct-11	Equip	FARM SUPPLY	6,900.00	Waived	1/2/12	F	6,900.00
Our Project	3524	12/1/11	Oct-11	Equip	FARM SUPPLY	6,900.00	Waived	1/2/12	F	6,900.00
Our Project	3524	12/1/11	Oct-11	Equip	LILLIAN RENTALS	374.99	Waived	1/2/12	F	374.99
Our Project	3524	12/1/11	Oct-11	Equip	LILLIAN RENTALS	650.00	Waived	1/2/12	F	650.00
Our Project	3524	12/1/11	Oct-11	Equip	OFFICE TRAILERS INC.	1,600.00	Waived	1/2/12	F	1,600.00
Our Project	3524	12/1/11	Oct-11	Equip	OFFICE TRAILERS INC.	4,639.28	Waived	1/2/12	F	4,639.28
Our Project	3524	12/1/11	Oct-11	Equip	OFFICE TRAILERS INC.	385.00	Waived	1/2/12	F	385.00

Our Project	3524	12/1/11	Oct-11	Equip	PEMBROOK TOOL	11.76	Waived	1/2/12	F	11.76
Our Project	3524	12/1/11	Oct-11	Equip	SADY EQUIPMENT	424.02	Waived	1/2/12	F	424.02
Our Project	3524	12/1/11	Oct-11	Equip	S & X ASSOCIATES	450.00	Waived	1/2/12	F	450.00
Our Project	3524	12/1/11	Oct-11	Equip	TILLEY RENTALS	340.00	Waived	1/2/12	F	340.00
Our Project	3524	12/1/11	Oct-11	Equip	TILLEY RENTALS	285.00	Waived	1/2/12	F	285.00
Our Project	3524	12/1/11	Oct-11	Equip	UNITED	(121.76)	Waived	1/2/12	F	(121.76)
Our Project	3524	12/1/11	Oct-11	Equip	MILNER RENTALS	15,000.00	Waived	1/2/12	F	15,000.00
Our Project	3524	12/1/11	Oct-11	Equip	STEVES CRANES	1,696.44	Open	1/2/12	no waiver	-
Our Project	3524	12/1/11	Oct-11	Equip	ARC WELDERS INC.	576.40	Open	1/2/12	no waiver	-
Our Project	3524	12/1/11	Oct-11	Equip	HERB EQUIPMENT	3,556.74	Open	1/2/12	no waiver	-
Our Project	3524	12/1/11	Oct-11	Sub	MID AMERICA	16,266.00	Open	1/2/12	no waiver	
Our Project	3524	12/1/11	Oct-11	Sub	DOVER PIPE FABRICATION	4,800.00	Open	1/2/12	no waiver	
Our Project	3524	12/1/11	Oct-11	Sub	Ace Painting Co.	41,695.00	Open	1/2/12	no waiver	-
Our Project	3524	12/1/11	Oct-11	Sub	Miller	52,045.00	Open	1/2/12	no waiver	
Our Project	3524	12/1/11	Oct-11	Sub	Manview	136,184.02	Waived	1/2/12	F	136,184.02
Our Project	3524	12/1/11	Oct-11	sub	National Insulation	44,380.00	Waived	1/2/12	F	44,380.00
Our Project	3524	12/1/11	Oct-11	Sub	Rocky Taylor	82,900.00	Waived	1/2/12	F	82,900.00
Our Project	3524	12/1/11	Oct-11	Sub	Triangle	84,730.00	Waived	1/2/12	F	84,730.00
Our Project	3524	12/1/11	Oct-11	Sub	United HVAC	192,000.00	Waived	1/2/12	F	192,000.00
Our Project	3524	12/1/11	Oct-11	Sub	United HVAC	5,849.81	Waived	1/2/12	F	5,849.81
Our Project	3524	12/1/11	Oct-11	Sub	United HVAC	65,500.00	Waived	1/2/12	F	65,500.00

Our Project	3524	12/1/11	Oct-11	Sub	Valley Builders	70,685.80	Waived	1/2/12	F	70,685.80
Our Project	3524	12/1/11	Oct-11	Sub	Venus Concrete	-27,000.88	Waived	1/2/12	F	-27,000.88
Our Project	3524	12/1/11	Oct-11	Sub	Yellow Consulting	164,886.55	Waived	1/2/12	F	164,886.55
Our Project	3524	12/1/11	Oct-11	Sub	VH Builders	(5,018.70)	Waived	1/2/12	F	(5,018.70)
Our Project	3524	12/1/11	Oct-11	Sub	United HVAC	75,000.00	Waived	1/2/12	F	75,000.00

Lien Waivers that have not been received can also be "aged" to determine the elapsed time from 60 days after the invoice date, total elapsed days between 30 and 59 days, and total lapsed time over 60 days by using the following formulas. Those waivers not received within a reasonable amount of time and exceeding 60 days need to be expedited.

Today's date is the formula - =now(). The subsequent formulas compare the due date by line item to today's date to calculate the data in each of the three columns. Today's date is in cell O2, thus the comparison shown in $O$2.

12/5/2011	< Today's Date	
Open Invoice Status		
Total Elapsed Days From 60 Days After Inv Date	Total Elapsed Days 30 to 59	Total Elapsed Days 60 or Greater
0		
0		
0		
0		
0		

Total Elapsed Days from 60 Days after Inv. Date Formula
"=IF(j5="Waived",0,+$O$2-(c5+60))"
"=IF(j6="Waived",0,+$O$2-(c6+60))"
"=IF(j7="Waived",0,+$O$2-(c7+60))"
"=IF(j8="Waived",0,+$O$2-(c8+60))"
"=IF(j9="Waived",0,+$O$2-(c9+60))"

Total Elapsed Days 30 to 59 Formula
"=IF(AND(O5>29,O5<60),"Yes","")"
"=IF(AND(O6>29,O6<60),"Yes","")"
"=IF(AND(O7>29,O7<60),"Yes","")"
"=IF(AND(O8>29,O8<60),"Yes","")"
"=IF(AND(O9>29,O9<60),"Yes","")"

Total Elapsed Days 60 or Greater Formula
"=IF (O5>59, "YES","")"
"=IF (O6>59, "YES","")"
"=IF (O7>59, "YES","")"
"=IF (O8>59, "YES","")"
"=IF (O9>59, "YES","")"

These formulas for aging lien waivers are normally oriented on the worksheet in the columns at the top of the Lien Waiver Record Log but were formatted on separate pages in order to fit for illustration purposes. Again, the Lien Waiver Record Log is copied and pasted from the Invoice Workbook submitted by the prime contractor each month for Material, Subcontractors, and Third Party Equipment Rentals.

CHAPTER 17 -
CONSUMABLE ITEMS

Consumable miscellaneous items are not directly billable to the owner for reimbursement if the contract has a small tools/consumable adder. These suggested items are included in a small tools/consumable adder, say $4.00 per craft hour billed and are valued at less than $750.00 each. This method of reimbursement avoids handling small individual invoices for multiple small dollar items.

Current Description

ABSORBENT OIL	CONSUMABLE
ACID MURATIC 50%	CONSUMABLE
ADAPTER 3/4" PIPE-GARDEN HOSE	CONSUMABLE
ADAPTER CAP JACKSON	CONSUMABLE
ADAPTER CORE DRILL	CONSUMABLE
ADAPTER HOOD TO HARD HAT	CONSUMABLE
ADAPTER HOUGAN BIT	CONSUMABLE
ADAPTER INERT GAS HOSE	CONSUMABLE
ADAPTER MILLER TO PORTA MIG	CONSUMABLE
ADAPTER SOCKET 3/8" & 1/2"	CONSUMABLE
ADAPTER STUD 300 CC/CV	CONSUMABLE
AIR COMPRESSED F/HORN	CONSUMABLE
ALCOHOL ISOPROPYL QT	CONSUMABLE
ANCHOR METAL ROOF SPIDER	CONSUMABLE
ANCHOR NAILIN ZAMAC	CONSUMABLE

ANTENNA RADIO	CONSUMABLE
APRON RUBBER	CONSUMABLE
ARBORS	CONSUMABLE
BAG BOLT	CONSUMABLE
BAG DUFFLE ARMY	CONSUMABLE
BAG SAND EMPTY/FULL	CONSUMABLE
BAND SWEAT	CONSUMABLE
BANDING 3/4" - 1 1/4" - 2" ROLLS	CONSUMABLE
BAR CHAIN SAW	CONSUMABLE
BARRELL BARRICADE	CONSUMABLE
BARRICADE STREET (A-FRAME; FLASHING; 24" & 36")	CONSUMABLE
BASE MAG WHITE FACE SCALE	CONSUMABLE
BATTERY (AA; AAA; C; D; 6V; 9V)	CONSUMABLE
BATTERY DRILL 12V - 24V	CONSUMABLE
BATTERY NA3003 LEVEL	CONSUMABLE
BATTERY RADIO	CONSUMABLE
BIT AUGER SHIP	CONSUMABLE
BIT BURR DIE GRINDER	CONSUMABLE
BIT CORE DIAMOND 1/2" - 18"	CONSUMABLE
BIT HOUGEN 1" & 2" DEPTH	CONSUMABLE
BIT HSS	CONSUMABLE
BIT HSS #'s	CONSUMABLE
BIT HSS LETTERS	CONSUMABLE
BIT HSS METRIC	CONSUMABLE
BIT HSS MRS-TAPERS	CONSUMABLE
BIT REBAR CUTTER	CONSUMABLE
BIT ROCK THRD CARB	CONSUMABLE
BIT ROUTER CARB	CONSUMABLE
BIT SCREWGUN PHILLIPS	CONSUMABLE
BIT SCREWGUN STRAIGHT SLOT	CONSUMABLE
BIT SCREWGUN TORX	CONSUMABLE
BIT SDS	CONSUMABLE
BIT SDS MAX	CONSUMABLE
BIT SHEETER	CONSUMABLE

BIT SPEED	CONSUMABLE
BLADE 5" DRY DIAMOND	CONSUMABLE
BLADE BANDSAW	CONSUMABLE
BLADE BRUSH CUTTING FOR WEEDEATER	CONSUMABLE
BLADE CHAIN SAW	CONSUMABLE
BLADE CIRC SAW	CONSUMABLE
BLADE COMBINATION FINISH MACHINE	CONSUMABLE
BLADE CONCRETE	CONSUMABLE
BLADE DIAMOND 12" - 30"	CONSUMABLE
BLADE DIAMOND DRY	CONSUMABLE
BLADE DIAMOND DRY QUICKIE SAW	CONSUMABLE
BLADE FEIN SAW	CONSUMABLE
BLADE FINISH FOR FINISH MACHINE	CONSUMABLE
BLADE FLOOR SCRAPER	CONSUMABLE
BLADE HACK SAW	CONSUMABLE
BLADE METAL	CONSUMABLE
BLADE METAL CARB.	CONSUMABLE
BLADE METAL QUICKIE SAW	CONSUMABLE
BLADE METAL SAWSALL	CONSUMABLE
BLADE PLANER	CONSUMABLE
BLADE PLASTIC for weedeater	CONSUMABLE
BLADE RADIAL ARM SAW	CONSUMABLE
BLADE RAZOR FLOOR/PAINT SCRAPER	CONSUMABLE
BLADE SHOE FINISH MACHINE	CONSUMABLE
BLADE UTILITY KNIFE	CONSUMABLE
BLADE WOOD QUICKIE SAW	CONSUMABLE
BLADE WOOD SAWSALL	CONSUMABLE
BLANKET INSULATED	CONSUMABLE
BLANKET MOVING	CONSUMABLE
BOARD KNEE	CONSUMABLE
BOLT CARRIAGE	CONSUMABLE
BOLT LAG	CONSUMABLE
BOLT LONG	CONSUMABLE
BOOTS 2 BUCKLE	CONSUMABLE

BOOTS 5 BUCKLE	CONSUMABLE
BOOTS HIP	CONSUMABLE
BOOTS RUBBER KNEE	CONSUMABLE
BOTTLE SAMPLE	CONSUMABLE
BOTTLE SPRAY 1 QT	CONSUMABLE
BOX ELECTRIC W/4 OUTLETS	CONSUMABLE
BOX LOCKOUT	CONSUMABLE
BOX MORTAR MIXER	CONSUMABLE
BOX SAND SIFTER	CONSUMABLE
BRACKET TANK SCAFFOLD	CONSUMABLE
BRICK RUB CONCRETE	CONSUMABLE
BROOM	CONSUMABLE
BRUSH HAND WIRE	CONSUMABLE
BRUSH LONG HANDLE MIXER	CONSUMABLE
BRUSH PAINT	CONSUMABLE
BRUSH PARTS CLEANING	CONSUMABLE
BRUSH SCRUB BLOCK	CONSUMABLE
BRUSH SCRUB Long Handle	CONSUMABLE
BRUSH SCRUB F/FLOOR BUFFER	CONSUMABLE
BRUSH VACUUM CLEANER	CONSUMABLE
BRUSH WIRE CUP - GRINDER	CONSUMABLE
BRUSH WIRE FOR FLOOR MACHINE	CONSUMABLE
BRUSH WIRE WHEEL FOR GRINDER	CONSUMABLE
BUCKET BOLT CANVAS	CONSUMABLE
BUCKET FINISHER 3 GAL	CONSUMABLE
BUCKET FIRE EXTINGUISHER	CONSUMABLE
BUCKET METAL 5 GAL	CONSUMABLE
BUCKET PLASTIC 1 QT - 5 GAL	CONSUMABLE
BULB FLASHLIGHT	CONSUMABLE
BULB FLORESCENT LIGHT	CONSUMABLE
BURLAP	CONSUMABLE
BUSHING BRASS	CONSUMABLE
CABLE BATTERY JUMPER	CONSUMABLE
CABLE BEAMGUARD SAFETY POST	CONSUMABLE

CABLE BLACK NEOPRENE 1/0 & 2/0	CONSUMABLE
CABLE CONTROL WIRE FEEDER F/LN	CONSUMABLE
CABLE LOAD LINE F/ROUSTABOUT	CONSUMABLE
CAN EMPTY 1-5 GAL	CONSUMABLE
CAN OIL SQUIRT	CONSUMABLE
CAP REBAR IMPALEMENT #3-#8	CONSUMABLE
CARIBINER	CONSUMABLE
CART CARPETED FURNITURE 4 WHL	CONSUMABLE
CARTRIDGE F/1/2 MASK	CONSUMABLE
CEMENT CONTACT	CONSUMABLE
CHAIN	CONSUMABLE
CHAIN SURVEY 100'	CONSUMABLE
CHAIR BOSEN	
CHAIR SCREED	CONSUMABLE
CHALK BOX	CONSUMABLE
CHALK POWDER	CONSUMABLE
CHAPS 36"L	CONSUMABLE
CHISEL COLD	CONSUMABLE
CHISEL F/AIR CHIPPING HAMMER	CONSUMABLE
CHISEL F/AIR SLAG HAMMER	CONSUMABLE
CHISEL F/B & D MACHO	CONSUMABLE
CHISEL F/JACKHAMMER	CONSUMABLE
CHISEL F/PAV BREAKER	CONSUMABLE
CHISEL F/RIVET BUSTER	CONSUMABLE
CHISEL F/SDS MAX	CONSUMABLE
CHISEL HAND	CONSUMABLE
CHOKER HAND SPLICE	CONSUMABLE
CHOKER TOOL TIE OFF	CONSUMABLE
CHUCK 1/4" COLLET SLICE TORCH	CONSUMABLE
CHUCK F/SCREWGUN	CONSUMABLE
CHUCK GUN WITH SLEEVE FOR STUD WELDING	CONSUMABLE
CLAMP CABLE FIST GRIP	CONSUMABLE
CLAMP HOSE	CONSUMABLE
CLAMP TORCH HOSE	CONSUMABLE

CLIP BELT RADIO	CONSUMABLE
CLIP TANK SCAFFOLD	CONSUMABLE
CLOTH EMERY	CONSUMABLE
CLOTH KROCUS	CONSUMABLE
COLLAR F/RIVET BUSTER	CONSUMABLE
CONE SAFETY 12" - 36"	CONSUMABLE
CONNECTOR BUG-O-TRACK	CONSUMABLE
CONNECTOR DOUBLE BALL	CONSUMABLE
COOLANT ANTI-FREEZE	CONSUMABLE
COOLER WATER 3 -10 GAL	CONSUMABLE
CORD DROP LIGHT 25'	CONSUMABLE
CORD ELECTRIC 2' W/3 OUTLETS	CONSUMABLE
CORD ELECTRIC EXT 10/3 & 12/3	CONSUMABLE
CORK MISC SIZES	CONSUMABLE
COUNTERSINK	CONSUMABLE
COUPLER TORCH HOSE	CONSUMABLE
COUPLING BSS PIPE	CONSUMABLE
COUPLING DRILL STEEL	CONSUMABLE
COUPLING HOSE	CONSUMABLE
COUPLING QUICK	CONSUMABLE
COUPLING SNAP	CONSUMABLE
COVER PAINT ROLLER	CONSUMABLE
COVERPLATE LENS PLASTIC	CONSUMABLE
CUP PAPER 7 OZ (250 CUPS)	CONSUMABLE
DECAL DANGER HIGH VOLTAGE	CONSUMABLE
DEGREASER	CONSUMABLE
D-ICER	CONSUMABLE
DIE F/WHITNEY PUNCH	CONSUMABLE
DIE SET RIDGID #194	CONSUMABLE
DIP NOZZLE	CONSUMABLE
DISC ALUM PILE HAMMER	CONSUMABLE
DISC ASCON PILE HAMMER	CONSUMABLE
DISC CONCRETE GRINDING	CONSUMABLE
DISC CUTOFF	CONSUMABLE

DISC DIAMOND 4" 1-2 ROW	CONSUMABLE
DISC DIAMOND 5" CUTOFF WHEEL	CONSUMABLE
DISC GRIND 5" SS TIGER	CONSUMABLE
DISC KIT 7" DISC PAD & WRENCH	CONSUMABLE
DISC METAL GRINDING	CONSUMABLE
DISC MICARTA PILE HAMMER	CONSUMABLE
DISC SANDING	CONSUMABLE
DISC SILICONE	CONSUMABLE
DISPENSER CUP	CONSUMABLE
DISPENSER SALT TABLET	CONSUMABLE
DRESSING BELT SPRAY	CONSUMABLE
EDGER CONCRETE	CONSUMABLE
ENGRAVER ELECTRIC	CONSUMABLE
ETHER STARTING FLUID	CONSUMABLE
EXCITER BRUSH SET	CONSUMABLE
EYE WASH BOTTLE	CONSUMABLE
FAN BOX 20" - 24"	CONSUMABLE
FAN HI VELOCITY	CONSUMABLE
FAN PEDESTAL	CONSUMABLE
FAN ROUND TILT 24"	CONSUMABLE
FEEDER MM-90 110V GUN LINER	CONSUMABLE
FEEDER ROUND BAIL	CONSUMABLE
FILE 3-CORNER 10"	CONSUMABLE
FILE BASTARD 1/2 ROUND	CONSUMABLE
FILE BASTARD FLAT	CONSUMABLE
FILE BASTARD KNIFE	CONSUMABLE
FILE CHAIN SAW	CONSUMABLE
FILE SMOOTH FLAT	CONSUMABLE
FILTER F/ DEFUMER	CONSUMABLE
FILTER FURNACE	CONSUMABLE
FILTER OIL	CONSUMABLE
FILTER SHOP VAC CARTRIDGE	CONSUMABLE
FILTER TEST	CONSUMABLE
EXTINGUISHER ABC FIRE	CONSUMABLE

EXTINGUISHER CO2 FIRE	CONSUMABLE
EXTINGUISHER-FIRE WATER	CONSUMABLE
FITTING HOSE WATER	CONSUMABLE
FITTING PROPANE HOSE	CONSUMABLE
FITTING SERVICE ENTRANCE CABLE	CONSUMABLE
FLAG ESCORT	CONSUMABLE
FLAG F/SIGNALMAN on hwy	CONSUMABLE
FLAG - GOLF CART	CONSUMABLE
FLAG UNITED STATES	CONSUMABLE
FLASHLIGHT	CONSUMABLE
FLOAT PUMP 110V	CONSUMABLE
FLOAT RUBBER	CONSUMABLE
FUNNEL	CONSUMABLE
GAS TANNER GAL.	CONSUMABLE
GASKET FORM-A #2 PERMATEX	CONSUMABLE
GASKET HOSE	CONSUMABLE
GATE CHAIN LINK ON PIPE	CONSUMABLE
GATORADE MIX PKT 2-1/2 GAL	CONSUMABLE
GAUGE FEELER 001-030 (32PCS)	CONSUMABLE
GAUGE FILLET WELD	CONSUMABLE
GAUGE RAIN	CONSUMABLE
GAUGE WIND METER	CONSUMABLE
GLOVES JERSEY	CONSUMABLE
GLOVES KEVLAR (ANSELL 80-600)	CONSUMABLE
GLOVES LATEX	CONSUMABLE
GLOVES RIGGING	CONSUMABLE
GLOVES RUBBER KNIT WRIST	CONSUMABLE
GLOVES WORK LEATHER	CONSUMABLE
GLUE	CONSUMABLE
GLUE LIQUID NAIL	CONSUMABLE
GLUE WELD CRETE	CONSUMABLE
GOGGLES BURNING	CONSUMABLE
GOGGLES CLEAR	CONSUMABLE
LENS GOGGLES	CONSUMABLE

HOW TO DETECT CONSTRUCTION FRAUD

GOGGLES MONO F/DUST	CONSUMABLE
GREASE 1200	CONSUMABLE
GREASE CABLE & CHAIN SPRAY	CONSUMABLE
GROOVER F/CONCRETE	CONSUMABLE
GUARD SHOE (PR)	CONSUMABLE
GUARD WHEEL F/MAKITA GRINDER	CONSUMABLE
GUN CAULK (SMALL-LARGE)	CONSUMABLE
GUN GREASE F/CARTRIDGE	CONSUMABLE
HAMMER BALLPEIN 16 OZ	CONSUMABLE
HAMMER BRASS 18 OZ.	CONSUMABLE
HAMMER BUSH	CONSUMABLE
HAMMER CLAW 16 OZ	CONSUMABLE
HAMMER RUBBER	CONSUMABLE
HAMMER SLEDGE # 2 - #4	CONSUMABLE
HAMMER STAPLER	CONSUMABLE
HAMMER WOOD MALLET	CONSUMABLE
HANDLE AIR ARC	CONSUMABLE
HANDLE BROOM	CONSUMABLE
HANDLE FILE	CONSUMABLE
HANDLE GRINDER 5" Makita	CONSUMABLE
HANDLE PAINT ROLLER	CONSUMABLE
HANDLE PICK	CONSUMABLE
HANDLE SLEDGE HAMMER	CONSUMABLE
HANDLE SLICE TORCH	CONSUMABLE
HANDLE WINCH	CONSUMABLE
HARDNER BODY FILLER	CONSUMABLE
HARNESS CRADLE 5423NS	CONSUMABLE
HASP	CONSUMABLE
HEAD AIR ARC ASSY	CONSUMABLE
HEAD GUN PAK5	CONSUMABLE
HEATER 110V PORTABLE	CONSUMABLE
HINGE	CONSUMABLE
HITCH PIN	CONSUMABLE
HOE GARDEN TYPE	CONSUMABLE

HOLDER PAINT ROLLER 18"	CONSUMABLE
HOLDER SOAPSTONE	CONSUMABLE
HOLDER TAPE LEATHER	CONSUMABLE
HOLDER TIE (OLD DOG)	CONSUMABLE
HOOK 5-10 TON	CONSUMABLE
HOOK GRAB 3/8"	CONSUMABLE
HOOK GUY CABLE	CONSUMABLE
HOOK SAFETY 5 - 10 TON	CONSUMABLE
HOOK BELT SAFETY	CONSUMABLE
HORN AIR	CONSUMABLE
HORN BULL	CONSUMABLE
HORSE SAW	CONSUMABLE
HOSE F/BARRELL PUMP	CONSUMABLE
HOSE F/PORTA POWER 6'	CONSUMABLE
HOSE GREASE FLEX 12"	CONSUMABLE
HOSE PROPANE 1/4"	CONSUMABLE
HOSE SOAKER	CONSUMABLE
HOSE WHIP 25' PAK5	CONSUMABLE
HOUSING WIRE REEL	CONSUMABLE
ICE MELT	CONSUMABLE
INSECTICIDE	CONSUMABLE
JAWS BOLT CUTTER #1	CONSUMABLE
KEYS	CONSUMABLE
KEY CHUCK	CONSUMABLE
KEYSTOCK SQUARE	CONSUMABLE
KIT HOSE REPAIR	CONSUMABLE
KIT LATCH 4 1/2 TON ALLOY	CONSUMABLE
KIT LOCKOUT	CONSUMABLE
KIT RATCHET REPAIR	CONSUMABLE
KIT SPARE PARTS 125 PRO CUT	CONSUMABLE
KIT SPARE PARTS 60 PRO CUT	CONSUMABLE
KIT SPARE PARTS PAK 5	CONSUMABLE
KIT WATER F/QUICKIE SAW	CONSUMABLE
KIT WATER TANK	CONSUMABLE

HOW TO DETECT CONSTRUCTION FRAUD

KNIFE CARPET	CONSUMABLE
KNIFE MACHETE	CONSUMABLE
KNIFE PUTTY	CONSUMABLE
KNIFE UTILITY	CONSUMABLE
LATCH SAFETY f/chain hoist	CONSUMABLE
LENS F/SANDBLASTER	CONSUMABLE
LEVEL EYE	CONSUMABLE
LEVEL SMART 48"	CONSUMABLE
LEVEL TORPEDO	CONSUMABLE
LEVER SLICE TORCH ASSY	CONSUMABLE
LEVER TORCH	CONSUMABLE
LIGHT BARRICADE BLINKER	CONSUMABLE
LIGHT POWER DC 600	CONSUMABLE
LIGHTER SINGLE-3 FLINT	CONSUMABLE
LINER HAT FLEECE LINED	CONSUMABLE
LINER PAK 10	CONSUMABLE
LINER RATCHET HARD HAT	CONSUMABLE
LINK CHAIN	CONSUMABLE
LOCKOUT F/ELECTRIC BOXES	CONSUMABLE
MAGNET HORSESHOE	CONSUMABLE
MAGNET POCKET	CONSUMABLE
MASK CPR MOUTH BARRIER	CONSUMABLE
MENDER HOSE SPLICE	CONSUMABLE
METER AMP	CONSUMABLE
METER VOLT	CONSUMABLE
MIRROR CONVEX ROUND	CONSUMABLE
MIRROR W/ HANDLE	CONSUMABLE
MIXER EPOXY 21"	CONSUMABLE
MOP COTTON	CONSUMABLE
MOP DUST 24"-48" W/FRAME/HANDLE	CONSUMABLE
MOP DUST REFILL 36"	CONSUMABLE
MOP DUST SPRAY (ENDUST)	CONSUMABLE
MOP SPONGE	CONSUMABLE
TRAP MOUSE	CONSUMABLE

MUFF EAR F/NOISE #310	CONSUMABLE
MUZZEL DUST 5" GRINDER	CONSUMABLE
NEEDLES F/SCALER	CONSUMABLE
NEVER SEIZE	CONSUMABLE
NIPPLE BSS PIPE	CONSUMABLE
NIPPLE INERT GAS HOSE	CONSUMABLE
NIPPLE TORCH HOSE 1/4"	CONSUMABLE
NOZZLE AIR SPRAY	CONSUMABLE
NOZZLE Alumina –tig welding	CONSUMABLE
NOZZLE BRASS	CONSUMABLE
NOZZLE EPOXY	CONSUMABLE
NOZZLE F/PORTA MIG	CONSUMABLE
NOZZLE FIRE HOSE	CONSUMABLE
NOZZLE HOSE PISTOL GRIP	CONSUMABLE
NOZZLE PROTEX SPRAYER	CONSUMABLE
NOZZLE WATER HOSE	CONSUMABLE
NUT INERT GAS HOSE	CONSUMABLE
NUT TORCH HOSE FUEL	CONSUMABLE
NUT TORCH TIP	CONSUMABLE
OIL 15W 40	CONSUMABLE
OIL BAR & CHAIN SAW	CONSUMABLE
OIL GEAR 80W QT	CONSUMABLE
OIL HYD 46AW	CONSUMABLE
OIL PENETRATING	CONSUMABLE
OIL THREAD CUTTING	CONSUMABLE
OIL TRANS FLUID TYPE ATF	CONSUMABLE
OIL TWO CYCLE 50:1 PINT	CONSUMABLE
OIL WD40 SPRAY--16OZ	CONSUMABLE
OIL ZEP 2000	CONSUMABLE
O-RING F/IMPACT	CONSUMABLE
PAD KNEE - PAIR	CONSUMABLE
PAD NYLON F/FLOOR MACHINE	CONSUMABLE
PAD SCOTCH BRITE 6"X9" V-FINE	CONSUMABLE
PAD SHOULDER HARNESS	CONSUMABLE

	PAD STEELWOOL F/FLOOR SCRUBBER	CONSUMABLE
	PADLOCK LOCKOUT	CONSUMABLE
	PADS SANDING ORBITAL 80 GRIT	
	PAINT SPRAY	CONSUMABLE
	PAINT THINNER	CONSUMABLE
	PAN DUST	CONSUMABLE
	PINS DOWEL SET	CONSUMABLE
	PIPE STOVE STRAIGHT	CONSUMABLE
	PISTON RIVET BUSTER	CONSUMABLE
	PIVOT ASSEMBLY	CONSUMABLE
	PLIERS BATTERY	CONSUMABLE
	PLIERS IRON WORKER	CONSUMABLE
	PLIERS KLEIN	CONSUMABLE
	PLIERS NEEDLE NOSE	CONSUMABLE
	PLIERS SIDE CUT	CONSUMABLE
	PLIERS SLIP JOINT	CONSUMABLE
	PLIERS TWISTER	CONSUMABLE
	PLIERS VISE GRIP	CONSUMABLE
	PLIERS WELDER	CONSUMABLE
	PLUG SPARK	CONSUMABLE
	PLUG WATER	CONSUMABLE
	PLUM BOB	CONSUMABLE
	POINT F/AIR CHIPPING HAMMER	CONSUMABLE
	PULLER CARPET	CONSUMABLE
	PUMP AIR BICYCLE	CONSUMABLE
	PUNCH & DIE SET	CONSUMABLE
	PUNCH CENTER	CONSUMABLE
	PUNCH F/RIVET BUSTER	CONSUMABLE
	PUNCH PIN	CONSUMABLE
	PUNCH SOLID	CONSUMABLE
	PUNCH TRANSFER SET	CONSUMABLE
	PUNCH WHITNEY	CONSUMABLE
	RAGS	CONSUMABLE
	RAINJACKET	CONSUMABLE

RAINPANT	CONSUMABLE
RAINSUIT	CONSUMABLE
RAKE ASPHALT	CONSUMABLE
RAKE LEAF	CONSUMABLE
RAPAROUND PIPE	CONSUMABLE
RATCHET 1/4 - 1/2" DR	CONSUMABLE
REAMER	CONSUMABLE
REDUCER ENAMEL PAINT	CONSUMABLE
REEL F/TIE WIRE	CONSUMABLE
RESPIRATOR DISPOSABLE	CONSUMABLE
ROD BRASS	CONSUMABLE
ROLLER PAINT W/HANDLE	CONSUMABLE
ROPE MANILA	CONSUMABLE
ROPE NYLON	CONSUMABLE
ROPE POLYPRO	CONSUMABLE
ROUND SOLID BRASS 1"	CONSUMABLE
RUBBER F/RIVET BUSTERS	CONSUMABLE
RUBBERBAND F/BANDSAW	CONSUMABLE
RULE 6' WOOD (CARPENTER-ENGINEER)	CONSUMABLE
SALT ROCK	CONSUMABLE
BELT DRIVE SANDER BOSCH	CONSUMABLE
SANDPAPER	CONSUMABLE
SANDPAPER BELT 3" X 24"	CONSUMABLE
SANDPAPER DISC	CONSUMABLE
SAW HAND	CONSUMABLE
SAW HOLE	CONSUMABLE
SAW KEYHOLE	CONSUMABLE
SCABBARD F/WRENCH	CONSUMABLE
SCALE WHITE FACE 10" - 20"	CONSUMABLE
SCRAPER HAND W/RAZOR	CONSUMABLE
SCRAPER PAINT	CONSUMABLE
SCRAPER WINDSHIELD LG HANDLE	CONSUMABLE
SCREW SET K-126	CONSUMABLE
SCREW TORCH BODY	CONSUMABLE

SCREWDRIVER	CONSUMABLE
SCREWDRIVER PHILLIPS	CONSUMABLE
SCREWDRIVER TORX SET	CONSUMABLE
SET TAP & DIE	CONSUMABLE
SHACKLE 1/2" F/BEAMGUARD POST	CONSUMABLE
SHACKLE 3/16" - 7/8"	CONSUMABLE
SHIELD SIDE CLIP ON f/glasses	CONSUMABLE
SHIELD SLICE TORCH	CONSUMABLE
SHOE F/6' STEP LADDER	CONSUMABLE
SHOE PIPE BRACE	CONSUMABLE
SHOE SAFETY F/STAGING REPAIR	CONSUMABLE
SHOT ALL COLORS	CONSUMABLE
SHOT BAG F/BLASTER	CONSUMABLE
SIGNS	CONSUMABLE
SLEEVE F/RIVET BUSTER	CONSUMABLE
SLEEVE GUN CHUCK STUD D	CONSUMABLE
SLEEVE GUN PAK 10	CONSUMABLE
SLEEVE KEVLAR 14" PR.	CONSUMABLE
SLING NYLON	CONSUMABLE
SLING F/WHEELBARROW	CONSUMABLE
SLING NYLON	CONSUMABLE
SNIPS TIN	CONSUMABLE
SOAP LIQUID CLEANER DEGREASER	CONSUMABLE
SOAPSTONE FLAT	CONSUMABLE
SOCKET 1/2" DR (REG. & METRIC)	CONSUMABLE
SOCKET 1/2" DR HEX (REG. & METRIC)	CONSUMABLE
SOCKET 3/8" DR (REG. & METRIC)	CONSUMABLE
SOCKET 3/8" DR HEX (REG. & METRIC)	CONSUMABLE
SOCKET SCREWGUN	CONSUMABLE
SOCKET TORCH AIR HOSE 3/8"	CONSUMABLE
SOCKET TS GUN INNER	CONSUMABLE
SODA BAKING (1# BOX)	CONSUMABLE
SOFTENER METAL CABLE	CONSUMABLE
SOFTNER PLASTIC F/SLINGS	CONSUMABLE

SOLVENT STODDARD	CONSUMABLE
SPADE	CONSUMABLE
SPIRITS MINERAL	CONSUMABLE
SPLICER TORCH HOSE	CONSUMABLE
SPONGE	CONSUMABLE
SPRAYER PLASTIC 3 GAL	CONSUMABLE
SPREADER FOUR LEG	CONSUMABLE
SPREADER TWO LEG	CONSUMABLE
SPRING DOOR	CONSUMABLE
SPRING F/AIR CHIPPING HAMMER	CONSUMABLE
SPRINKLER LAWN	CONSUMABLE
SQUARE CARPENTER FRAME	CONSUMABLE
SQUARE COMBINATION	CONSUMABLE
SQUARE COMBINATION #33H EDP#50	CONSUMABLE
SQUARE TRI	CONSUMABLE
SQUEEGEE FLOOR	CONSUMABLE
STAKE SLOPE	CONSUMABLE
STAMPS STEEL	CONSUMABLE
STAND BARRELL 24" HIGH	CONSUMABLE
STAND BARRICADE	CONSUMABLE
STAND FLAG CRANE	CONSUMABLE
STAND LIGHT W/SIGNAL LIGHTS	CONSUMABLE
STATION HAND WASH	CONSUMABLE
STATION LOCKOUT F/20	CONSUMABLE
STEEL DRILL	CONSUMABLE
STEELWOOL	CONSUMABLE
STEM SCREWGUN	CONSUMABLE
STENCIL 1" & 2" LETTERS	CONSUMABLE
STICK TEMP	CONSUMABLE
STONE CUP GRINDING 4"	CONSUMABLE
STONE GRIND BENCH 6"X 1"	CONSUMABLE
STONE RUBBING FLAT	CONSUMABLE
STOPPER SEWER	CONSUMABLE
STRAP CHIN-HAT	CONSUMABLE

STRAP CROSS OVER BEAM	CONSUMABLE
STRAP NYLON 27' W/BINDER	CONSUMABLE
STRAP RUBBER 24"	CONSUMABLE
STRING LINE weed trimmer	CONSUMABLE
STUD GUN CONNECTOR EC 200	CONSUMABLE
STYROFOAM	CONSUMABLE
SWITCH STUDGUN	CONSUMABLE
TAG DO NOT OPERATE	CONSUMABLE
TAG FIRE EXTINGUISHER	CONSUMABLE
TAG SCAFFOLD	CONSUMABLE
TAGS BRASS 1"	CONSUMABLE
TAGS LOCKOUT	CONSUMABLE
TAGS RED F/REPAIR	CONSUMABLE
TAGS WHITE	CONSUMABLE
TAMPER F/PAVE BREAKER	CONSUMABLE
TAP BOTTOM	CONSUMABLE
TAP STARTER	CONSUMABLE
TAPE BLUE 3" X 1000'	CONSUMABLE
TAPE CARPET	CONSUMABLE
TAPE CAUTION YELLOW 3" X 1000'	CONSUMABLE
TAPE CLEAR REINFORCED 1"	CONSUMABLE
TAPE DANGER RED 3" X 1000'	CONSUMABLE
TAPE DUCT	CONSUMABLE
TAPE F/LABELING DYMO	CONSUMABLE
TAPE FRICTION	CONSUMABLE
TAPE MASKING	CONSUMABLE
TAPE NONSKID	CONSUMABLE
TAPE REFLECTOR	CONSUMABLE
TAPE REINFORCED	CONSUMABLE
TARP CANVAS	CONSUMABLE
TARP NYLON	CONSUMABLE
TARP PLASTIC	CONSUMABLE
TARP RED MESH 8'X 22'6"	CONSUMABLE
TARP SUPER POLY 30'X 30'	CONSUMABLE

TEE BSS 1 1/4"	CONSUMABLE
TEE BSS PIPE	CONSUMABLE
TESTER CIRCUIT	CONSUMABLE
TESTER CORD GFCI	CONSUMABLE
TESTER POLARITY	CONSUMABLE
TESTER VOLTAGE	CONSUMABLE
THERMOMETER	CONSUMABLE
THINNER LAQUER	CONSUMABLE
TIP CONTACT TWEKO 1/16"	CONSUMABLE
TIP CUTTING ACET & HPG	
TIP F/PROTEX SPRAYER	CONSUMABLE
TIP GREASE GUN	CONSUMABLE
TIP HEATING ROSEBUD	CONSUMABLE
TIP PROPANE	CONSUMABLE
TIP SCARFING	CONSUMABLE
TIRE FOAM FILLED F/GOLF CART	CONSUMABLE
TUBE F/WHEELBARROW	CONSUMABLE
TIRE PICKUP TRUCK	CONSUMABLE
TIRE F/WHEELBARROW	CONSUMABLE
TIRE FOAM FILLED F/WHEELBARROW	CONSUMABLE
TOOL SETTING F/RED HEAD	CONSUMABLE
TROWEL MARGIN	CONSUMABLE
TUBING CLEAR	CONSUMABLE
TUMBLER PADLOCK 412 #21	CONSUMABLE
TWINE NYLON	
UNION BSS PIPE	CONSUMABLE
VALVE AIR THROTTLE	CONSUMABLE
VALVE BALL	CONSUMABLE
VALVE CHECK f/oxy-acet line	CONSUMABLE
VALVE GATE	CONSUMABLE
VEST WORK /LIFEJACKET	CONSUMABLE
VISOR CLEAR FACE SHIELD	CONSUMABLE
VISOR SHADED Face shield	CONSUMABLE
VISQUEEN 4 - 8MIL	CONSUMABLE

VISQUEEN FIRE RETARDENT	CONSUMABLE
VISQUEEN REINFORCED	CONSUMABLE
WAND CMI PIN	CONSUMABLE
WASHER AIR HOSE 3/4" CP	CONSUMABLE
WATER IN BOTTLES	CONSUMABLE
WEDGE LOG SPLITTING	CONSUMABLE

CHAPTER 18-
SUGGESTED SMALL TOOLS

Notes:
$xxx. will be added to each craft hour worked to compensate for small tools. The following items will not be directly billed to owner. This is not an all-inclusive list. This list is not intended to cover materials in place that are part of the permanent structure. Items on list are valued at $750 or less. Safety supplies such as hard hats, ear protection, and eye protection are directly billable if the contract specifies safety supplies.

DESCRIPTION

AIR MOVER COPUS ELEC –(FAN)	SMALL TOOL	
AIR TANK AUXILIARY	SMALL TOOL	
AIR TOOL CLEANER	SMALL TOOL	
AUGER - 6 IN	SMALL TOOL	
AUGER EARTH 10" & 12"	SMALL TOOL	
AXES	SMALL TOOL	
BACKBOARD FOR STOKES STRETCHER	SMALL TOOL	
BACKFLOW PREVENTER	SMALL TOOL	
BAR CROW OR PINCH 18" - 48"	SMALL TOOL	
BAR HICKEY REBAR	SMALL TOOL	
BELT DRIVE SANDER BOSCH	SMALL TOOL	
BENCH WOOD F/TRAILER	SMALL TOOL	
BENDER - TUBING	SMALL TOOL	
BOX GANG SMALL 24"X 24"X 48" **or Smaller**	SMALL TOOL	
BOX MITRE W/SAW	SMALL TOOL	

BOX TOOL	SMALL TOOL	
BREAKER PAVEMENT 25# & 35#	SMALL TOOL	
BUCKET MOP W/RINGER LARGE	SMALL TOOL	
BURNER PROPANE LEAD	SMALL TOOL	
CABLE & HOSE F/PORTA MIG	SMALL TOOL	
CAGE PROPANE TANK	SMALL TOOL	
CAGE TANK 3 BOTTLE	SMALL TOOL	
CAGE TANK PICKING 10 BTLS	SMALL TOOL	
CAN SAFETY EMPTY 5 GAL	SMALL TOOL	
CART DOCK 4 WHL 30"X 60"	SMALL TOOL	
CART DOLLY F/ 55 GAL DRUM	SMALL TOOL	
CART HAND 2 WHEEL	SMALL TOOL	
CART HAND OXY/ACET BOTTLE	SMALL TOOL	
CART LIQUID OXYGEN	SMALL TOOL	
CART PAINT STRIPE	SMALL TOOL	
CART REFRIGERATOR	SMALL TOOL	
CART TANK W/24" STEEL WHEELS	SMALL TOOL	
CART TRASH 1/2 – 1 1/2YD	SMALL TOOL	
CHAIN BINDER 3/8" X 20' W/HOOK	SMALL TOOL	
CHAIR STACK	SMALL TOOL	
CHARGER BATTERY	SMALL TOOL	
CHUCK JACOBS F/HOUGAN DRILL	SMALL TOOL	
CLAMP C 2" - 14"	SMALL TOOL	
CLAMP PLATE 1/2 - 4 TON	SMALL TOOL	
COMEALONG 3/4TON 5'LENGTH	SMALL TOOL	
COMEALONG 3/4TON 15'LENGTH	SMALL TOOL	
COMEALONG 3/4TON 20'LENGTH	SMALL TOOL	
COMEALONG 3/4TON 25'LENGTH	SMALL TOOL	
COMEALONG 3/4TON GLIDE	SMALL TOOL	
COMEALONG 1 1/2TON 5L	SMALL TOOL	
COMEALONG 1 1/2TON 15L	SMALL TOOL	
COMEALONG 1 1/2TON 20L	SMALL TOOL	
COMEALONG 2TON 15L	SMALL TOOL	
COMEALONG 3TON 5L	SMALL TOOL	

HOW TO DETECT CONSTRUCTION FRAUD

COMEALONG 3TON 15L	SMALL TOOL	
COMEALONG 3TON 20L	SMALL TOOL	
COMEALONG CABLE	SMALL TOOL	
COMEALONG CONCRETE W/HANDLE	SMALL TOOL	
COMPOUND SWEEPING (OIL - WAX)	SMALL TOOL	
COMPRESSOR AIR 110 ELEC	SMALL TOOL	
COMPRESSOR F/NAILER ELEC	SMALL TOOL	
CUP GLASS SUCTION	SMALL TOOL	
CUTTER BANDING	SMALL TOOL	
CUTTER BELT 36"	SMALL TOOL	
CUTTER BOLT 12" - 48"	SMALL TOOL	
CUTTER CABLE	SMALL TOOL	
CUTTER PIPE	SMALL TOOL	
CUTTER PIPE 1/2"-2"	SMALL TOOL	
CUTTER TILE VINYL	SMALL TOOL	
CUTTER WEED	SMALL TOOL	
DIGGER POST HOLE	SMALL TOOL	
DOLLY DRY WALL	SMALL TOOL	
DOLLY FIFTH WHEEL	SMALL TOOL	
DRILL AIR 1/2"	SMALL TOOL	
DRILL AIR 1/2" R.A.	SMALL TOOL	
DRILL AIR 3/8"	SMALL TOOL	
DRILL AIR 1 1/4"	SMALL TOOL	
DRILL AIR 1/2"	SMALL TOOL	
DRILL BATTERY 1/2" 14V	SMALL TOOL	
DRILL BATTERY 1/2" 18V	SMALL TOOL	
DRILL BATTERY 3/4" 12V	SMALL TOOL	
DRILL BATTERY 3/8" 12V	SMALL TOOL	
DRILL BATTERY 3/8" 18V	SMALL TOOL	
DRILL DRIVER BATTERY 3/8"	SMALL TOOL	
DRILL ELEC 1"	SMALL TOOL	
DRILL ELEC 1/2"	SMALL TOOL	
DRILL ELEC 1/2" R.A.	SMALL TOOL	
DRILL ELEC 1/4"	SMALL TOOL	

DRILL ELEC 3/4"	SMALL TOOL	
DRILL ELEC 3/8"	SMALL TOOL	
DRILL ELEC 3/8" R.A.	SMALL TOOL	
DRILL MAG SMALL	SMALL TOOL	
DRILL PRESS 12"	SMALL TOOL	
DRIVER POST	SMALL TOOL	
DRIVER POST AIR OPER	SMALL TOOL	
EDGE STRAIGHT 72" STEEL	SMALL TOOL	
EDGE STRAIGHT ALUM 6' - 24'	SMALL TOOL	
EXTENSION 1"DR SOCKET	SMALL TOOL	
EXTENSION 1/2"DR SOCKET	SMALL TOOL	
EXTENSION 1/4"DR SOCKET	SMALL TOOL	
EXTENSION 3/4"DR SOCKET	SMALL TOOL	
EXTENSION 3/8"DR SOCKET	SMALL TOOL	
EXTENSION AUGER 2 MAN	SMALL TOOL	
EXTENSION CORE DRILL	SMALL TOOL	
EXTENSION DRILL BIT	SMALL TOOL	
EXTENSION NOSE 12"X1"DR	SMALL TOOL	
EXTENSION PAINT ROLLER	SMALL TOOL	
EYE LIFTING SWIVEL	SMALL TOOL	
FAN 30" - 36"	SMALL TOOL	
FAN 40" - 48"	SMALL TOOL	
FANS, HEPA W/ FILTER	SMALL TOOL	
FLOAT CHANNEL RADIUS 10'	SMALL TOOL	
FLOAT CONTROL SYSTEM	SMALL TOOL	
FORMS CLEANING - BARREL SPRAYER	SMALL TOOL	
FUEL TANK STAND	SMALL TOOL	
GAUGE 10,000 PSI F/PORTA POWER	SMALL TOOL	
GAUGE ACETYLENE & OXYGEN	SMALL TOOL	
GAUGE AIR PLASMA ARC PAK 5	SMALL TOOL	
GAUGE CO2	SMALL TOOL	
GAUGE FLO METER F/ARGON-CO2-HE	SMALL TOOL	
GAUGE THICKNESS	SMALL TOOL	
GRAB ROPE F/5/8" ROPE	SMALL TOOL	

HOW TO DETECT CONSTRUCTION FRAUD

GRASSHOPPER	SMALL TOOL	
GREASE GUN W/COMPRESSOR	SMALL TOOL	
GRINDER 5"	SMALL TOOL	
GRINDER 7" B&D	SMALL TOOL	
GRINDER AIR 5"	SMALL TOOL	
GRINDER AIR 9"	SMALL TOOL	
GRINDER BENCH	SMALL TOOL	
GRINDER CONCRETE	SMALL TOOL	
GRINDER DIE 2"	SMALL TOOL	
GRINDER ELEC 6"	SMALL TOOL	
GRINDER ELEC 7" - 9"	SMALL TOOL	
GRINDER PENCIL	SMALL TOOL	
GUN COMPLETE AIR ARC	SMALL TOOL	
GUN DISPENSER EPOXY	SMALL TOOL	
GUN GREASE AIR	SMALL TOOL	
GUN HEAT	SMALL TOOL	
GUN MIG MAGNUM	SMALL TOOL	
GUN RIVET	SMALL TOOL	
GUN RIVET POP	SMALL TOOL	
GUN SPOOLMATIC CABLE	SMALL TOOL	
GUN STAPLE W/COMP	SMALL TOOL	
HAMMER AIR CHIPPING	SMALL TOOL	
HAMMER ROTO AIR 3/4"	SMALL TOOL	
HAMMER ROTO BATTERY 24V	SMALL TOOL	
HAMMER SLEDGE # 6 - #20	SMALL TOOL	
HANDLE MACHINE ROLLER	SMALL TOOL	
HANDLE SOFT CUT SAW	SMALL TOOL	
HANDLE T TAP ADJ	SMALL TOOL	
HEADSET RADIO	SMALL TOOL	
HEATER KEROSENE	SMALL TOOL	
HEATER LP GAS 70,000	SMALL TOOL	
HEATER PROPANE/NATGAS 375000BTU	SMALL TOOL	
HEATER PROPANE TANK TOP DUAL	SMALL TOOL	
HEATER PROPANE VENTLESS	SMALL TOOL	

HEATER RADENT UPRIGHT W/HSE RE	SMALL TOOL
HEATER SALAMANDER F/PROPANE	SMALL TOOL
HOIST CHAIN 1 1/2TON 20' LENGTH CHAIN	SMALL TOOL
HOIST CHAIN 1 1/2TON 25'LENGTH	SMALL TOOL
HOIST CHAIN 1/2TON 15'LENGTH	SMALL TOOL
HOIST CHAIN 1/2TON 20'LENGTH	SMALL TOOL
HOIST CHAIN 1/2TON 25'LENGTH	SMALL TOOL
HOIST CHAIN 1/2TON 40'LENGTH	SMALL TOOL
HOIST CHAIN 1/2TON 50'LENGTH	SMALL TOOL
HOIST CHAIN 1TON 15'LENGTH	SMALL TOOL
HOIST CHAIN 1TON 20'LENGTH	
HOIST CHAIN 1TON 30'LENGTH	SMALL TOOL
HOIST CHAIN 1TON 40'LENGTH	SMALL TOOL
HOIST CHAIN 1TON 50'LENGTH	SMALL TOOL
HOIST CHAIN 1TON 60'LENGTH	SMALL TOOL
HOIST CHAIN 1TON-100'LENGTH	SMALL TOOL
HOIST CHAIN 2TON 20'LENGTH	SMALL TOOL
HOIST CHAIN 2TON 25'LENGTH	SMALL TOOL
HOIST CHAIN 2TON 30'LENGTH	SMALL TOOL
HOIST CHAIN 2TON 40'LENGTH	SMALL TOOL
HOIST CHAIN 2TON 50'LENGTH	SMALL TOOL
HOIST CHAIN 2TON 60'LENGTH	SMALL TOOL
HOIST CHAIN 3/4TON 6'LENGTH	SMALL TOOL
HOIST CHAIN 3/4TON 20'LENGTH	SMALL TOOL
HOIST CHAIN 3TON 15'LENGTH	SMALL TOOL
HOIST CHAIN 3TON 20'LENGTH	SMALL TOOL
HOIST CHAIN 3TON 30'LENGTH	SMALL TOOL
HOIST CHAIN 3TON 40'LEENGTH	SMALL TOOL
HOLSTER RADIO	SMALL TOOL
HOOD SANDBLAST AIR	SMALL TOOL
HOSE AIR	SMALL TOOL
HOSE AIR FLEX	SMALL TOOL
HOSE ARGON	SMALL TOOL
HOSE DISCHARGE	SMALL TOOL

HOSE EXHAUST BLOWER	SMALL TOOL	
HOSE FIRE	SMALL TOOL	
HOSE SANDBLAST 1 7/8"	SMALL TOOL	
HOSE SUCTION SECTION	SMALL TOOL	
HOSE VACUUM CLEANER	SMALL TOOL	
HOSE WATER	SMALL TOOL	
IMPACT AIR 1/2"	SMALL TOOL	
IMPACT AIR 3/4"	SMALL TOOL	
IMPACT AIR 3/4" SPLINE	SMALL TOOL	
IMPACT AIR 3/8"	SMALL TOOL	
IMPACT ELEC 1/2" – 3/4"	SMALL TOOL	
JACK FLOOR 2TON – 4- 50 TON	SMALL TOOL	
JACK HYDRAULIC 8 - TON	SMALL TOOL	
JACK PLATFORM 3500	SMALL TOOL	
JACK PLATFORM 5000	SMALL TOOL	
JACK SCREW	SMALL TOOL	
JACK TRACK 5TON	SMALL TOOL	
JACK TRACK 10TON	SMALL TOOL	
JACK TRACK 20TON	SMALL TOOL	
JACK TRANSMISSION	SMALL TOOL	
JACKHAMMER 19#	SMALL TOOL	
JACKHAMMER 28#	SMALL TOOL	
JACKHAMMER 35#	SMALL TOOL	
JACKHAMMER 55#	SMALL TOOL	
JACKHAMMER DRILL	SMALL TOOL	
LADDER EXT FIBERGLASS 16' - 40'	SMALL TOOL	
LADDER JACK F/SCAFFOLD	SMALL TOOL	
LADDER STEP FIBERGLASS 3' - 16'	SMALL TOOL	
LADDER STRAIGHT 6' - 24'	SMALL TOOL	
LADDER TANK FIBERGLASS	SMALL TOOL	
LEVEL ALUMINUM 18" - 96"	SMALL TOOL	
LEVEL - BAZOOKA PLUMB BOB	SMALL TOOL	
LEVEL COMPUTERIZED STANLEY	SMALL TOOL	
LEVEL PLUMB POINTER 3	SMALL TOOL	

LEVEL SCALE	SMALL TOOL	
LEVEL STAND W/ADJ JACK	SMALL TOOL	
LEVEL WOOD 24" - 48"	SMALL TOOL	
MAGNET 1 1/2 - 3 TON	SMALL TOOL	
MAGNET 36" WIDE PULL TYPE	SMALL TOOL	
MATS OUTRIGGER	SMALL TOOL	
MICROPHONE RADIO HAND	SMALL TOOL	
MICROMETER (if valued under $1,000)	SMALL TOOL	
MULE DOCK TWO WHEEL	SMALL TOOL	
NAILER AIR BRAD	SMALL TOOL	
NAILER AIR COIL	SMALL TOOL	
NAILER AIR FINISH	SMALL TOOL	
NAILER AIR FRAMING	SMALL TOOL	
NAILER AIR STRIP	SMALL TOOL	
NAILER FRAME PULSE	SMALL TOOL	
NAILER TRIM PULSE	SMALL TOOL	
OVEN ROD 10#, 50#, 300#	SMALL TOOL	
PICK	SMALL TOOL	
PLANE CONCRETE	SMALL TOOL	
PLANE ELEC 3 1/4" – 3"	SMALL TOOL	
PORTA POWER GAS	SMALL TOOL	
PORTA POWER PUMP LARGE	SMALL TOOL	
PORTA POWER PUMP SMALL	SMALL TOOL	
POT LEAD MELTING	SMALL TOOL	
POWER DRIVE 700	SMALL TOOL	
PRISM R.ANGLE FOR TRANSIT	SMALL TOOL	
PRISM ROUND W/STAND F/Total Station	SMALL TOOL	
PULLER CABLE - SMALL	SMALL TOOL	
PUMP 2" AIR	SMALL TOOL	
PUMP BARRELL ELECT W/HOSE	SMALL TOOL	
PUMP BARRELL F152	SMALL TOOL	
PUMP OIL ELEC	SMALL TOOL	
PUNCH BUTTON METAL	SMALL TOOL	
PUNCH HAND BUTTON	SMALL TOOL	

HOW TO DETECT CONSTRUCTION FRAUD

RAKE ROCK	SMALL TOOL	
RAM 5TON TOE LIFT	SMALL TOOL	
RAM 25TON TOE LIFT	SMALL TOOL	
RAM 25TON X 18"	SMALL TOOL	
RAM 30TON X 2"	SMALL TOOL	
RAM 30TON X 4"	SMALL TOOL	
RAM 30TON X 7"	SMALL TOOL	
RAM 30TON X 9"	SMALL TOOL	
RAM 30TON X 15"	SMALL TOOL	
RAM 50TON X 2"	SMALL TOOL	
RAM 50TON X 5"	SMALL TOOL	
RAM 50TON X 7"	SMALL TOOL	
RAM 50TON X 9"	SMALL TOOL	
RAM 50TON X 11"	SMALL TOOL	
RAM 50TON X 18"	SMALL TOOL	
RAM 55TON X 2"	SMALL TOOL	
RAM 55TON X 7"	SMALL TOOL	
RAM HYD 5 - 25 TON	SMALL TOOL	
RAMPS LOADING	SMALL TOOL	
RATCHET 3/4" - 1" DR	SMALL TOOL	
RATCHET AIR 1/2"	SMALL TOOL	
RATCHET STEAMBOAT 1 3/8" X 24"	SMALL TOOL	
REGULATOR PROPANE GAUGE	SMALL TOOL	
ROLL A LIFT 2000#	SMALL TOOL	
ROLLER AND SWIVEL	SMALL TOOL	
ROLLER MACHINE 3 3/4TON	SMALL TOOL	
ROLLER MACHINE 5TON	SMALL TOOL	
ROLLER MACHINE 6TON	SMALL TOOL	
ROLLER MACHINE 7 1/2TON	SMALL TOOL	
ROLLER MACHINE 10TON	SMALL TOOL	
ROLLER MACHINE 15TON POLY	SMALL TOOL	
ROUTER	SMALL TOOL	
ROUTER PLUNGE	SMALL TOOL	
ROUTER TRIM	SMALL TOOL	

SANDBLASTER 300	SMALL TOOL	
SANDER BELT	SMALL TOOL	
SANDER ORBITAL ELEC	SMALL TOOL	
SANDER PALM	SMALL TOOL	
SAW AIR	SMALL TOOL	
SAW BENCH	SMALL TOOL	
SAW CHAIN ELEC 14", 16"	SMALL TOOL	
SAW CHAIN GAS 14"	SMALL TOOL	
SAW CHAIN GAS 16" – 24" BAR	SMALL TOOL	
SAW CHOP 14"	SMALL TOOL	
SAW CIRC BATT 18V 5-3/8"	SMALL TOOL	
SAW CIRC ELEC	SMALL TOOL	
SAW CIRCULAR ELEC 7 1/4" – 16"	SMALL TOOL	
SAW HACK FRAME W/O BLADE	SMALL TOOL	
SAW JIG	SMALL TOOL	
SAW LAMINATE TRIMMER	SMALL TOOL	
SAW MITER	SMALL TOOL	
SAW MITER COMPOUND 10" – 12"	SMALL TOOL	
SAW MITRE BOX 10", 12", 15"	SMALL TOOL	
SAW PORTA BAND	SMALL TOOL	
SAW QUICKIE 12" – 14"	SMALL TOOL	
SAW QUICKIE AIR 12"	SMALL TOOL	
SAW RADIAL ARM 10" – 14"	SMALL TOOL	
SAW RAIL W/GUIDE	SMALL TOOL	
SAW RECIPRICAL AIR	SMALL TOOL	
SAW SABER	SMALL TOOL	
SAW SABER AIR	SMALL TOOL	
SAW SPIRAL	SMALL TOOL	
SAW TABLE 10"	SMALL TOOL	
SAWS ALL	SMALL TOOL	
SAWS ALL BATTERY	SMALL TOOL	
SCALE 24 X 30 PLATFORM	SMALL TOOL	
SCALE DYNOMETER 5000#	SMALL TOOL	
SCALE DYNOMETER 20000#	SMALL TOOL	

SCRAPER FLOOR 8"	SMALL TOOL	
SCRAPER LONG HANDLE	SMALL TOOL	
SCREWGUN 2000 RPM	SMALL TOOL	
SCREWGUN 2500 RPM	SMALL TOOL	
SCREWGUN 4000 RPM	SMALL TOOL	
SCREWGUN 5300 RPM	SMALL TOOL	
SCREWGUN AIR	SMALL TOOL	
SCREWGUN AUTOTRAX	SMALL TOOL	
SCREWGUN QUICK DRIVE	SMALL TOOL	
SCRIBE AIR	SMALL TOOL	
SHACKLE 1" - 3"	SMALL TOOL	
SHACKLE SHEET PILE	SMALL TOOL	
SHEAR 12 – 14 GAUGE ELEC	SMALL TOOL	
SHEAR 14 GAUGE GAS	SMALL TOOL	
SHEAR 16 18 GAUGE ELEC	SMALL TOOL	
SHEAR 18 GAUGE DBBL/CUT	SMALL TOOL	
SHOVEL ROUND POINT		
SHOVEL SCOOP ALUM #16714	SMALL TOOL	
SHOVEL SHARPSHOOTER	SMALL TOOL	
SHOVEL	SMALL TOOL	
SIREN ELECTRIC WARNING	SMALL TOOL	
SOCKET #4 & #5 SPLINE DR	SMALL TOOL	
SOCKET 1 1/2" DR (REG. & METRIC)	SMALL TOOL	
SOCKET 1" DR (REG. & METRIC)	SMALL TOOL	
SOCKET 1" DR HEX (REG. & METRIC)	SMALL TOOL	
SOCKET 3/4" DR (REG. & METRIC)	SMALL TOOL	
SOCKET 3/4" DR HEX (REG. & METRIC)	SMALL TOOL	
SPOOLER / CABLE	SMALL TOOL	
SPREADER BROADCAST	SMALL TOOL	
SPREADER WALK BEHIND	SMALL TOOL	
SQUARE DRYWALL T	SMALL TOOL	
STABILIZER TRIPOD	SMALL TOOL	
STAND BANDING	SMALL TOOL	
STAND PIPE	SMALL TOOL	

STAPPLER AIR 1"	SMALL TOOL	
STATION EYE WASH	SMALL TOOL	
STATION PICKING F/OXY & ACET	SMALL TOOL	
STENCIL MACHINE	SMALL TOOL	
STUDGUN	SMALL TOOL	
TABLE PICNIC	SMALL TOOL	
TAMPER AIR HAND HELD	SMALL TOOL	
TAPE MEASURE	SMALL TOOL	
THREADER PIPE W/HANDLES	SMALL TOOL	
TONG ICE	SMALL TOOL	
TOOL CLAMPING P-1	SMALL TOOL	
TORCH 500,000 BTU W/10' HOSE &		
TORCH CUTTING		
TORCH HELIARC COMPLETE	SMALL TOOL	
TORCH PROPANE SET W/GAGE, TIPS	SMALL TOOL	
TORCH ROSEBUD COMPLETE #3 #4	SMALL TOOL	
TORCH SLICE 10" COMPLETE		
TRIMMER LAMINATE	SMALL TOOL	
TRIPLE SHEAVE - LARGE	SMALL TOOL	
TRIPOD LEVELING NEW	SMALL TOOL	
TROLLY BEAM	SMALL TOOL	
TROLLY HOIST 1/2T	SMALL TOOL	
UNIVERSAL 1"DR	SMALL TOOL	
UNIVERSAL 3/4"DR	SMALL TOOL	
UNIVERSAL SPLINE	SMALL TOOL	
VACUUM CARPET	SMALL TOOL	
VACUUM SHOP	SMALL TOOL	
VIBRATOR 110V	SMALL TOOL	
VIBRATOR AIR VICE GRIP	SMALL TOOL	
VISE BENCH	SMALL TOOL	
VISE PIPE	SMALL TOOL	
WEED EATER STIHL	SMALL TOOL	
WHEEL WELL 12"	SMALL TOOL	
WHEELBARROW	SMALL TOOL	

WINCH ELEC 1000#	SMALL TOOL	
WINCH MANLIFT	SMALL TOOL	
WINDER CABLE W/POWER PAC	SMALL TOOL	
WRENCH ADJUSTABLE 15" - 24"	SMALL TOOL	
WRENCH CHAIN 18", 24"	SMALL TOOL	
WRENCH COMBINATION 1 1/16" - +		
WRENCH COMBINATION - 23MM - +	SMALL TOOL	
WRENCH FIRE PLUG		
WRENCH FLARE	SMALL TOOL	
WRENCH HEX 1 1/8" - +	SMALL TOOL	
WRENCH HEX* 24MM - +	SMALL TOOL	
WRENCH PIPE 18" - 48"	SMALL TOOL	
WRENCH SLUG 1 1/16" - +	SMALL TOOL	
WRENCH STRAP 18"	SMALL TOOL	
WRENCH TORQUE 1/2" 250#	SMALL TOOL	
WRENCH TORQUE 1/4"	SMALL TOOL	
WRENCH TORQUE 3/8" 100#	SMALL TOOL	

CHAPTER 19 -
GLOSSARY:

Accruals – The monthly and/or annual identification of project costs that needs to be identified in the current reporting period regardless of when actually paid. This reports for accounting purposes liabilities of the owner anticipated to be expended in the following month or within six months of year end reporting.

Addendum – a modification to the bidding documents or contract to describe additions, deletions, clarifications, or corrections. An addendum becomes contractual after the Contract is executed.

Alliance - A consortium or partnership of contractors and owners working together for the common purpose on a large project such as a nuclear project or common industry advancement that should benefit all parties. Caution: Most employees of an Alliance will still have loyalties to their own companies rather than a new allegiance to a temporary partnership.

Application for Payment – the Contractor's summary requesting reimbursement for the amount of completed portions of the work as well as for materials, equipment delivered and stored prior to being installed in the Project. The Application for Payment may also include sub-tier contractor payments for completed work and/or materials they have procured for the benefit of the project but not yet incorporated in the work.

Apprentice - a craft employee training in a qualified four year program who are eventually promoted to journeymen after being a first year apprentice, second year apprentice, third year apprentice, and fourth year apprentice.

Bid – A contractual proposal to perform the work or a portion of the work for an amount of money or a projected target amount based on available information in the bidding documents. The award of the bid usually results in issuing a contract or letter of intent for the contractor to proceed with mobilization.

Bidding Documents – Drawings, schematics, site project maps, and other documentation prepared by the owner or owner's architect that describes in sufficient detail information that is necessary in order for potential contractors to review and prepare their bids to accomplish the project. These documents are the basis for formulating the schedule, timeline, potential risks, and resources needed to define the project.

"Boilerplate" Specification – That contract language that covers a multitude of common and "standard" conditions such as who (owner or contractor) is responsible for general site conditions such as electricity, phones, construction trailers, trash removal, etc. These general provisions deal with procedure. Boilerplate terms should not be used to justify a design oversight. These cover a standard condition; don't let the general language be used to strain an interpretation for work that was missed by the designer.

Builder's Risk Insurance – A specialized specific form of property insurance which provides for loss or damage to the work during the course of construction caused by the contractor. It does not replace the normal coverage provided by the owner for General Liability, Property, or Workmen's Comp.

Building Permit – A permit issued by the governmental authority in the county or township of the project allowing construction to proceed in accordance with approved drawings and specifications. Normally the building permit is obtained by the owner at his expense and is not the responsibility of the contractor. Some projects require a different permit for each element of a project such as chimneys, buildings, and collection ponds.

Cash Discount – A seller's incentive for the buyer to make prompt payment within a stipulated period of time after the invoice date of the transaction. This amount, which can vary from 1% to 5% of the net amount excluding sales taxes, can be deducted from the invoice amount by the buyer when writing the check if the terms of the purchase order are followed. If the contract provides advance payments from the owner and the contract is Cost plus fees, this cash discount should be passed to the owner since he is entitled to the lower price. The discount reduces the cost of the material and reflects actual cost.

Cash Neutral – A contractual mechanism of providing the prime contractor funds in advance on a monthly basis using the owner's money to pay all labor, material, subcontractor's, overhead, and other obligations so that the contractor does not incur any borrowing costs funding the project. A cash advance is provided from the owner at the beginning of every month based on cash flow estimates provided by the prime contractor. The advance is reconciled to actual funds expended when the following month's Application for Payment is rendered. The cash "position" of the prime contractor is referred to as neutral because he is not risking his own funds.

Certificate of Insurance – A document issued by an Insurance Agency attesting to the insurance in effect, dates of coverage, and amounts in force for a company or contractor. Certain types of insurance for specific projects should name the owner as a secondary beneficiary. For long term projects expanding several years, new copies of certificates should be requested and retained on file as proof of coverage to replace any expired certificates. These certificates provide proof that insurance payments were actually made and coverage is in force.

Change Order – A deviation from the original scope of work. This may be additional enhancements not originally anticipated during design or a deletion of work. It may be due to an agreed substitution of materials, improvement in design, extension of contract schedule due to unforeseen delays, blanket approval of overtime work to meet deadlines, etc. It should be agreed to in writing as a contract modification. There is no inherent right of the owner to change the work and no changed work should be performed without a properly executed Change Order except in the case of an emergency to prevent loss of life, injury, or property damage.

Contingency Allowance – An amount of money included in the project budget that provides for unpredictable or unforeseen items of work or changes that were required by the owner.

Contract – A legally enforceable agreement between two or more parties or persons. A "meeting of the minds" where an agreement is made detailing the terms, remuneration, and type of product or service that must be delivered between the parties to satisfy the written agreement. Failure to perform or provide the product or service would result in a breach of contract.

Contract Award – A communication which could be written or oral from the owner to the contractor accepting a bid for work. This creates a legal obligation between the parties to proceed. In some cases, the contractor may begin the mobilization, procuring materials, and/or soliciting bids from subcontractors before a legal contract is in place.

Contract - Firm Price – An agreed upon total price the owner and contractor established in advance in order to complete the project. A firm price does not require documentation of costs such as material, labor, or equipment. The contractor pockets any excess between the firm price agreed to and his actual costs. This "turnkey" contract requires no accountability or auditing unless claims for extra cost are submitted that were unforeseen or were the responsibility of the owner.

Contract - Lump Sum – Same as Firm price contracts.

Contract - Maximum Not to Exceed – An agreed to price with an incentive to share cost savings between the owner and contractor.

Contract - Time and Material – A reimbursable contract for all direct and indirect costs associated with the project including all fees and adders. All expenditures need to be documented. This type of contract is also referred to as Cost plus Fee Agreement. The owner assumes the risk of project completion for unforeseen events such as strikes, inclement weather, or material shortages.

Contractor – A person or entity that is responsible for performing the scope of work identified in the owner-Contractor Agreement.

Craft labor – Union or non-union field personnel responsible for installation of material, equipment, and buildings at the project.

Critical Path Schedule – A schedule that identifies all essential events in the sequence of installation necessary to meet completion schedule. Milestones that would severely impact costs and accomplishing other completion milestones and dates if they cannot be installed in the sequence specified. Non-critical path items would not impact completion if they are delayed or not performed.

Disputes – Typically a disagreement between parties where contract terms are not specific and different interpretations evolve.

Dispute Clause – The dispute clause in the contract provides the specific procedure for resolution of serious problems. It may detail a progressive series of steps, such as appealing to higher authorities, or may describe the ultimate option of arbitration.

Direct Costs – Expenditures made for the direct benefit of the owner to complete the project. This includes craft labor payroll costs, material costs, sub-tier contractor costs, and equipment costs.

Double Dip – For the purposes of this book, the term implies billing for the same item twice in two different ways such as through a direct reimbursement of a supplier invoice and indirectly as a component of a rental rate or fee, such as paying for gasoline deliveries for jobsite equipment which also includes a fuel component in the rental rate.

Drawings – Graphic blueprints or pictorial documents providing the design, dimensions, and locations of the buildings, equipment, and specific features of a project. These provide details, elevations, and diagrams of plumbing, electrical, entrances and exits, placement of machinery and are usually created by a design architect or engineer.

Due Diligence - A legal term that requires both owner and contractor(s) to execute the contract using qualified and experienced personnel in the most effective and prudent manner to manage and complete the project expeditiously. Time is of the essence attitude where the contractor is acting as the owner's agent on his behalf to produce the expected benefits at the lowest cost.

Extra – A term to describe an item of work that usually involves additional costs not contemplated at the signing of the original contract scope of work.

Fee – Compensation for organizing, staffing, and expertise to accomplish the project.

Fee - Overhead – The agreed to percentage, say 15%, applied with each monthly billing as a percentage of all costs incurred at the project during a specific time period that recovers overhead costs. This overhead fee compensates the contractor for other miscellaneous items to continue his business, such as home office staff costs.

Fee – Profit – The agreed to percentage, say 10%, applied to all direct costs with each monthly billing as a percentage of all costs incurred at the project during a specific time. Under a fixed fee contract the profit fee could be paid based on a pre-scheduled monthly payout regardless of expenditures or percentage complete.

F.I.C.A. - Federal Insurance Corporation of America – **Social Security.** Weekly amounts withheld from employee and subcontractor employee's gross wages that are collected and remitted to the Federal government with matching funds from the employer.

Force Majeure – This is a term given to delays that are the fault of neither party to the contract. These are unforeseeable and beyond the control of either party such as strikes, severe weather, and acts of God. These delays usually permit the contractor to file for an extension of time, but will not allow either party to be compensated for the time or expenses. The owner correspondingly cannot seek actual or liquated damages.

General Conditions – Provisions that are common to many construction projects that describe the rights, responsibilities, and relationships of all parties. General Conditions may provide responsibility for potable water, temporary construction toilets, trash removal, storage yard locations, parking locations for construction workers, and general site conditions that are considered when submitting a bid to the owner.

Guaranteed Maximum Contracts – a contract that provides for the contractor to be reimbursed for Cost of the Work plus Fee which together shall not exceed the established guaranteed Maximum Price. The Guaranteed Maximum Price is subject to adjustment by change order just like change orders affect a lump sum contract. Guarantee Maximum Contracts usually include a savings sharing provision whereby the contractor and owner share in the savings on a specified percentage basis or 25% to contractor and 75% to owner. Savings is usually defined as the difference between the cost plus fee and the guaranteed max.

Home Office Costs – Staff costs and administrative expenses at the contractor's normal place of business regardless of project location. Home Office costs are not directly billable but reimbursed through an overhead adder expressed as a percentage with each monthly invoice.

Incentive Bonuses – A contractual obligation that rewards the contractor for meeting schedule milestones, safety milestones, or cost savings that are specifically identified and can be measured on a periodic basis.

Indirect Costs – Pensions, insurance, taxes, vacations, sick leave, holiday pay, and incentive pay that are obligations by federal, state, or union contract mandates for personnel directly attributable to the project.

Journeyman – a craft employee who has completed a four apprenticeship and is qualified to perform all duties in his craft. A non-supervisory position reporting to a foreman in his respective craft such as a laborer, carpenter, electrician, ironworker, millwright, painter, or truck driver paid by the contractor on the weekly craft payroll.

Labor – The actual cost per hour paid by the contractor for those workers who are directly engaged in the project at the site location.

Labor Burden – the employer's net actual cost of payroll taxes (FICA, SUTA, FUTA), net actual cost for employer's cost of union benefit adders, and net actual cost to employer for worker's compensation insurance.

Letter of Intent – A formal written document from the owner to the contractor indicating an intention to enter into a formal agreement, which sets forth the general terms of the contract.

Litigation – When disputes cannot be resolved between owner, prime contractor, or sub-tier contractors where attorneys are required from all parties to resolve.

Low Bid – A bid price that is the lowest among competing contractors for performing the work.

Lump Sum Contract – an agreed upon price for all costs and fees incurred during construction. The risk of excessive delays and unanticipated events is born by the contractor. As a result the quoted price may be higher than time and material contracts to compensate the contractor for potential unknown events. The lump sum contract may be modified by change orders if agreed upon unforeseen events take place or if the owner desires changes of scope or enhancements of the original drawings. These change notices are tracked separately and added to the lump sum progress payments.

Mechanic's Lien – A security interest in a particular real estate that has been improved in order to secure payment for labor and material used in the property's improvements. The lien provides for the right to sell the property to which the lien attaches if the debt is not paid.

O.S.H.A. – Occupational Safety and Health Administration

Overhead Costs – Home office burden, electricity, phone, fax machines or other items needed to administer the execution of the contract.

Overhead Fee – Usually a percentage adder to all actual costs incurred that reimburses the contractor for his home office costs. If all actual costs for the month are billed at $100,000, an overhead fee of 15% would be added to the invoice or an additional $15,000 would be paid to compensate for home office costs.

Percentage of Completion – An engineering analysis of project status compared to total completion such as 50% complete after examining all materials installed in place compared to the amount of work remaining to be done. It can be expressed as a percentage of funds compared to budget or amount of installed assets.

Performance and Payment Bonds – The performance bond (an insurance policy) protects the owner from the contractor's failure to complete the contract by indicating that a financially responsible party (an insurance agency) stands behind the contractor to the limit of the amount of the bond. These are usually a project cost paid for by the owner. Most performance bonds will require such a guarantee for 100 percent of the contract amount. The Miller Act of 1969 requires performance bonds on all government projects. Proof that the bond was actually obtained should always be required by the owner.

Prequalification of Bidders – The review process of qualifying bidders on the basis of their experience, availability, and capability for installing the project. Past performance on other projects, researching newspaper articles, and credit worthiness are to be considered. Interviews with company employees having worked on previous projects should be performed and documented to avoid repeating the same prior disputes.

Prime Contractor - The primary business entity responsible to the owner for completion of the overall project with all contractor site personnel and subcontractors reporting to the Prime Contractor.. Other contractors with expertise in electrical, plumbing, drywall, or painting schedule their work through the prime contractor and submit their costs plus fees to the prime contractor, who in turn, includes these costs with his expenses plus fees.

Progress Payment – Monthly payments made during the project progress for the completion of work performed during the immediate prior month. It may be for material purchased and stored but not installed for items that may require long lead time in order to assure availability and avoid delays.

Project Cost – Total cost of the Project including all construction, professional and legal fees, land cost, furnishings and equipment, financing, and other indirect costs for temporary storage, office space, and tools not incorporated into the project but necessary for completion.

Property Insurance – Recovery for loss or damage to the work at the site caused by fire, lightning, vandalism, and malicious mischief. Usually the owner provides property insurance for his normal day to day operations. A deductible may be in place to avoid nuisance claims of small amounts.

Public Liability Insurance – Recovery for negligent acts resulting in bodily injury, disease, or death of persons other than employees of the insured, and/or property damage.

Punch List items – A final list of corrective actions required by the contractor to remedy after owner and contractor "walk through" the project in order for the owner to accept final completion and release final payment.

Reimbursable Expenses – Funds expended by the contractor and his sub-tier contractors supplying labor, materials, or professional services directly used for the benefit of the owner (that must be documented as proof of payment) and in terms with the contract.

Release of Retention – The final payment to contractors where the contract requires a withholding of percentage of completion payment after completion and acceptance of the work. After the release of retention is made, the contractor has been paid 100 percent of his quoted fixed price.

Retention – A contractual agreement for the owner to "hold back" from the contractor or keep a portion of the money due during each monthly progress payment to assure satisfactory acceptance of the work. Upon completion and acceptance of the project, the final retention is paid to the contractor (usually 10 percent of the contract total amount) after all punch list items and disputes have been resolved. Should the contractor default on the contract, the owner may use the retention held to obtain another contractor to complete the work. Retention is often used in the place of Performance and Payment Bonds.

Satellite Tool Rooms – One or more tool rooms located near the construction activity to expedite checking out material and tools. These remote tool rooms are away from the general warehouse where it would be impractical and time consuming to issue and return the more expensive tools on a daily basis.

Scope of Work – The scope of work that must be completed in order to fulfill contractual obligations that must be clearly and completely defined. The scope will be interpreted as work that is plainly and obviously necessary for a complete installation.

Security – The safeguarding of owner assets through security fencing, locks, guards, and controlled access to the project. Site security is normally the responsibility of the owner that require all contractors compliance with established security rules.

Specifications – Written requirements for material, equipment, construction systems, standards, and workmanship.

Sub-Tier Contractor – A contactor experienced in a trade or specialty that coordinates his work with the prime contractor according to the project schedule. He independently hires his own crews to perform their work and is responsible for payroll, material, taxes, and other costs directly related to the project.

Successful Bidder – the contractor chosen by owner for winning the contract as either lowest price or best qualified to perform the work.

Superintendent – The site representative who is a lead contractor employee responsible for all field supervision and completion of the work. The Superintendent is also responsible for site Safety requirements established by O.S.H.A. and the owner.

Third Party Rentals – The leasing of construction equipment, office equipment, or anything required for a short term duration needed for a specific purpose obtained from a leasing company and not provided by the owner or contractor. The economic benefits of leasing an item outweigh the benefits of maintenance, depreciation, and owning the item after project completion are all to be considered. Usually the leasee (owner) is responsible for scheduled maintenance, oil changes, damages, vandalism, and fuel when the item in on the project.

Work Around – An alternative work flow plan to be utilized if unforeseen circumstances prevents the normally schedule plan of the day. This allows a "back-up" plan utilizing existing resources, such as available labor and material, to continue working and avoid delays and increased costs to the project.

Worker's Compensation Insurance – an employer's insurance policy for compensation in the event of personal injury, sickness, disease or death occurring on the project site.

Work in Progress – That portion of the work that continues and has not been accepted by the owner for testing or operations. Some projects may have multiple stages or line items that can be accepted upon completion by the owner and "turned over" for operational purposes.

Made in the USA
Middletown, DE
18 April 2019